Grampy

Air Mail

The
Cautious Investor's
GUIDE TO PROFITS
in
PRECIOUS
METALS

ALSO BY DANIEL M. KEHRER

*Pills and Potions: New Discoveries About Prescription
and Over-the-Counter Drugs*
with JAMES KEHRER

DANIEL M. KEHRER

The
Cautious Investor's
GUIDE TO PROFITS
in
PRECIOUS
METALS

Times
BOOKS

Library of Congress Cataloging in Publication Data
Kehrer, Daniel M.
The cautious investor's guide to profits in
precious metals.
Bibliography: p.
Includes index.
1. Precious metals.   2. Metals as an investment—
United States.   I. Title.
HG261.K44   1986   332.63   85-40269
ISBN 0-8129-1233-0

Manufactured in the United States of America
9 8 7 6 5 4 3 2
First Edition

Designed by Giorgetta Bell McRee/Early Birds

FOR KAYE, FOREVER

*A Beacon
in the Night,
When I Am Lost,
Brings Comfort
and Love.*

CONTENTS

CHARTS, TABLES, AND ILLUSTRATIONS

WHERE TO FIND IT:
Helpful Precious Metals Investment Directories

PART I

Why Precious Metals?

CHAPTER 1

A New View for
a New Generation

- **A Balanced View**
- **After Gold Prohibition**
- **Exploratory Investing: A Blossoming New Menu**
- **Things to Come**
- **Your Precious Metals Game Plan**
- **Voodoo Economics**

Every investment book should begin with a confession. Here's mine:

I have no idea what will happen in the future to the prices of the precious metals you'll read about—gold, silver, platinum, and palladium. (Palladium, a sister metal of platinum, is the newest darling of the field.)

I do not belong to the precious metals promotional fraternity that year after year churns out bubbly literature on precious metals, recommending that you rush out and invest your hard-earned cash. That group *always* says prices are going up because they have a vested interest in saying so. And they have no qualms about quoting prices they claim will be achieved.

The trouble is, those predictions are no more accurate than picking numbers out of a hat. Sure, predictions come true *sometimes*. And a broken clock is right twice a day.

Nor is mine the opposite view that says it's all a hoax. The anti-gold and -silver folks claim that high precious metals prices result from an elaborate world conspiracy that lines the pockets of the promoters and bilks unsuspecting investors.

A BALANCED VIEW

This book is intended to be a balanced view of a booming investment choice for Americans—not totally unbiased perhaps, but a view that weighs the dangers of choosing precious metals against the potential benefits. Ultimately, only you, the investor, can make the decisions for your financial future. Your choices are presented in a straightforward "how-to" approach without the sugar coating that accompanies most investment literature. This study is practical, not promotional.

As editor in chief of a nationally circulated personal finance/ investment magazine, I've seen all too much rah-rah investment "advice" slide across my desk (and into the round file). On the topic of precious metals, straight talk for the intelligent individual consumer/investor is the rarest commodity of all.

If you've purchased precious metals in the past and are looking for a pat on the back—reinforcement that you will soon become rich— don't expect to find it here. Such cheerleading is readily available from the gold and silver promoters, who will gladly sell it to you.

Precious metals—gold in particular—need *not* be viewed as modern-day religious icons promising financial salvation. They needn't substitute for a political statement.

There may be ideological reasons for owning gold and silver instead of exclusively paper-based investments. Or you may want precious metals as disaster insurance. But don't confuse those purposes with *investing* in gold, silver, platinum, and palladium. There is a difference.

You *invest* for financial protection and to make a profit. And to make a profit you must one day sell all or part of what you own. An investor needs flexibility and discipline to sell, as well as buy, when the time is right.

This is a view of the changing role of precious metals, which are emerging as a mainstream American financial choice for the future.

A New View, A New Generation

Planning your financial future is tough. Investing successfully is even tougher. The explosion of choices facing money-conscious Americans today brings new meaning to the word "confusion." Personal finance has become *the* preoccupation of the decade. Younger Americans, older Americans, people in all stages of their financial lives are becoming more militant toward money . . . more liberated . . . more concerned with financial and investment freedom and choices.

In this new financial climate, precious metals have come front and center. They were once shunned as too risky, too specialized, too difficult for the average individual. But there has been an awakening toward the possibilities of investing in gold and silver—and more recently, platinum and palladium. These investments are not just for the rich or for the survivalists who hide their gold in caves. With a sensible approach, they can be for just about anybody.

Evidence of this change abounds. Your local bank may now offer precious metals. A few years ago that was unheard of. American businesses and consumers now realize that precious metals can play a legitimate role in an overall financial plan—perhaps only a very minor supporting role for some, much larger for others. In today's dangerous financial climate, one key to financial success is to diversify investments. Precious metals offer a prime opportunity to do so.

Ways to invest in precious metals have become far more accessible to the average investor. Gold, silver, platinum, and palladium—although still considered risky and out of bounds for some people—have grabbed seats next to stocks, bonds, real estate, and other traditional investments in today's financial auditorium. The big brokerage firms, banks, mutual funds, insurance companies, and others have warmed up to precious metals. They are names you will recognize—Merrill Lynch, E. F. Hutton, Dean Witter, Brink's, Prudential-Bache, PaineWebber, Shearson Lehman Brothers, Citibank, Security Pacific, and First National Bank of Chicago, among hundreds of others.

In recent years new precious metals investment products aimed at consumers have sprouted like weeds on a newly seeded lawn. The key word there is *investment*. Buying jewelry made from these metals is not considered an investment.

Promoters spotted a huge and largely untapped market among American individuals hungry for new financial ideas. But that also attracted the frauds and cheats. Precious metals reputations in the 1970s and 1980s were not unstained. You'll read about this darker side to precious metals as well.

AFTER GOLD PROHIBITION

It is understandable that American attitudes have lagged behind world attitudes toward precious metals. They were shaped by the legacy of prohibition—not the short-lived ban on alcohol that most people think of, but a much longer (forty-year) ban on an equally addictive element, gold. From 1934, when Franklin Roosevelt decreed the ban against owning gold, until December 31, 1974, it was *illegal* to own gold bullion in the United States.

The precious metals business in this country only recently entered its second decade. Partly because it's still an adolescent, the field is fraught with many dangers for investors.

Precious metals represent the only "international" investment most folks will ever make. Gold, silver, platinum, and palladium are *world* commodities. Prices are linked partly to what happens in the U.S. economy, but they also move with the whims of investors *worldwide*. In precious metals, what happens along the Danube or the Amazon can be as important as what happens along the Potomac.

EXPLORATORY INVESTING: A BLOSSOMING NEW MENU

If you have avoided precious metals because of scary rhetoric, it may be time to reconsider. If you already have experience in precious metals, you will be surprised by the rush of new developments and strategies available. Only a few years ago the menu was limited. Now there are dozens of ways to approach the four precious metals, and hundreds of variations on those themes. They range from the utterly simple to the ultra-risky.

You can get started in precious metals for as little as you like—$100 will get you going in a special program at a major brokerage firm. For less than $50 you can start by purchasing ounces of silver bullion. There's no trick to it. The risks can be as low or high as you choose.

Depending on how you approach precious metals, they can offer financial peace of mind (the long-term, buy-it-and-forget-about-it view) or they can rob you blind. Gold, silver, platinum, and palladium can make your heart race, your blood boil, your pocketbook plump or empty.

THINGS TO COME

Here are some of the developments you'll read about:

- The instant diversity and safety of precious metals mutual funds.
- The pros and cons of different forms of bullion bars, ingots, and coins of all sizes for all budgets.
- The simplicity of precious metals certificates and how the plans differ; where you can get started for under $500; programs that let you pay by credit card; how to avoid sales taxes and storage headaches; plans that let you transfer funds directly from a bank account or money market fund into precious metals.
- The dangers of leverage contracts, and other precious metals pitfalls to avoid.
- The metals merchants—who they are, how they work, where to find them, and what they do and do not offer. Also, the latest trend—discount precious metals brokers.
- The special risks of precious metals investing, and how to assess your own risk profile.
- Investing in gold and silver mining stocks. Choices range from "blue chip" mines to super-speculative penny mining shares.
- How rare (numismatic) coins can offer a gold and silver "double play."
- Special tax considerations of precious metals investing.
- Using your home computer to help track the metals and keep tabs on your investment portfolio.

- Background about each of the metals showing the whys and wherefores of supply, demand, and price changes.
- How you can set up an investment plan tailored to your personal financial needs.
- Tips on storing your investment, and how you can buy and hold precious metals outside the United States if you wish.
- The ins and outs of precious metals "options"—a sophisticated device that lets you gamble for bigger profits over the short term (less than a year). Options offer a way to profit even when prices are *falling*. Plus, the dangerous game of commodity futures.
- You'll find specific lists of names, addresses, and telephone numbers of places to find further information and to follow up as you pursue precious metals on your own.
- A selection of charts and tables to help put it all in perspective.

YOUR PRECIOUS METALS GAME PLAN

A conservative approach to gold is to view it as a "financial constant"—as investment insurance and not a money-making machine. In years past, gold's strength was not in making everyone rich but in guarding *long-term holders* against becoming poor. Gold, and to a lesser extent the other precious metals, can be *protectors* as well as creators of wealth by being used in different ways.

VOODOO ECONOMICS

When precious metals are "hot," there will be no shortage of headlines in newspapers, magazines, and investment advisory newsletters. The only sane advice is to ignore them all. This is surely voodoo economics at its finest. I have an assortment on my desk at the moment; all from the same general time period. This is how they read:

**FADING GLOW OF PRECIOUS METALS
REBOUND SEEN FOR GOLD**

LOST LUSTER OF PRECIOUS METALS
NEW LIFE FOR PRECIOUS METALS
$4,000 GOLD BY 1987?
THE CRASH IN GOLD
PRECIOUS METALS: A TIME TO BUY!

Attempts to foretell precious metals prices in the 1980s have reached epidemic proportions. The predictions fly like political promises in an election year. It's best to treat them with equal reverence.

For the Fun of It

Gold ideologues would cringe at the thought, but precious metals investing today can even be *fun*. No other investment is quite like it. Gold and silver have historical pedigrees that stretch back thousands of years. Platinum and palladium offer "ground floor" entrance to the new "twenty-first century" high-tech precious metals.

Coins made of precious metals are as much objects of art as they are money. Some items are so aesthetically pleasing that owners refuse to give them up. The range of choices—from mining shares to bullion bars, mutual funds to silver options—makes it exciting.

After all the warnings and all the balancing, you may find precious metals an addictive sort of investment. In any market where prices swing up and down—be it for walnuts or woolens, pears or precious metals—there is a profit to be made, if you are willing to accept the risk.

The market has made it simple. Gold is a phone call away. There is a lure of owning gold, silver, platinum, or palladium—both discomforting and comforting at the same time. Millions of financially aware Americans are now looking into precious metals as one sound element of a well-thought-out investment plan for the remainder of this century . . . and beyond.

CHAPTER 2

Gold Basics: What's the Fuss?

- **Gold's Amazing Physical Prowess**
- **Monetary Gold: Government Stocks and Government Rules**
- **Supply and Demand**
- **The Investor Demand Triumvirate**
- **Tracking the Price of Gold**

Gold is rare. It's also incredibly handy for industrial and other commercial uses. And people *believe* it is valuable, so they buy it. These three attributes have made gold a unique commodity. The main concerns for today's investors and other "users" of gold are: Where has gold been, where might it be going, and why?

To understand what changes gold has been through, and where its future as an investment may be headed, you'll want to know something about what drives the world's gold market. That's what this chapter is about. If you want to get right to the investment angles, and don't want to bother with gold market basics (including a few fascinating facts about the metal), move on to the nuts and bolts. This sets the stage for what is to come.

Other things on this earth are more rare than gold. Platinum, for example, is a hundred times more scarce, yet it commands a price roughly the same as gold. (Super Bowl tickets also come to mind, but that's something else again.)

Gold is not just another world commodity like soybeans, sugar, copper, or lumber. It has star quality. Though it reacts to supply and demand, like other commodities, some ingredients of that demand make a strange brew indeed.

GOLD'S AMAZING PHYSICAL PROWESS

How rare is gold? If you could gather together all the gold mined in recorded history, melt it down, and pour it into one giant cube, it would measure only about eighteen yards across! That's all the gold owned by every government on earth, plus all the gold in private hands, all the gold in rings, necklaces, chains, and gold art. That's all the gold used in tooth fillings, in electronics, in coins and bars. It's everything that exists aboveground now, or since man learned to extract the metal from the earth. All of it can fit into one block the size of a single house. It would weigh about 91,000 tons—less than the amount of steel made around the world *in an hour*. That's rare.

To reach the gold, some mines now stretch more than 2 miles underground. The world's easy-to-find gold is long gone. Today it takes an average of 4 tons of gold-bearing rock to produce a single ounce of gold—much more at some low-grade mines.

But rarity is only part of the equation. Gold is remarkably versatile and useful. It is the most pliable of any metal, a property called malleability. If gold could be chewed like bubble gum, with a one-ounce stick you'd be able to blow a bubble the size of a small kitchen. Gold can be pounded into sheets so thin it would take a quarter-million of them to make a stack an inch thick.

The Science of Gold

A scientist would tell you that gold can perform these amazing feats of agility because of its uniquely arranged atoms—perfect 79/118/79 measurements. That's a nucleus of 79 protons and 118 neutrons surrounded by 79 electrons. These atoms have an almost unhealthy affinity for one another, refusing to break away even under the direst of circumstances (like repeated blows of the gold artisan's hammer). That stretching ability is also known as ductility. A single ounce of gold can produce *50 miles* of superfine gold wire.

In addition to gold's amazing ability to stretch, the metal is nearly indestructible. It doesn't corrode, not even with most acids. It won't tarnish or rust and is unaffected by the weather. Even air pollution doesn't phase it, except perhaps for a coating of soot. More than any other metal, gold is able to resist chemical reactions with other elements. Salt water won't hurt it. Gold doubloons recovered from sunken wrecks still glisten. Gold artifacts buried for thousands of years haven't a trace of tarnish.

Industrial Prowess

For today's high-technology users of gold, the metal's prowess as an electrical and thermal conductor makes it highly prized. A microscopic circuit etched with liquid gold can replace miles of conventional wiring in a computer. Manufacturers count on gold to provide the absolute best, most trouble-free electrical contact points for their products. The electronics industry worldwide gobbles up over 100 tons of the metal for use in telephone equipment, televisions, calculators, computers, and other products. You can credit gold for the high reliability of most such products.

Gold is used increasingly in architecture, not only as a decoration but also to increase energy efficiency. Glass in some buildings is now tinted with a coating of gold two-millionths of an inch thick. The gold cuts glare and lets in light but blocks the heat-producing infrared rays from the sun.

Even modern medicine has turned to gold. Some of the latest drugs developed to treat arthritis contain large amounts of gold—as much as 50 percent of the drug. The gold-based arthritis medications show promise of becoming the first drugs actually able to halt or even reverse the progress of some types of arthritis.

These uses remain tiny compared to the amount of gold the world uses each year in jewelry—nearly 700 tons at last count in non-Communist countries. Nearly 60 tons of gold end up in the mouths of people around the world (dentistry usage); about 200 tons are used for official gold coins; 35 tons for gold medallions and other gold medals; and another 60 tons for decorative purposes (such as gold-plated cigarette lighters and tableware).

More Efficient Use

Industrial users of gold have smartened up. Lately they've figured out ways to use this high-priced raw material much more sparingly. Back when oil was cheap, nobody thought much of wasting it. Only after the price shock did Detroit start designing more fuel-efficient engines. Gold too was once cheap, pegged at less than *$40 per ounce* back in the early 1970s. At that price, industrial users could afford to slop it on their products like paint.

When the price soared things changed. Users invented ways to radically reduce the microscopic thickness of gold plating on electronic devices. Instead of coating an entire device with gold, the metal is applied to selected areas only. The result has been a much more efficient use of gold in industry, although total usage has grown because many more products are being made.

MONETARY GOLD: GOVERNMENT STOCKS AND GOVERNMENT RULES

Gold is not just a lovely decorative metal that has dubious value, like a designer fashion. It has been thought of as money almost as long as the concept of money itself has existed. Gold has literally thousands of uses, and in the late twentieth century it has emerged as an indispensable industrial commodity.

In the past, most of the world's supply of this yellow metal ended up in government stockpiles around the world. Since the late 1950s, however, there has been a massive shift. Most gold produced around the world now goes to private investment and industry. And since 1968, when the major world powers agreed for a time to stop hoarding all the newly mined gold, the metal has become a free market commodity.

Think of it. After thousands of years of changing hands mostly as money, gold has begun to float as a free market commodity only since the late 1960s. Little wonder there is so much debate about its place in tomorrow's economy.

According to U.S. government figures, one-third of all the gold that has been mined in the world is still in government vaults. The U.S. government today owns about 263 million ounces of gold (at $500 per ounce, that's worth about $132 billion, enough to cover only a tiny part of the national debt. Oddly, however, Uncle Sam still values his gold hoard at a mere $42 per ounce, the last "official" government-set price).

U.S. gold holdings are actually way *down*. Back in 1950, the United States held a cache of 650 million ounces. That shrank to a little over 500 million ounces in 1960, to 315 million ounces in 1970, and on down to today's level. The accompanying table shows you how other governments have handled their gold stockpiles.

The Biggest Deregulation of All

When there was still a monetary gold standard (with currency backed by a set amount of gold), governments held the gold price stable and filled their vaults with the metal. Before 1968 there was little need to import gold into the United States. By law, individuals were prohibited from owning it, so there was no demand for bullion or coins to be met. Gold for commercial use was available from U.S. Treasury stockpiles.

But on March 18, 1968, when Uncle Sam closed his gold sales "window," commercial users suddenly faced the cold hard free market world of gold. Only then did the first gold wholesale operations begin in the United States. Rhode Island Hospital Trust National Bank was one of the first. RIHT isn't exactly a household name, but this commercial bank controls almost half of the commercial gold market in the United States. Other major players in the United States now are J. Aron & Company, Republic National Bank, Morgan Guaranty, Crédit Suisse, Mocatta Metals, Johnson Matthey, and Engelhard, among others.

When the old gold system completely unraveled, governments threatened to wave their collective magic wand and declare that gold was no longer money, then sell off most of what they owned to com-

Central Bank Gold Reserves by Country and Region

Million Troy Ounces

	1950	1960	1970	1980	1981	1982	1983	1984
Industrial								
United States	652.0	508.7	316.3	264.3	264.1	264.0	263.4	263.1
Canada	16.6	25.3	22.6	21.0	20.5	20.3	20.2	20.2
Australia	2.6	4.2	6.8	7.9	7.9	7.9	7.9	7.9
Japan	0.2	7.1	15.2	24.2	24.2	24.2	24.2	24.2
Austria	0.2	8.4	20.4	21.1	21.1	21.1	21.1	21.1
Belgium	16.8	33.4	42.0	34.2	34.2	34.2	34.2	34.2
Denmark	0.9	3.1	1.8	1.6	1.6	1.6	1.6	1.6
France	18.9	46.9	100.9	81.9	81.9	81.9	81.9	81.9
Germany	–	84.9	113.7	95.2	95.2	95.2	95.2	95.2
Italy	7.3	63.0	82.5	66.7	66.7	66.7	66.7	66.7
Netherlands	9.0	41.5	51.1	43.9	43.9	43.9	43.9	43.9
Norway	1.4	0.9	0.7	1.2	1.2	1.2	1.2	1.2
Spain	3.2	5.1	14.2	14.6	14.6	14.6	14.6	14.6
Sweden	2.6	4.9	5.7	6.1	6.1	6.1	6.1	6.1
Switzerland	42.0	62.4	78.0	83.3	83.3	83.3	83.3	83.3
United Kingdom	81.8	80.0	38.5	18.8	19.0	19.0	19.0	19.0
Other	1.6	2.7	1.5	1.4	1.7	1.7	1.7	1.7
European Monetary Cooperation Fund	–	–	–	85.6	85.7	85.7	85.7	85.7
TOTAL	857.1	982.5	911.9	873.0	872.9	872.6	871.9	871.6

SOURCE: *International Monetary Fund*

mercial users. But the United States, which started selling heavily again in 1972, and the International Monetary Fund were the only ones to actually do that. In recent years government ownership around the globe has steadied or increased slightly. All other governments either held on to their gold stocks or added to them. Only Third World nations facing staggering debts have been forced to sell gold at times to avoid defaulting on loans.

The nations of the world would have to be crazy to give up their gold at this point. According to Crédit Suisse, gold now represents the single most valuable asset owned by the central banks of the world. By no means have the politicians lost interest in it.

SUPPLY AND DEMAND

In a free market, supply and demand will always balance, one way or another. Those forces apply to gold and the other precious metals. If supply is larger than demand, the price will drop until it looks cheap enough that demand picks up the slack. Likewise, when there is more demand than supply, the price rises.

The Supply Side

The world's gold supply comes from four basic sources:

(1) New mine production.

(2) Gold from "secondary" sources, which means gold recovered from scrap industrial uses, old jewelry, and other "scrap."

(3) Gold sales by Communist nations—the Soviet Union (the world's second largest gold producer), China, and North Korea. This is notoriously hard to predict.

(4) Sales by Western governments.

Mining Supply

If you combine all of those sources of supply for gold, the amount of new metal becoming available has been remarkably stable since the late 1970s.

But in the 1980s, mines are producing more gold than they have in years. Whether that trend continues will depend on what happens to the price of gold. If it doesn't rise substantially, the trend could slow or even reverse in the 1990s.

New technologies have lowered the cost of mining gold, which, combined with a high market price, can make it an attractive enterprise. In coming decades, we may see the last untapped source of gold conquered—the oceans, where millions of ounces lie in seafloor sediments. So far, cost and environmental barriers to retrieving that gold have been too great.

The amount of gold mined around the world fell steadily through the 1970s—from about 49 million ounces in 1970 to only 40 million ounces in 1980. That includes production in Communist countries. Counting only non-Communist production (supply studies usually separate the two), mining production fell 25 percent during the 1970s, from 40 million ounces to 30 million ounces, then jumped back up to 35 million ounces by the mid-1980s.

Who's Got the Gold?

The world's leading gold-producing nation by far is South Africa, claiming two-thirds of the Western world's output. The Soviets are in second place. Canada is the third largest gold-producing nation—but a distant third. Canadian mines produce only about 10 to 15 percent as much as South African mines. Canada, nevertheless, saw an explosive gold rush in the early 1980s as new deposits were discovered and output soared. (Chapter 15 provides more details on investment potential here and elsewhere in gold mining stocks.)

Fourth place is a close race among Brazil, China, and the United States. Production in Brazil and the United States has soared in recent years, even more so in Brazil, where a Wild West–style gold rush was on. U.S. gold production is only about 4 percent of total world output.

Other major gold-producing nations include Australia, the Philippines, Papua New Guinea, Chile, Zimbabwe, Colombia, the Dominican Republic, Ghana, Peru, and Mexico. The accompanying table shows how they stack up.

Top Ten Gold-Producing Nations

Thousand Troy Ounces

	1980	1981	1982	1983	1984	1985	1986 Projected	1987 Projected
(1) South Africa	21,631	21,122	21,355	21,846	21,880	21,863	22,023	22,184
(2) Soviet Union	8,300	8,425	8,550	9,100	9,200	9,400	9,600	9,700
(3) Canada	1,563	1,673	2,081	2,363	2,615	2,862	3,117	3,323
(4) United States	970	1,378	1,466	1,957	2,129	2,567	2,987	2,973
(5) Brazil	1,127	1,177	1,447	1,728	1,630	2,042	2,443	2,624
(6) China	1,500	1,745	1,770	1,830	1,900	2,000	2,150	2,300
(7) Australia	548	591	867	941	1,151	1,636	1,657	1,648
(8) Papua New Guinea	457	553	563	588	577	1,083	1,069	1,077
(9) Philippines	666	753	830	802	842	866	866	902
(10) Chile	216	400	546	571	553	581	588	594

SOURCE: The Gold Institute

In the decade from 1975 to 1985, gold from the mines of the world accounted for about 65 percent of the supply entering the market each year. The rest came from scrap or from sales by the Soviet Union and other governments.

South Africa's lead in gold production has narrowed. Its share of the world gold mining pie has been shaved from 75 percent in the 1970s to near 60 percent in the 1980s. That's more the result of increased production elsewhere rather than a drop in gold coming from South Africa. The South Africans themselves predicted increasing production until 1990, even though the U.S. Bureau of Mines, among others, anticipated ". . . a steady decline in metal production from South Africa beginning about 1987."

A Cautious Investor's Tip: The U.S. Bureau of Mines publishes a profile of the gold market each year. For a free copy you can write to: Bureau of Mines, U.S. Department of the Interior, Publications Distribution Branch, 4800 Forbes Avenue, Pittsburgh, PA 15213.

While mines produced more gold in recent years, less has become available from secondary sources. When gold topped $800 per ounce in 1980, people everywhere scoured attics, basements, and grandma's hope chest for old gold items to cash in. Recovery of scrap gold mushroomed. Now there are fewer people with old jewelry still lying around. Industrial users are becoming more efficient; much less gold can be recovered from discarded equipment. While supplies from mining grew, supplies from scrap fell.

Red Gold Supplies

Soviet and other Communist nation sales are the perennial wild card of the gold supply picture. Crédit Suisse, one of the largest Swiss banks and a world leader in the gold market, calls Soviet gold sales a "puzzle." According to the bank, two contrasting theories have tried to explain this source of gold:

• The first says that the Soviets usually market their gold in preplanned amounts, without regard to the price or other market considerations.

• The second holds that gold sales are geared precisely to the Soviet government's foreign exchange needs, and it sells when it needs the cash (to buy grain, for example) and can get the best price.

According to Crédit Suisse, Soviet tactics in recent years seem to confirm the latter theory. And since sales depend on the USSR's cash needs and not on how much gold its mines are actually producing, "Soviet influence upon the state of the gold market and the level of prices is difficult to assess."

J. Aron & Company, a major U.S. wholesale precious metals supplier that closely follows the markets, agrees. In one of its periodic *Gold Review and Outlook* reports, the firm says, "It is extremely difficult to project possible gold exports by the Soviet Union, North Korea and other centrally planned economies. . . ."

However inaccurately Communist nation gold sales are predicted, the gold market does react to this factor. When the Soviets are expected to "dump" large amounts of gold on the market, prices can drop precipitously, even though some experts feel such fears are groundless.

When the Soviets sell, they do it through a Swiss bank, like most other governments. It's easy since the Soviets have set up their very own Swiss bank to do it for them—Wozchod Handelsbank in Zurich, which is linked to the State Bank in Moscow.

The Demand Side

The demand side of the fence gets more interesting. This is where investors come in. And this is where gold has undergone its radical transformation over the last several decades. Governments and industry no longer call all the shots. As Crédit Suisse put it, "The gold market has recently been caught up in a broad wave of popular participation." Here's why:

• Restrictions against private gold ownership have been lifted. While the players include most industrialized nations and many developing countries, the United States now absorbs a quarter of total current production.

• Rising incomes, fear of inflation, and international political tensions have led to wider public interest in owning gold—attracting ever larger numbers of investors with modest and even very modest means.

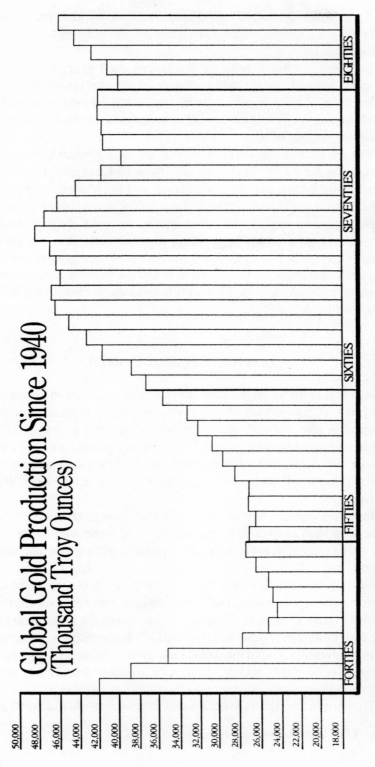

Global Gold Production Since 1940
(Thousand Troy Ounces)

SOURCES: Consolidated Gold Fields, U.S. Bureau of Mines; J. Aron and Co., The Gold Institute, Int'l Gold Corp.

As a group, the world's gold investors now wield ultimate control over the price of gold, forcing governments and industry to watch from the sidelines.

In terms of pure volume of gold taken each year, industrial and jewelry demand (called fabrication demand) can outmuscle the demand for gold from investors. Total fabrication demand in recent years has been around 36 million ounces, compared to investment demand of under 20 million ounces.

The jewelers of the world, however, are selling much less gold than they did in the 1970s. They now sell 10- or 12-karat gold items instead of 14- and 18-karat to keep it affordable. Just as industrial users of gold have learned to cut back, so have the jewelers. Even though people are spending more money than ever before on gold jewelry, and the amount of gold used has been rising, it is still well below what it once was. Also, while consumers in some countries once bought gold jewelry as an investment, they have now shifted to more clearly defined types of investment gold. This shift has cut the demand for gold jewelry worldwide.

Investor Demand Crucial

Investment demand has become the most crucial factor in determining the price. A comparison of industrial and jewelry demand to investor demand is like that between a big ocean liner and a tiny speedboat. Huge numbers of investors stand ready at any given moment to move into or out of gold and other precious metals if their expectations shift. The big industrial users must play catch-up once prices have already moved.

Investors fall into two groups: those that view gold as something to hold long term as financial "insurance," and those who move in and out of the market to make a "quick" profit (anything less than several years).

Few people realize how large this group has become. "One common misconception is that relatively few investors are involved in this market," says J. Aron & Company, a division of the investment banking firm Goldman, Sachs in New York. "A surprisingly broad spectrum of investors around the world view gold as an integral part of their investment portfolio, and the number of investors sharing this view is increasing steadily."

This firm's specialists estimate that investors worldwide own more than 700 million ounces of gold. Both the United States, where gold ownership for individuals was legalized in 1975, and Japan, where restrictions were eased in 1978, are still largely virgin territory for gold investment. Millions of individuals have moved into gold since those years, but millions more have waited on the sidelines.

THE INVESTOR DEMAND TRIUMVIRATE

The question of what influences today's gold price boils down to this: Why do investors think the way they do?

No one can answer the question completely. Even the term "investor" leaves room for interpretation. Investors in precious metals are a diverse group, including individuals of all occupations and income levels in all areas of the United States and the world . . . bankers and traders who invest as part of their business . . . and institutional investors who manage other people's money.

But gold's performance in recent years has left little doubt about which key factors play a role in influencing the price:

- The level of interest rates.
- Strength or weakness of the U.S. dollar.
- Expectations for inflation.

These three items constantly shift, and they may not carry equal weight in investors' minds. The year 1984 is but one example of how these factors can work. During that year inflation in the United States remained extremely low—about 4 percent. People believed inflation would remain under control for the time being. Interest rates dropped but were still considered high by long-range standards.

There is an important difference between "real" and "nominal" interest rates. The real interest rate takes into account the effects of inflation. If inflation is low, a high nominal rate (before adjusting for inflation) will look even higher in real terms. But if inflation is high at the same time interest rates are high, the real rate of interest after taking inflation into account will appear much lower. That in turn would make an investment such as gold look more attractive. A high nominal interest rate is not important. A high real interest rate will draw investors into interest-bearing investments and away from gold. Such was the case in 1984. As a result, the price of gold took a dive.

The Dollar's Role

An even greater force in the market that year was the phenomenal strength of the U.S. dollar around the world. Low inflation, high interest rates, and a strong dollar knocked gold right off its rocker. With every blip upward for the dollar on the financial radar, gold dipped a little further. When the dollar reversed course, gold would recover.

But that was only one year. There is no rule that the dollar and gold both can't do well at the same time. For example, from mid-1982, when gold hit bottom, until early 1983 the price of gold went on a giddy upward ride—at the same time the U.S. dollar experienced a sharp rise. So gold and the dollar don't always move against each other.

When inflation picks up and interest rates fall, gold often improves dramatically. And, if history holds true, the U.S. dollar would, at such times, become less attractive overseas.

A Different Foreign View

What few people realized in the days when the dollar reigned supreme and gold looked cheap was that the picture appeared much different when viewed from outside the United States. The *world* price of gold is always set in U.S. dollars. Gold that looked cheap in U.S. dollars would look much more expensive if your paycheck came in German marks or French francs, for example. Just as a strong dollar makes it cheap for Americans to vacation in Paris and expensive for Parisians to visit New York, it makes gold look cheap to Americans and expensive to the French. When the dollar is down, this pendulum swings in the other direction.

While American investors flocked to buy gold coins at bargain basement prices in the early 1980s, investors and industrial users of gold in some other countries found themselves priced out of the market because their currencies were so low compared to the U.S. dollar.

Consider the South Africans. During the early 1980s, the South African rand (their "dollar") plunged in value against the U.S. dollar— from $1.30 per rand to 60 cents at one point. While the price of gold in dollars was falling, the price of gold in terms of the rand actually went up. In 1985, when gold hit its lowest point in years, as measured in U.S. dollars, the gold price in marks and pounds was running close to record levels.

Why is this important? Because it affects demand for gold among investors in other countries. British investors balk at gold when the pound is low, making the dollar price of gold look high. When the dollar falls, gold looks cheaper (even if it has gone up in dollar terms) and demand from these investors picks up once again as well. The same applies elsewhere.

For this reason, precious metals watchers now closely track what the metals are worth in other currencies as well as in U.S. dollars. It can give a radically different impression of what is happening in the gold market *outside* the United States.

Another year, another set of worldwide economic circumstances would completely reshuffle the supply/demand cards, dealing investors a vastly different hand to play. There is no formula. A big increase in mine supply might set the pace one year; a weak dollar the next; high inflation another time; and Soviet gold sales still another.

Were supplies to increase tremendously, it might look bad for gold. But investors can snap up all that gold and demand more if they have the right motivation. As one expert puts it, "It is not the size of the surplus alone that matters, but its size relative to the intensity of investor interest at the moment in time."

Some gold market veterans have given up trying to interpret the yearly supply/demand projections. Like most statistics, these can be interpreted any way your heart desires.

Letting the Big Kids Play

Investor demand is what counts, say these voices. And not just individual investors. If the big *institutional* investors—the pension funds and insurance companies—ever pin their sights on gold, the market would have yet another major new player.

Up to this point, institutional investors who control billions of dollars in assets have stayed away from gold. At first they did so by law. Then, after the U.S. courts seemed to relax restrictions against institu-

Factors That Influence the Price of Gold

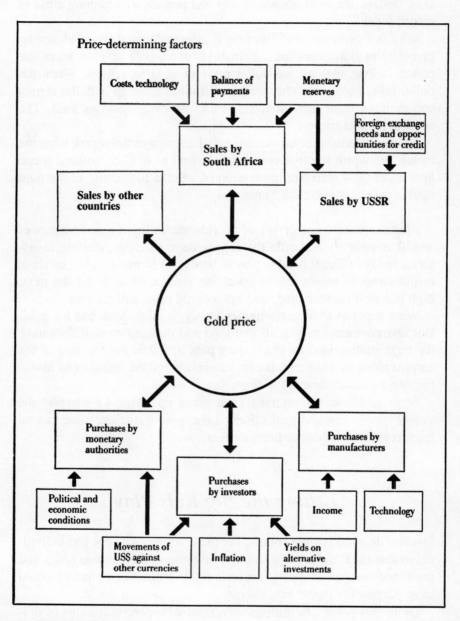

Price-determining factors

Costs, technology

Balance of payments

Monetary reserves

Foreign exchange needs and opportunities for credit

Sales by South Africa

Sales by other countries

Sales by USSR

Gold price

Purchases by monetary authorities

Purchases by investors

Purchases by manufacturers

Political and economic conditions

Movements of US$ against other currencies

Inflation

Yields on alternative investments

Income

Technology

SOURCE: Crédit Suisse

tions investing funds in precious metals, they still avoided gold by choice.

The law says that pension fund managers, and others who invest money belonging to individuals or groups (such a person is called a fiduciary), must do so "prudently." Until lately, gold was not considered by most conservative institutional money managers to be a prudent investment.

That is changing, ever so slowly. More managers now believe that it is prudent to balance off their investments with a small amount of precious metals. If ever this vast amount of institutional money casts a more covetous eye on gold, the results could be explosive. As long as there are better, higher-paying, and safer places for their money, they are not likely to rush in to embrace gold. But the door has been left ajar, and managers of some institutional investment portfolios have a Plan B ready to use when the time is right.

Upsetting Supply and Demand?

Here are a few things that could upset the supply/demand balance of gold in either direction:

• A resumption of gold sales by the United States, the International Monetary Fund, or other world bodies.
• Large gold sales by countries facing huge debts they cannot pay.
• Unexpected Soviet gold dumping.
• Large "dishoarding" of scrap gold following a rapid increase in the price.
• Somebody discovers an acceptable substitute for gold in industrial uses. (So far that hasn't happened. Industry has found ways to use less gold, but no other metal or combination of metals can yet match gold's desirable properties.)

TRACKING THE PRICE OF GOLD

If you want to see how the gold price has performed in the past, there is little need to look beyond 1968. When the official gold price was hiked from $20.67 per ounce to $35 per ounce in 1934, it stayed there until 1968.

During the 1930s and 1940s, gold poured into the U.S. Treasury at that price. During the 1950s and 1960s, when the United States still promised to exchange gold for dollars, foreign central banks vigorously accepted that kind offer. Only in 1971, after half of the nation's stock was siphoned off, did officials finally end gold convertibility.

Long before that time, gold was threatening to burst from its artificial price container. National governments conspired to hold the price down to $35 an ounce—ultimately without success. While the price was artificially set by governments at that level, gold as an international commodity commanded a far higher price. When gold was later unleashed into a free market it had much catching up to do.

A group of seven nations calling itself the International Gold Pool set a two-tier system for gold prices in 1968. Governments would trade gold at $35 per ounce, while all other gold would be allowed to move with supply and demand.

And move it did, to *yearly averages* of $58 per ounce in 1972; $97 in 1973; $160 in 1974; $193 in 1978; $307 in 1979; and $612 in 1980 before starting a multiyear slide into the latter half of the 1980s, with intermittent ups and downs along the way.

The U.S. dollar was devalued twice in the early 1970s, raising the *official price* of gold to $38 in 1972 and to $42.22 in 1973. According to the U.S. Bureau of Mines, the United States today remains the only holder of large gold reserves in the world that still values them officially at $42.22 per ounce.

With that second devaluation in 1973, the President was given the power to allow private ownership of gold for the first time since President Franklin Roosevelt banned it in 1934. But it didn't actually happen until December 31, 1974.

By 1985 the gold market was beginning to settle down. Gold prices were once far more jittery than they are now, although they still can take a wild swing now and again when investors get especially nervous. But back in the late seventies and early eighties, the gold market would jump at every sound. A political crisis somewhere in the world would send gold soaring $25, $50, or more in a single trading session. Today such huge ''bad news'' moves in gold are less frequent, though not unheard of.

When the Russians shot down a Korean airliner; when the United States invaded Grenada; when India's prime minister was assassinated, the gold market hardly rippled. A few years earlier such events might have touched off a near panic in the market.

Tracking the Price of Gold

U.S. $ Per Troy Ounce

	1977	1978	1979	1980	1981	1982	1983	1984
January								
High	136.10	176.60	237.80	825.00	597.00	402.40	510.10	379.20
Low	127.30	166.90	217.60	575.50	501.70	370.00	450.50	365.90
Average	132.38	173.44	227.06	671.82	556.29	383.90	482.52	370.58
February								
High	144.20	183.50	254.20	713.00	518.70	386.10	508.40	401.80
Low	132.80	174.00	231.40	615.00	481.50	360.50	400.50	377.20
Average	136.88	178.44	246.31	664.46	503.57	374.34	488.32	387.00
March								
High	153.70	189.70	249.80	648.00	544.50	361.80	436.70	404.60
Low	143.10	175.60	234.80	463.00	458.70	312.80	410.00	386.00
Average	148.61	183.45	241.25	553.65	498.63	329.95	420.84	394.62
April								
High	152.80	180.60	247.00	538.50	526.60	369.70	445.00	387.40
Low	145.80	167.40	230.80	487.10	473.90	326.30	421.70	376.10
Average	149.19	174.47	239.42	513.66	494.55	350.71	433.27	381.36

	1977	1978	1979	1980	1981	1982	1983	1984
May								
High	148.90	184.20	276.80	545.20	491.50	345.40	443.90	389.70
Low	142.60	169.10	245.60	505.50	465.30	322.20	412.00	371.20
Average	146.30	176.26	257.61	515.60	479.35	334.22	436.89	377.68
June								
High	144.20	186.60	284.00	650.00	474.70	336.40	423.00	395.60
Low	137.10	180.50	272.60	559.00	423.50	298.00	402.10	368.50
Average	141.27	183.68	279.30	603.28	458.06	315.68	412.95	377.62
July								
High	147.00	204.00	306.70	678.50	418.00	366.50	430.60	370.70
Low	140.30	182.90	282.20	608.50	400.20	303.00	412.80	333.70
Average	143.71	189.81	295.63	642.63	408.39	341.05	423.55	345.94
August								
High	147.30	215.40	320.00	645.50	435.80	430.50	425.70	354.00
Low	142.80	198.40	281.40	603.20	388.50	330.50	409.90	339.00
Average	145.62	205.96	302.26	626.75	411.97	367.17	416.72	347.68
September								
High	154.60	219.10	399.00	715.00	467.50	486.00	416.90	347.75
Low	146.20	206.00	321.40	637.80	426.90	393.30	401.90	335.25
Average	150.36	212.89	358.25	676.45	444.52	434.39	411.30	341.09

October								
High	165.50	245.00	416.00	686.70	451.70	454.80	403.20	348.50
Low	153.80	220.10	366.80	623.50	423.00	386.40	376.20	333.50
Average	159.71	228.18	389.00	660.12	436.86	423.29	394.20	340.17
November								
High	168.20	223.00	419.10	648.00	430.60	442.60	403.00	350.45
Low	155.00	192.50	367.20	602.50	393.80	403.30	375.20	329.00
Average	162.36	204.64	391.33	622.02	412.17	415.23	382.31	340.86
December								
High	166.50	227.00	517.80	628.70	422.50	461.90	403.40	332.00
Low	155.60	195.80	426.00	544.00	393.30	431.70	372.60	307.50
Average	160.88	209.11	466.39	593.29	409.21	444.87	386.63	319.74
Annual								
High	168.20	245.00	517.80	825.00	597.00	486.00	510.10	404.60
Low	127.30	167.40	217.60	463.00	388.50	298.00	372.60	307.50
Average	148.11	193.36	307.82	611.98	459.02	376.23	424.12	360.29

SOURCE: *Handy & Harman*

Nevertheless, when a combination of events converge, the market can get crazy. In 1985, for example, just when everyone was writing gold's obituary, the market turned in its biggest one-day jump (about $35) since the halcyon days of 1980. That move was sparked by concerns over the U.S. banking system, a weakening dollar, and the fact that gold was already looking mighty cheap to many investors.

After years of hearing people cry wolf, gold buyers have simply stopped listening. Now they react to more pragmatic shifts—in inflation, interest rates, and other supply/demand factors.

Individual investors acquired a good deal of market savvy over the first decade that gold ownership was allowed after 1975. They buy when the price is right. Nothing shows that better than monthly sales figures for gold bullion coins such as Krugerrands—a key barometer of individual investor interest in the gold market.

In the last few months of 1981 and first two months of 1982, while the price of gold was dropping from $425 to $375, purchases of Krugerrands were dropping from about 400,000 ounces per month to 300,000 ounces.

In March 1982 the price of gold plunged to nearly $300 per ounce. But gold coin sales went in the opposite direction, more than doubling to 665,000 ounces. Investors clearly saw a bargain, and they were right.

In April the price jumped back up again. Coin sales tumbled to 142,000 ounces. As the price rose, coin sales fell even further later that year, until November. That month the price of gold dropped and investors again went in to buy with their wallets open.

The Gold "Constant" Destroyed?

Two all-time favorite arguments of gold promoters are that the metal has remained a monetary constant and that it has been a "store of value" for thousands of years. They have all kinds of charts to prove it. But charts can mislead. It all depends on what time period you wish to look at. For periods longer than eight or ten years, the argument holds. For any less time, you run into trouble.

Gold in the first half of the 1980s was no constant. Nor was it much of a store of value as the price bounced between $285 and $800 per ounce. Few investors who bought at $600 only to stare a $300 price in the face five years later would say they had purchased protection for their assets and purchasing power.

Who Sets the Price?

There is no single answer to this question. The daily price of gold moves like a slow wave around the world's time zones, between markets . . . back and forth, up and down. In recent years, New York has bullied the rest of the world to grab a leading a role in world gold trading. Other trading centers include London, Zurich, Hong Kong, Singapore, Tokyo, Chicago, and Winnipeg (Canada). In all, there are fifteen major trading centers for gold around the world. In the United States, the Commodity Exchange, Inc. (COMEX), in New York, is a key price-setting center.

But there still are only two leading "primary" trading centers, London and Zurich. A primary market receives the newly mined gold and releases it to the rest of the world markets. New York is a big market only on paper.

Zurich claims to be the most important primary market for gold trading in the world. It is through Zurich that the world's two largest gold-producing nations—South Africa and the Soviet Union—deal most of their gold.

The London Fix

But the London gold market remains the most visible to millions of American investors. That's where the twice-daily ritual the world knows as the London Fix is performed. What they "fix" is the price of gold, and those prices are then used as indicators for other traders around the world. The gold price you read in the newspaper may be the London fixing price.

Every business day—once in the morning, again that afternoon—representatives from five elite gold trading firms in London powwow to decide on a price for their gold. The five firms that participate are Mocatta & Goldsmid Ltd. (founded 1684); Sharps, Pixley Ltd. (a subsidiary of Kleinwort, Benson Ltd.) founded about 1750; N. M. Rothschild & Sons Ltd. (founded 1804); Johnson Matthey Bankers Ltd. (founded 1817); and the "youngster" of the crowd, Samuel Montagu & Co., Ltd. (founded 1853).

Five individuals from these firms meet privately in a discreet room at N. M. Rothschild in London. It's all very "starched collar" but still has the air of a college fraternity ceremony with all its flag waving and special hand signals. The meeting chairman suggests different prices, until the number of buyers represented by these traders, and the number of sellers, balances. At that point, the price is "fixed."

But don't be confused. The price of gold is anything but fixed. Once this price is announced in London, traders elsewhere around the world set about changing it. The London Fix is a key indicator of the market direction, but by no means is it immovable.

CHAPTER 3

Silver: Some Basics for Investors

- **A Short Silver Price History**
- **Silver Battles: Ripoff or Opportunity?**
- **The Silver Saga in the United States**
- **Where the Silver Comes From**
- **The Silver Surplus**
- **Silver Manipulations**
- **Whither Silver Now?**

Silver is different in critical ways from gold. For one, it is vastly more plentiful. Silver is more of an industrial metal than gold, but its price still reacts to investor whims. Silver is a hybrid-type metal, sharing characteristics with gold and displaying some of its own quirks as a commodity. Its price has proven to be more jumpy than gold's, although at times it has been called gold's poodle—wherever gold's price goes, silver's is sure to follow.

A SHORT SILVER PRICE HISTORY

The ups and downs of silver's price closely track the ups and downs of gold since 1970. That year the price of silver averaged $1.77. It dipped in 1971 to an average price of $1.54, then tripled in price by 1974, when it averaged $4.70 per ounce. For the next four years silver was relatively stable. The fireworks started again in 1978. Silver began the year at $4.91 per ounce and ended at just over $6.00.

In 1979 the dam broke. The price of silver climbed steadily, ending the decade of the seventies at $28 per ounce under some highly unusual circumstances. The cash price hit the outlandish $48 mark on January 21, 1980 before the bubble burst. By the end of that year, the price had crashed to $15.65, and the slide continued in 1981, ending that year at $8.25. June 21 marked the other end of the price pendulum, as silver bottomed out at $4.88.

That was considered incredibly cheap and it did not last long. Within six months, the price had doubled once again, to over $10 per ounce. In 1983 it closed in on $15 per ounce again, but that didn't last. Again silver lived up to its reputation as a volatile metal, losing more than 50 percent of its price by 1985, when it fell below $6.00 per ounce.

One example illustrates how the market can react to inflationary expectations, in this case linked to the price of oil: In 1982, when OPEC reduced the price of a barrel of oil from $34 to $29, inflation expectations also dropped. The price of silver plunged 32 percent in just twelve days, from $14.74 to $10.02.

SILVER BATTLES: RIPOFF OR OPPORTUNITY?

Silver has become a battleground among competing special interests, leaving investors to scratch their heads wondering what to believe. The folks who produce silver—the silver mining companies—would like everyone to believe that prices are headed up, up, up. They are joined by the brokers, the dealers, and sundry silver promotion bulls.

In the other corner are the companies that *use* silver in their products—photographic companies, electronics manufacturers, makers of

Tracking the Price of Silver

U.S. $ Per Troy Ounce

	1977	1978	1979	1980	1981	1982	1983	1984
January								
High	4.52	5.03	6.75	48.00	16.75	8.32	13.86	8.58
Low	4.30	4.83	5.96	33.65	12.72	7.81	10.86	7.90
Average	4.41	4.94	6.25	38.25	14.75	8.03	12.40	8.18
February								
High	4.72	5.04	7.93	39.00	14.05	8.66	14.75	9.81
Low	4.45	4.84	6.66	31.00	12.37	7.80	10.95	8.70
Average	4.54	4.94	7.42	35.08	13.02	8.27	13.96	9.13
March								
High	4.96	5.47	7.76	36.70	13.25	7.82	11.28	10.04
Low	4.71	4.93	7.12	11.10	11.52	6.90	10.13	9.35
Average	4.84	5.28	7.45	24.13	12.34	7.21	10.62	9.65
April								
High	4.87	5.40	7.85	16.40	12.27	7.59	12.37	9.62
Low	4.68	4.90	7.28	13.10	10.90	6.14	10.80	8.90
Average	4.78	5.12	7.49	14.50	11.44	7.31	11.69	9.22

	1977	1978	1979	1980	1981	1982	1983	1984
May								
High	4.80	5.41	8.77	13.55	11.34	6.89	13.60	9.26
Low	4.50	4.95	7.95	10.80	10.31	6.26	12.06	8.63
Average	4.69	5.12	8.37	12.53	10.85	6.67	12.98	8.97
June								
High	4.58	5.47	8.76	17.65	10.86	6.06	12.63	9.45
Low	4.32	5.23	8.30	14.18	8.57	4.89	11.09	8.33
Average	4.45	5.32	8.54	15.74	10.00	5.58	11.75	8.74
July								
High	4.62	5.61	9.56	16.95	9.10	7.31	12.42	8.30
Low	4.39	5.16	8.55	15.15	8.29	5.57	11.30	6.90
Average	4.50	5.33	9.14	16.05	8.63	6.50	12.09	7.42
August								
High	4.57	5.89	10.47	16.33	9.64	8.31	12.75	7.92
Low	4.33	5.35	8.74	15.57	8.30	6.22	11.52	7.09
Average	4.45	5.51	9.33	15.89	8.93	7.14	12.10	7.61
September								
High	4.66	5.70	16.85	24.25	11.32	9.31	12.32	7.63
Low	4.43	5.43	10.91	16.23	8.75	7.64	11.23	7.02
Average	4.54	5.58	13.15	20.14	10.04	8.73	11.92	7.26

October								
High	4.86	6.30	18.00	21.80	9.63	10.34	10.43	7.66
Low	4.63	5.66	15.45	18.47	8.96	7.96	8.71	7.14
Average	4.77	6.06	16.78	20.18	9.25	9.46	9.84	7.32
November								
High	4.95	6.05	18.77	19.65	9.25	10.83	9.69	7.80
Low	4.69	5.67	15.87	17.68	8.03	9.29	8.34	7.03
Average	4.83	5.88	16.60	18.65	8.55	9.89	8.84	7.49
December								
High	4.79	6.08	28.00	18.85	8.92	11.21	9.97	7.15
Low	4.61	5.84	18.75	14.32	7.95	10.07	8.54	6.26
Average	4.71	5.93	21.79	16.39	8.43	10.59	9.12	6.69
Annual								
High	4.96	6.30	28.00	48.00	16.45	11.21	14.74	10.04
Low	4.30	4.83	5.96	10.80	7.95	4.89	8.34	6.26
Average	4.62	5.43	11.02	20.63	10.52	7.95	11.44	8.14

SOURCE: *Handy & Harman*

silverware and jewelry. They argue that silver prices are rigged by the speculators and silver promoters.

Eminent economist John Kenneth Galbraith was right when he said that Americans have an inordinate desire to get rich quickly with a minimum of physical effort. That's why investor fantasies are still fueled by those peak prices of 1980—the $50 silver, $800 gold, $1,000 platinum. "If only they get to that point again" is a common investor lament. But those levels were reached under extraordinary circumstances, and it will take extraordinary circumstances to bring them back again.

The Consumption Myth

Silver bulls once argued that prices *must* go up because the world consumes much more silver than it produces. In the early 1980s that was proven wrong. It's a superficial reading of the supply and demand statistics and ignores silver recycling and other "secondary" sources of silver supplies. Silver is now a surplus metal.

The industrial silver users who make bigger profits when the price of silver is low are on the other side. They seem to believe that if they repeat out loud the words "Silver is not a good investment" often enough, everyone else will finally believe it and stop buying silver as an investment. Here's a closer look at different points of view toward silver as an investment today:

Ripoff of Innocent Victims?

Some industrial users of silver claim that they—and investors too—are the innocent victims of a well-orchestrated effort by silver promoters to manipulate the price of the metal and line their own pockets.

The price of silver *can* be manipulated. It has often happened in the past. The government, corporations, and mining interests have done it. Even super-rich individual investors have done it. But in what direction? With so many manipulators manipulating, it starts to balance out.

The government once did everything it could to prop up the price of silver. Then later on it tried its best to drive it down. Corporate interests have played the manipulation game—up and down. Private individuals—namely, the Hunts of Texas—manipulated up and were more successful at it than anyone could have imagined, at least for a short while. The commodity exchanges in the United States discovered they could get in on the manipulation game too. It was their pin that popped the Hunt brothers' silver-lined balloon in 1980. (More on this episode later.)

The silver users say there is far more silver "out there" than the investment bulls are willing to admit. Recycling has meant that much less silver is actually being *consumed*.

And there is a big difference between silver "use" and silver "consumption." Consumption means it is gone—used up. Silver *use* means it can be recovered—recycled. And that is precisely what's happening in the world's largest silver-using industry—photography.

Self-Serving Stands

Each side in the running, sometimes acrimonious silver controversy makes self-serving arguments. *The Silver Mania* (published in 1984) by W. J. Streeter, an executive in the photographic industry, says so right up front. But this book makes points that silver investors ignore at their own peril. If nothing else, it balances off the bubbly projections you hear from the brokers, dealers, and assorted members of the great silver promotion fraternity.

Industrial users of silver have adjusted to radically higher silver prices since the early 1970s. They blame almost everyone for the "silver mania" that pushed up the price (and pushes it down at times just as easily)—the government, politicians, and silver promoters. They also blame television, newspapers, and magazines for "reporting unquestioningly the self-serving propaganda" of brokers and dealers who fan the flames of distortion to earn larger profits from commissions that investors like you pay. And they will forever blame the Hunts, who inspired a price explosion the likes of which may never be seen again.

Silver Supply Shift

The key to comprehending worldwide supply and demand for silver is to understand recycling. Just as the world discovered energy conservation, it has also discovered conservation of other natural resources that are more expensive than they once were. Count silver in that group.

Silver fresh from the mine shaft was long considered *the* source of world supply. But that "primary" silver alone now makes up only about half—at times much less—of what fills silver demand each year. Companies that make photographic films, X-ray labs, and printing firms that use silver-based methods all have become proficient at recapturing silver. Market watchers who once counted that silver as "used"—missing and presumed dead—now come to discover it is not gone after all.

A huge amount of silver is involved. Add this "secondary" silver to world supplies and suddenly a decades-long silver supply shortfall becomes a large and growing surplus, ready to meet needs of industry and investors.

But much still depends on market conditions—a fact to which users would like to close their eyes. Like it or not, expectations of investors and speculators around the world will continue to dictate the price much the same way as they do for gold.

THE SILVER SAGA IN THE UNITED STATES

U.S. government meddling in the silver market stretches back throughout the nation's history. From today's vantage point, however, the most significant moves started in the 1930s, when individual ownership of gold was banned.

In 1933 and 1934 the government passed laws creating silver certificate money (a kind of forerunner of today's private precious metals certificates). Silver holdings in the United States were nationalized, and the government proceeded to buy up all the silver. Uncle Sam wanted to control the price and to have enough silver to back up the silver certificate money that was being printed.

The U.S. Treasury had the silver market in a stranglehold. By the 1950s, the government owned a whopping hoard of *2 billion* ounces. Compare that to today's U.S. silver stockpile of about 137 million ounces. Silver was so plentiful that during World War II it was used to mint nickels.

Then came changes. The price of silver was too low for many mines to profit, so they closed. But the economy was booming. Industry's demand for silver had to be met. By 1960 the United States had to stop stockpiling silver and start selling it—and sell it did. Within a few years the government's pile was nearly wiped out.

In the early 1960s the government suspended sales from its stockpile and prices started to climb. But that was also bad. Once it reached $1.29 per ounce, the silver in a silver dollar would be worth more than the coin's $1 face value (each coin has less than one ounce). At $1.38 per ounce, the silver content of dimes and quarters also passed the critical point and became worth more than the face value of those coins.

So in 1963 the United States started printing one-dollar Federal Reserve notes that could not be cashed in for silver. And shortly after that, with the Coinage Act of 1965, silver disappeared from quarters and dimes. The silver content of half-dollars was reduced to 40 percent—the so-called Kennedy Clad (a silver layer stuck to copper and nickel) half-dollars, minted until 1970.

The government was unable to keep the price of silver down by unloading large amounts from the national stockpile. But the Feds kept on selling through the 1960s, at times disposing of 2 million ounces at a crack in weekly auctions.

The Great Debate: To Sell or Not to Sell

The official government position is that there is no need to stockpile silver for national defense. That has sparked a running debate: What should be done with the remaining 137 million ounces in Uncle Sam's basement. Should it be sold off? If that happens, it could depress the market—and millions of investors as well. The industrial users would love it because their profits would rise. Mining and investor interests have argued against it.

In cash-starved Washington, that cache of silver is a tempting morsel. Congress approved additional sales of silver in 1981. The government was to auction off 100 million ounces by 1985. In late 1981, Uncle Sam sold off 2 million ounces of silver (at an average price of $9.37), but that was it. Irate mining companies fearing a profit squeeze squawked. Senator James McClure of Idaho (a big silver mining state) convinced Congress to change its position. Further silver sales by the government were halted.

The game continues. Lawmakers from silver mining states block silver sales and those from states with silver manufacturing interests push for the sales. Senator John Chafee of Rhode Island (a big jewelry-making center) said he'd like to sell *all* the silver to create jobs for his constituents.

Silver remains a political football. In the hands of the politicians the silver sales issue will again be used for dipping in the Washington pork barrel.

WHERE THE SILVER COMES FROM

In the early 1980s mine production of silver increased rapidly. It had bottomed in 1980—ironically the same year the price peaked—due to labor strikes and the fact that mines work their lowest-grade ores when prices are high, resulting in lower output. Unlike production of gold, platinum, and palladium, which is dominated by South Africa and the Soviet Union, silver is more evenly distributed around the globe, including much in the Americas. Here are the world's eight largest silver-producing countries, and their approximate shares of the pie as of 1985:

The Eight Largest Silver-Producing Nations

Country	Percent of Total
Mexico	16%
Peru	14%
Soviet Union	13%
United States	11%
Canada	10%
Australia	7%
Poland	5%
Chile	4%
50 other countries	20%

In the United States five large mining companies account for half the silver produced: Hecla Mining Co., ASARCO, Inc., Anaconda Co., Kennecott Corp., and Sunshine Mining. Anaconda and Kennecott both produce silver as a by-product of copper mining.

The expansion of silver mining output worldwide in the early 1980s was remarkable. But that's largely a matter of price. Silver mines are quick to shut when prices drop. And much of the world's silver is mined as a by-product of other metals—copper, zinc, lead, and nickel. Silver supplies from those sources are linked to other metal prices. When copper is down, the mines cut production, and by association, silver production is also cut. But when the price of copper (and the other metals) is up, it can subsidize production of silver, no matter what price it fetches in the market.

There are four types of silver mines: those that extract pure silver from high-grade ores; mines that extract pure silver from low-grade ores (at a higher production cost); mines that produce silver in roughly equal value proportions with other metals; and mines that produce silver as a minor by-product. In the United States, about half the silver comes from pure silver mines. Worldwide, only about a third comes from pure silver mine sources.

There are few reliable estimates of what it costs a mine to produce an ounce of silver. Each mine has different mining methods, ore grades, and other factors. Estimates of cost per ounce range from under $4 up to $12.

"Secondary" Silver

The other major source of silver is the "secondary supply," which accounts for at least 40 percent and at times more than 50 percent of supply. This includes scrap silver, silver from recycling, silver from melting old coins, and, curiously, silver sold by individuals in India and other South Asian nations.

Exporting silver from India is illegal, but it occurs anyway whenever the smugglers can get a good price on the international market. This "Indian Hoard" silver, as it is called, has long been considered a formidable force in the world market. Indians tend to hold silver in all its forms as a means of preserving wealth. When millions of these silver owners start to sell off their holdings, it can equal almost 10 to 20 percent of the world's total mine output for a year.

The amount of "scrap" silver entering the market from old silverware, old coins, and other sources depends mostly on price. When silver is up, the flood of secondary silver increases. When the price falls, so does scrap recovery. Industrial users continue to recycle regardless of small price changes.

Industrial demand for silver in the 1980s was growing, although over the longer term it was still down considerably from what it once was. New technologies of silver use and recovery are largely responsible. Photo films still use silver, but less of it. Little is wasted. Most experts believe that silver will still be used in films for many years since no substitute has been found to provide the same high-quality images.

Red Silver

Western analysts seem to know little for certain about silver production and consumption in the Communist nations. At times the Soviets export silver; other times they buy it. When they buy, the market considers that bullish and the price goes up.

The paucity of reliable information about silver in the Soviet Union, China, North Korea, and Poland—all major silver producers—makes this link to world prices little more than an elaborate guessing game, and one subject to wild rumors. Projections of supply and demand from this sector should be viewed with caution.

Investment Demand—the Great Equalizer

Investors around the world are the great silver market equalizer. The psychology mimics the gold market. In fact, silver rarely makes a major move alone. If investors believe inflation will pick up, that belief will translate into higher prices for all the precious metals.

The moves may vary in degree, depending on other factors. But, notes J. Aron & Company, "The expected rate of return on silver holdings is simply each investor's expectation of future price increases." When the price drops, investor demand can actually *increase*. Upward potential increases when the price drops. The result is that increased demand can become a self-fulfilling prophecy, either halting a slide or pulling the price back up.

THE SILVER SURPLUS

In the twenty-five years between 1960 and 1985, there were only two periods with a significant silver surplus—in the late 1960s when the U.S. Treasury was selling off huge amounts of the metal, and in the early to mid-1980s when mine production was up while industrial demand remained low.

J. Aron & Company, which publishes periodic research reports on silver, describes the investor role in silver:

> . . . the silver market has become more gold-like. In the gold market, jewelers and industrial users never consume all of the new metal entering the market; investors always absorb the additional gold, with the intensity of their demand relative to the quantity of metal available to them being a prime influence on the price. The fact that gold supplies exceed fabrication demand has never kept gold prices from rising sharply, nor will similar conditions make high or volatile silver prices impossible in the future.
>
> The growing importance of investors is probably the most significant change in the silver market. Investors have always played a central role, but . . . the character of their function in the silver market has been transformed.

Uses of Silver

These are the top commercial/industrial uses of silver in the United States, in order of importance:

photography
electrical contacts and conductors
brazing alloys and solders
sterling ware
jewelry
batteries
electronic-plated ware
catalysts
coins, medallions, and commemorative silver items
dental and medical use
mirrors

Photography is by far the largest silver user, accounting for 35 to 40 percent of total demand. The biggest industrial users of silver in the photo field are Eastman Kodak, Agfa-Gevaert, Fuji Photo, Ciba-Geigy, 3M, Polaroid, and Du Pont.

Growth in the photographic market has outpaced the industry's successful efforts to reduce the amount of silver it uses. Photo firms have slashed the amount of silver used in films, reduced the amount needed to develop that film, and sharpened their talent for recovering silver from spent photo materials—film, developing papers, and solutions.

The great fear among silver investors is elimination of silver from photography due to technological advances such as electronic photos. That would kill silver demand and presumably the price as well. But so far, photography remains a silver-based business. That's unlikely to change for the remainder of this century.

Is It All a Hoax?

Many reputable silver experts say the price is inevitably headed up over the long term. But a few dissenters claim the entire silver market is a cruel hoax perpetrated by greedy silver bulls, brokers, and dealers. They claim the price of silver rightly belongs at no more than $4 per ounce. Anything above $8 per ounce, they say, is market manipulation.

In this view, the "Invisible Hand"—the free market forces that tend to keep prices in line (first described by Adam Smith, father of modern economics)—will eventually force the price to those levels.

The trouble is, for every "expert" claiming silver is not a good investment, three claim that it is or will be. They need only cite the new control wielded by individual investors who will doubtless move in droves to buy silver at the next sign of a price boom. Even if silver is bountiful, when gold heads up, silver will follow.

SILVER MANIPULATIONS

The Soviets

The silver market has been manipulated so often that it is not difficult to believe it is happening again. The Soviets play the game well. In one instance, the Soviet Union started buying silver in Zurich. When word "got out," investors reacted by pushing up the price, as they often do on such news. But the Soviets had something else in mind. They had bought silver precisely to push up the price, for the rise in silver dragged gold up with it. A few days later, the Soviets were in the market selling their gold at the higher price, which is precisely what they wanted in the first place.

The Hunts

For many people, the name Hunt now conjures up visions of silver rather than ketchup. The Hunt brothers, Nelson Bunker and Herbert, once attempted to corner the world market in silver. By 1979 the Hunts already owned a large stake. In 1979 and 1980 they went wild buying silver futures contracts. The market went wild too.

In the futures business, scarcely anyone follows through and *buys* the commodity that the futures contract says they must buy. It's just not done. But rumors flew in 1980 that the Hunts and a few other wealthy buyers actually intended to take delivery of the silver they controlled.

Since futures contracts let any investor—you or the Hunts—control large amounts of the metal for a small down payment, the Hunts effectively "owned" the rights to more silver than the market could possibly have delivered all at once from its usual sources. That made some people panic. If the Hunts had demanded delivery, they would have cornered the market.

In January 1980, with silver at $35 per ounce, New York's Commodity Exchange Inc. (COMEX), where the Hunts were doing much of their trading, restricted the number of futures contracts that any individual could own. It didn't work. The Hunts got around it, and the price climbed to nearly $50 per ounce.

So, on January 21, after declaring an emergency, COMEX changed the rules of the game. They stopped *all* buying so the Hunts, or anybody else for that matter, could only *sell* their silver. And when they sold it would have to be to the big wholesale operators who control COMEX. The exchange had outmanipulated the manipulators.

As the price plunged, the Hunts lost *billions* of dollars. Casualties were many, including major brokerage firms that were buying for the Hunts; banks that had made loans to finance purchases; industrial users who nearly fainted from the price increases; and, of course, millions of investors who went along for the ride and got burned in the crash.

WHITHER SILVER NOW?

Proponents of the ''silver is bountiful'' view claim that in coming years, as the price drops, investors will begin to sell ''because their unrealistic expectations will not be realized.'' Even if they are right, however, it doesn't paint silver out of the individual investment picture. Like the weather, silver prices will continue to change. The lower they go, the more room there will be for an eventual upswing if you're willing to take the long view.

So long as silver is linked to the other precious metals in the collective mind of worldwide investors, and to inflation expectations, interest rates, and other outside influences, there will be moves up and moves down. And that will always have the makings of profit potential for astute investors who know the ''rules'' and the dangers.

The silver users themselves have predicted that new demand for silver ''will be impressive'' into the 1990s. That demand will come from economic growth, and from new uses for silver in electronics. Despite a bountiful supply, that still sounds like an argument for higher prices.

CHAPTER 4

Platinum and Palladium: The New Twenty-First-Century Precious Metals

- **What's Special About Platinum and Palladium?**
- **Platinum Versus Gold: The Price Ratio**
- **Platinum and Palladium Performance**
- **Precious (Industrial) Metals**
- **Russian Roulette: Or Who's Got the Platinum and Palladium?**
- **America's Stockpile Shortage**
- **No Surplus Here**
- **Newfound Investor Demand**

For millions of precious metals investors in the United States and around the world, platinum and palladium are the new kids on the block. They have become the precious metals of the high-tech generation—twenty-first-century investments.

Most people recognize platinum as a precious metal even more rare than gold. It is the "noble" metal. But *palladium*? Actually, it's a sister metal of platinum and the black sheep of our precious metals foursome.

Platinum and palladium are the most prominent members of the "platinum group," which in addition includes rhodium, ruthenium, iridium, and osmium. For practical purposes, platinum and palladium are the only two of interest to the cautious investor.

Investors in the United States have only recently discovered these metals. Their future looks bright—even more so than for the traditional investment precious metals, gold and silver. The relationship between platinum/palladium and silver/gold is clouded. They fall loosely into the same investment field of precious metals, but investors view these metals in very different lights.

Platinum and palladium joined the investment family on a grand scale only in the 1980s. But once individual investors started demanding the noble metals, brokers and dealers added them to their spice shelf of investment choices. Major brokerage firms that once offered only gold and silver have added platinum and sometimes palladium to the list.

Not long ago it was a hassle to invest in platinum or palladium because the choices were so limited, the market much smaller, and the dealers in the area more highly specialized. That's changing. Though platinum and palladium are still not as accessible as gold and silver, they are gaining rapidly.

One place you *won't* find platinum and palladium investments is at your local bank. Even though some commercial banks have moved strongly into precious metals, they are not permitted to offer platinum and palladium under current banking laws. That too could change.

WHAT'S SPECIAL ABOUT PLATINUM AND PALLADIUM?

• Platinum is an immensely strong metal—durable, virtually corrosion-proof, and stable even at extreme temperatures. That's why it was chosen as the material from which to construct the world's "official yardsticks"—the standard weights and measures.

• The Soviet Union, a leading producer of platinum metals, minted platinum coins between 1826 and 1846; and again to commemorate the 1980 Moscow Olympics.

• Platinum has a silky white sheen to it, much prized in jewelry in many parts of the world. Celebrated French jeweler Carl Fabergé made some of his famous eggs using platinum. Cartier used this metal in his watches. The Japanese adore platinum jewelry more than gold.

• Platinum is one of the world's most versatile metals, in addition to being one of the rarest. It is a much harder metal than gold or silver, with a considerably higher melting point (1,979° C, compared to 1,063° for gold). It is more durable than gold, yet still malleable. It's also a very dense metal. Says platinum refiner Johnson Matthey, "Because of its great density, greater than gold and twice that of lead . . . the amount of platinum which comes to the Western World market each year would occupy a *five-foot cube,* or could comfortably fit into the passenger compartment of a London taxi cab. Twenty-five of those taxis could hold the estimated total quantity (2,000 tons) of platinum mined and sold in all of history."

• It takes 4 tons of ore to produce one ounce of gold, but *10 tons* of ore to produce a single ounce of platinum.

How rare is this metal? Consider these average annual mine production results over a recent ten-year period, from the early 1970s to the early 1980s, for seven major metals:

Platinum Rarity: Seven Metals Compared

	Tons
Platinum	80
Gold	1,000
Silver	10,000
Uranium	25,000
Nickel	500,000
Copper	9,000,000
Iron	500,000,000

There is thought to be a fifty-five-year aboveground supply of gold sufficient to meet industrial needs, a two-year supply of platinum, and no additional supply of palladium.

PLATINUM VERSUS GOLD: THE PRICE RATIO

Some savvy market watchers have long used the platinum-to-gold ratio as a barometer of how the noble metal is doing. Platinum at times commands a premium over the price of an ounce of gold, while at other times it costs less.

Through most of the 1970s, the price of an ounce of platinum was higher than an ounce of gold. In 1974, for example, the average price of platinum was $200 per ounce; $159 for gold. In 1975, the first year Americans were again permitted to own gold, the yellow metal moved out front slightly. By 1978, however, platinum had gained the upper hand once again. Its average price that year was $261, compared to $193 for gold. The gap was even wider in 1979, when platinum averaged $441 and gold $307. In 1980 platinum topped out at $1,040 per ounce, some $200 per ounce higher than gold's 1980 peak.

In the early 1980s the situation reversed. Platinum started selling for less than gold. In 1981 and 1982 gold outpaced the noble metal. In 1983 the two ran about neck and neck, with platinum once again taking the lead by 1985, and so on.

While there probably is no fixed relationship that works to draw platinum and gold prices into a set alignment, some investors take it as a signal that platinum is a bargain whenever its price drops below gold's. Because of platinum's extreme rarity and primary use as an industrial commodity, many experts believe it should sell for a premium above the price of gold, whenever industrial demand is strong— which is to say, during periods of economic vitality in the United States and other industrialized nations.

PLATINUM AND PALLADIUM PERFORMANCE

Between 1982 and 1985 platinum and palladium proved just how well and how differently they could perform compared to their more popular competitors, gold and silver. From a low of $48 per ounce in 1982, palladium soared. It more than tripled in price to nearly $170 per ounce by 1984, when it took a breather. Platinum couldn't match that performance but still did better than gold and silver. At other times, however, depending on the many variables that affect metals prices, the results could be completely different.

Tracking the Prices of Platinum and Palladium

	Platinum	*Palladium*
1975		
High	178.00	117.00
Low	140.00	42.40
Average	153.16	68.25
1976		
High	183.50	62.00
Low	135.60	37.40
Average	154.86	47.76
1977		
High	186.20	59.50
Low	144.80	41.20
Average	159.15	49.69
1978		
High	384.90	86.70
Low	185.60	52.40
Average	261.34	63.71
1979		
High	716.00	230.50
Low	342.40	72.60
Average	440.79	117.49
1980		
High	1,040.10	317.50
Low	482.60	142.00
Average	681.49	198.87
1981		
High	593.50	147.00
Low	369.60	63.30
Average	445.31	93.66

	Platinum	Palladium
1982		
High	389.70	100.60
Low	243.60	48.90
Average	326.57	66.12
1983		
High	498.70	172.50
Low	377.10	88.60
Average	425.69	133.84
1984		
High	414.00	165.40
Low	286.10	121.50
Average	358.94	146.49

SOURCE: J. Aron & Company

Investors still play a minor (though increasing) role in the platinum and palladium markets. Investment demand accounts for roughly 42 percent of the gold market each year, 31 percent of the silver market, and a mere four-tenths of one percent of the platinum market. In the palladium market, investor demand doesn't even show up yet on the scale.

PRECIOUS (INDUSTRIAL) METALS

The key movers and shakers in the platinum and palladium markets are the industrial users: the auto and electronics industries, oil refiners, chemical companies, dental and medical fields, and the jewelry business. The United States is the world's largest user of these two metals.

In Japan platinum jewelry is king. In 1984, for example, demand for platinum jewelry there totaled nearly half a million troy ounces, compared to a paltry 10,000 ounces used for that purpose in the United States.

Industrial demand for platinum dates to the 1940s, when oil refiners started using it to improve the octane rating of gasoline. From there, demand took off. Overall demand for platinum in the industrialized Western nations doubled from 1950 to 1960, doubled again from 1960 to 1970, and doubled yet again from 1970 to 1980.

The auto industry today is the largest user of platinum in the United States. You might say that as GM goes so goes the platinum market. Until 1974 autos and platinum had little in common. Then along came the pollution control laws, and a new word entered the American lexicon: catalytic converter. This device cuts down on air pollutants. Each car made in the United States since that time must have one. Platinum (and sometimes palladium) is the catalyst in the catalytic converter.

But that market for platinum in the United States has pretty much matured. Any growth must come from overall growth in car sales. Not so outside the United States, where a vast potential new market for platinum in catalytic converters remains untapped. Most other nations have not yet adopted U.S.-style antipollution steps for auto exhaust. But many of them now realize that their countries are being choked by auto exhaust. Every step closer they come to requiring catalytic converters on their cars is considered a bullish move for platinum and palladium.

Precious metals analysts expect expanding demand from automakers worldwide to boost platinum and palladium prices into the 1990s. That may be an oversimplified view, however, since many other factors are involved.

The Oil Connection

Pollution control devices are not the only auto industry link to platinum and palladium. Oil is another. Both of these metals figure into the oil refining process, helping produce high-octane unleaded gasoline—the very fuel needed to operate all those converter-equipped cars.

This is also a key to understanding why platinum and palladium may react differently to inflationary expectations than will gold and silver. Low inflation usually reduces investor demand for gold and silver, and the prices of those two metals drop. But low inflation often *boosts* industrial recovery, and hence industrial demand for platinum and palladium. If the chain holds firm, that pushes the prices of these two metals up. Since investor demand is a much smaller piece in the platinum/palladium price puzzle, investor disillusionment with precious metals due to low inflation can have less of an effect on platinum and palladium.

The same reasoning applies for oil prices. Lower oil prices, often a bad omen for gold, can bring vitality to platinum sales. Cheaper gas means more driving, which means more people buying cars.

RUSSIAN ROULETTE:
OR WHO'S GOT THE PLATINUM
AND PALLADIUM?

One reason platinum and palladium prices bounce so readily is the precarious supply situation. Guess who controls a bear's share of the world's platinum and palladium? Yup . . . the Soviets . . . *and* the South Africans. The United States, which uses most of the world's supply but has precious little platinum and palladium of its own, must depend on those two nations. For two such vital strategic metals, that's not a healthy situation.

South Africa has a lock on supplying platinum to the non-Communist world. About 70 percent of the metal used by Westerners comes from that strife-filled nation. Most of the rest comes from the Soviet Union.

With palladium, the pecking order is reversed. The USSR supplies the world, *when it wants to*. That fact alone gives the market the jitters. Best estimates (no one's really sure) say that the Soviet Union satisfies 60 to 75 percent of the world's appetite for palladium. That situation adds an element of danger that makes an investment here seem like an adventure in international intrigue. But with greater risk comes greater profit potential.

South Africa is the second largest producer of palladium. Canada is third, but produces only a tiny amount of platinum and palladium by comparison.

The slightest hint or rumor that the Soviets are cutting or increasing their sales to the West can send prices and speculators scrambling. The Soviets can be expected to play the market to their maximum advantage. They may withhold metal to drive prices up but would not be expected to flood the market with palladium since they have a vested interest in preventing a market collapse.

Platinum Mining

South Africa has the only mines in the world that produce platinum and palladium as the primary metal. In the USSR and Canada platinum and palladium are mined as a by-product of nickel, although certainly a crucial by-product.

What's more, only *two* mining companies—Rustenburg Platinum

Mines Ltd. and Impala Platinum Ltd.—account for the vast majority of platinum that comes from South Africa. In effect, the Western industrialized nations depend on these two mines for most of their platinum.

The United States produces a minuscule amount of platinum and palladium, but, according to the U.S. Bureau of Mines, that amount is negligible compared with what is used here. And the United States would be hard-pressed to find a replacement for foreign platinum and palladium imports if supplies are ever curtailed. If that happens, hopes would fall to two areas: stepped-up recycling (that's already happening), and bringing into production as yet untapped platinum/palladium deposits in Montana and Minnesota.

Substitutes? The government says that for auto antipollution devices, platinum and palladium have little competition. Each car typically requires less than one-tenth of an ounce of the metal as a catalyst, so the amount this item adds to the sticker price is minimal. Silver and gold can be substituted in many electronics industry uses of platinum and palladium. But in oil refining, substitutes don't work as well.

AMERICA'S STOCKPILE SHORTAGE

To try to loosen the foreign stranglehold on America's platinum pipeline, the federal government has decided to create a stockpile. That way, if the Soviets pull the plug, or a revolution disrupts the mines in South Africa, there will at least be a *short-term* supply to fall back on. To that end, the United States has set goals for itself—stockpile goals meant to discourage any OPEC-like cartel from holding the nation hostage to platinum.

But the government has been well short of its goals, and going nowhere fast. In 1985, for example, the "U.S. Strategic Stockpile" of platinum and palladium looked like this:

"U.S. Strategic Stockpile" of Platinum and Palladium

Metal	Official Goal	In Stock	Shortfall
platinum	1.3 million oz.	450,000 oz.	850,000 oz.
palladium	3 million oz.	1.3 million oz.	1.7 million oz.

The amount of platinum and palladium in the strategic stockpile is less than half of the nation's goal. The supply outlook for these strategic metals is one reason Washington treads softly on the issue of economic sanctions against South Africa's apartheid government.

Private industry has its own stockpiles, but they wouldn't last long in an emergency. In fact, some industrial users have already let their stockpiles dwindle since the 1970s, believing the federal hoard can provide the needed cushion.

A cutoff of platinum from South Africa or palladium from the USSR would most certainly send the prices of those two precious/strategic metals soaring. Domestic production might increase; Canadian production would help, but not much.

A Sensitive Market

The markets in platinum and palladium, especially the latter, are far smaller and thinner than the markets in gold and silver. That means they are more sensitive to supply and demand disruptions.

But arguments that platinum and palladium are sensitive *only* to industrial demand, and not speculative demand from investors, ignore the coattail effect. Indeed, prices of these two metals will dance more rapidly to the industrial demand tune. But gold and silver cannot make a major move without dragging platinum and palladium along for at least part of the ride.

NO SURPLUS HERE

With gold and silver, there is usually plenty of metal left over to meet investment needs after commercial users have taken their share. With platinum and palladium, precious little, if any, is left. As these metals continue to attract attention from investors and speculators worldwide, prices could be forced higher.

The world's largest consumers of the metals are two industrial giants, Japan and the United States. The demand for platinum and palladium from these two nations, together with supply uncertainties in South Africa and the Soviet Union, makes the world market something of a seesaw. Demand down, supply up. Supply up, demand down. Demand down, supply down. You get the idea.

Platinum and palladium have also performed solo in recent years. A major precious metals research firm called the increase in palladium use in the early 1980s "dramatic" and "astounding." It was so strong, in fact, that available supplies were not enough. The shortage pushed the price up and forced the users of this metal to snitch from their rainy-day stockpiles. (The industry jargon for this is a "drawdown of market inventories.")

The electronics industry is the largest user of palladium, followed by dental/medical users, the auto industry, chemical industry, oil refiners, jewelers, and glassmakers.

The auto industry creates most of the demand by far for platinum, followed by petroleum, chemicals, electronics, glass, dental/medical, and jewelry. For many years total demand for platinum was greater than for palladium. The less expensive of the two metals, palladium, passed its higher-priced kin for the first time in 1981, according to U.S. Bureau of Mines figures.

Palladium Supply: Cutting It Close

Supply and demand for palladium has always been nip and tuck. As supplies became short and prices rose in the mid-1980s, more and more palladium was being recovered from scrap sources.

In the United States ever larger numbers of junked cars are equipped with platinum- or palladium-containing catalytic converters. Those cars will become a major source of "secondary" platinum and palladium supply in years to come, just as the move to tighten emission standards in other countries will create more demand for the metals. The amount of platinum and palladium recovered from scrap sources was expected to increase *tenfold* from 1985 to 1990. In just one year—1982 to 1983, for example—recycling of scrap palladium increased 63 percent worldwide.

Even if the supplies of platinum and palladium remain stable, a few metals experts forecast a doubling of demand for the two metals—largely due to increased interest among investors—between 1985 and 1990. These same crystal ball gazers predict that by the 1990s an ounce of platinum should be worth twice what an ounce of gold is worth, a more realistic reflection of its short supply compared to gold.

They also say that palladium, which has run about one-third to one-half the price of gold, should be selling for about the same price as gold.

Fuel Cells: New Platinum Boom?

The auto and electronics industries may demand more platinum and palladium in the 1980s and 1990s. But even that could be dwarfed if predictions of other new uses for the metals come true. Chief among them is the fuel cell, a batterylike device that would include an electrode coated with a catalyst made of palladium or platinum. Like most newfangled energy-saving inventions, however, development has been slower than expected. Lower oil prices removed the urgency. And there's no telling how much palladium or platinum would be used. A substitute might even be found before the device reaches full-scale commercial production, if at all. An increase in the price of platinum might conceivably render such a device uneconomical.

One possible "surprise" use of palladium: cigarette filters containing tiny amounts of palladium fibers that will do for cigarette smokers what catalytic converters do for the air in our cities.

Be careful about how much stock you put in predictions of ever greater demand for these metals due to advances in technology. The same technology that invents new products and uses for platinum and palladium can also find substitutes and ways for companies to use less.

NEWFOUND INVESTOR DEMAND

By the latter 1980s investment demand for these two metals—once a mere fly on the back of the platinum/palladium buffalo—had become more like a gang of fleas. The impact was being felt. Hundreds of thousands of ounces of platinum are now bought by investors yearly. The market buffalo who once wrote off the investors actively court them with platinum bars in small sizes, platinum coins, certificate and accumulation plans, and other enticements.

But although they are blood brothers, the market personalities of platinum and palladium differ in some important ways.

Platinum and palladium are not now, nor have they ever been, considered "monetary" metals. Unlike gold and silver, there are no huge stockpiles of these metals in government and central bank vaults hanging over the market like a sword of Damocles.

Of all the precious metals, palladium in the 1980s has become the hardest to come by. The world has used more of this metal than it has produced, causing a palladium deficit that drove up the price.

Palladium was being used in more and more industrial products as a substitute for the more expensive (for now) gold and platinum. And that's what resulted in the lightning quick 250 percent increase in the price of palladium from mid-1982 to the end of 1983.

As I write, today's newspaper has a story describing a new patent issued in Washington (#4,486,274) for a method of coating telephone parts with palladium. The process, patented by AT&T Bell Labs, was reportedly saving that industrial giant millions of dollars a year. It permits electronic equipment to be plated with "gold-flashed" palladium instead of with pure gold. According to this account, AT&T was able to reduce the amount of gold required by 95 percent. Bad news for gold; bullish news for palladium.

But if this upstart metal gets too expensive, it no longer will make sense to use it in place of gold or platinum, and the market would shift back in the other direction. That starts to happen when the price of palladium reaches more than 50 percent of the price of platinum. An ounce of platinum goes twice as far as an ounce of palladium.

Johnson Matthey, an international metals dealer, publishes a slick booklet titled *Platinum*, which reviews the world platinum situation yearly. Free for the asking from: Johnson Matthey, 100 High Street, Southgate, London, N146ET, England.

Pricing the Metals

Prices quoted for platinum and palladium can be confusing. You may still see as many as three different prices for the metals. The producer price, although not followed much anymore, was once set by the big platinum producers. It was the price their best customers would pay for platinum or palladium on long-term contracts. This price often bore little relation to the free market price of the metals.

There are also spot or dealer prices for the metal. They move up and down according to what the market dictates. One key price the market watches is the price set on the New York Mercantile Exchange (NYMEX) where platinum and palladium futures contracts are traded.

From a mid-1980s vantage point, the future for platinum and palladium looked to be the most robust of all the precious metals.

Where the Metals Come From: A Supply Comparison

GOLD			SILVER		
Mine Production:	63%		Mine Production:	56%	
Secondary Supply: (scrap recovery)	26%		Secondary Supply:	41%	
			Other:	3%	
Communist Sales:	11%				

PLATINUM			PALLADIUM		
Mine Production:	79%		Mine Production:	37%	
Secondary Supply:	8%		Secondary Supply:	12%	
Soviet Sales:	13%		Soviet Sales:	51%	

SOURCE: J. Aron & Company/Goldman, Sachs

Precious Metals Demand: Who Uses the Gold, Silver, Platinum, and Palladium?

GOLD			SILVER		
Jewelry Demand:	44%		Industrial Demand:	58%	
Investment Demand:	41%		Investment Demand:	31%	
Industrial Demand:	15%		Jewelry Demand:	8%	
			Coins:	3%	

PLATINUM			PALLADIUM		
Industrial Demand:	76%		Industrial Demand:	97%	
Jewelry Demand:	23.6%		Jewelry Demand:	3%	
Investment Demand:	0.4%		Investment Demand:	negligible	

SOURCE: J. Aron & Company/Goldman, Sachs

PART II

The Many Ways to Invest in Precious Metals

CHAPTER 5

The Quick List of Investment Choices

- **Gold's Selection Edge**
- **Ways to Invest: The Quick List**

Part of the fun in precious metals is choosing from the slick new menu of ways to invest. You can buy lumps of gold, silver, platinum, and palladium fashioned (the precious metals term is "fabricated") into a hundred sizes and shapes—something for everybody.

Choose from bullion bars, ingots, and coins . . . certificates that signal your ownership of a specified amount of metals . . . automatic purchase and "coin-of-the-month" clubs . . . plans that let you buy lots of gold with a small down payment . . . shares in companies that mine the metals . . . mutual funds that pool money from many investors like yourself to invest in mining companies and bullion . . . precious metals options . . . futures contracts . . . hybrid products that combine these features . . . and still more.

You can walk into a precious metals shop (a "dealer" or "broker"), plunk down your money, and walk out with your gold, silver, or whatever. You can buy over the telephone, often locking in the price as of that moment. You can invest through the mail, perhaps through your local bank or stockbroker, and manage it all on your personal computer from the comfort of your living room.

GOLD'S SELECTION EDGE

Gold, the most popular metal of the foursome, offers the widest select-tion. Silver is not far behind. If platinum is your choice, the pickings will be a bit slimmer. Since 1982, however, platinum's popularity has soared among individual investors in the United States. And that hasn't gone unnoticed by the companies that mine, fabricate, and sell this vital commodity. Platinum is rapidly gaining on gold and silver as an investment choice.

Increasing numbers of major precious metals dealers now offer palladium on their metals menus as well. You may see it classified as a *strategic metal*. In spite of palladium's low public profile, you should have little trouble satisfying an appetite for this particular metal.

WAYS TO INVEST: THE QUICK LIST

Here's a capsule version of today's new investment menu of gold, silver, platinum, and palladium. Each method is detailed in later chapters:

• **Bullion Bars, Wafers, Ingots,** or whatever other names they've thought up for these often rectangular blocks of gold, silver, platinum, and palladium. This is what you see in glossy photos of precious metals that adorn the dealer brochures. Sizes range from a few grams to the hard-to-lift gold bricks.

• **Bullion Coins** have become the bread and butter of the market, especially for small investors. The most widely recognized of all the gold bullion coins are the South African Krugerrand and the Canadian Maple Leaf. Silver and platinum bullion coins are also available. Be careful not to confuse *bullion* coins with *numismatic* or *rare* coins. They are two totally different items.

• **Bagged Coins or "Junk Silver"** are the coins you once carried in your pocket—the pre-1965 dimes, quarters, and half-dollars that were made of real silver (well, at least 90 percent silver). Now they offer a unique way to tap into the silver market.

• **Precious Metals Certificates** are the fastest, most convenient way to invest directly in precious metals. They've opened the doors to precious metals ownership for millions of individuals. Certificates offer all of the potential in owning metals but spare you the headaches of lugging the stuff around, storing it, paying taxes on it, insuring it, and making sure it's real. A precious metals certificate is a piece of paper that says you own a certain amount of metal. This dandy invention was originally called a *warehouse receipt* and also a *delivery order*. Those relics of industry jargon have largely fallen into disuse as far as consumers are concerned but still crop up on occasion.

• **Depository Receipts.** This is another piece of paper that says you own a certain amount of gold, similar to a precious metals certificate. It's also one of the safest ways for an investor to own gold. The main difference centers around whether it is "fungible" or not. If the term "fungible" worries you, the same concept is also known as "segregated" as opposed to "nonsegregated." It describes a minor but potentially crucial difference in how the company from which you bought the metal stores it for you.

• **"Designer Metals": Private Mint Medallions.** Many national governments have plunged headlong into the business of minting gold and silver coins to sell (at a profit) to investors. Canada, Mexico, the United States, the Soviet Union, South Africa, Austria, and Great Britain are just a few of the most prominent competitors. But governments don't have a monopoly on this market. Large private mints and metals firms also make and sell their own "brand name" or designer coins. Technically they should be called coinlike ingots or medallions since they cannot be spent like regular coins.

• **Automatic Purchase Plans.** The name says it. You set up an account, tell the dealer how much you wish to invest, and the firm will automatically buy gold, silver, platinum, or palladium for you on a set date as often as you like.

• **Low-Cost Accumulation Plans for Small Investors.** Some of the biggest-name brokerage firms on Wall Street (and Main Street) now offer precious metals purchase plans designed for small investors. Here you can start with as little as $100. A few commercial banks offer something similar, called a gold or silver passbook account. It works like a regular savings passbook account, except you're accumulating gold or silver instead of cash, and the account doesn't pay you any interest and isn't federally insured.

• **Rare Coins** —also known as *numismatic* coins. Precious metals purists don't normally consider an investment in rare coins as part of their world. Then again, coin collectors (who prefer the label "numismatists") consider an investment in these gold and silver rarities to be superior to precious metals alone. There's an overlap between these two fields that investors can exploit. Play it right and you could end up a double winner, tapping the best profit potential that precious metals *and* rare coins have to offer.

• **Leverage Contracts and Margin-Buying Plans.** This is easy. Avoid them. Under federal rules, only a handful of firms are specifically authorized to sell these contracts to investors. And even these firms have been under pressure to stop. But don't count on the protective arm of Uncle Sam to shield you from sleazy precious metals salesmen. Despite the rules, many so-called leverage firms have sprouted. Largely outcasts, they are some of the most unscrupulous operators around. They'll try to hook you with slick come-ons about huge profits with only a small amount of up-front money. Beware.

• **Hybrid Products.** The competition to snare your investment business is intense. And, as befits this slugfest atmosphere, the precious metals sales force keeps coming up with new products. Most are not new at all, but combine elements of other products into a single package. Included in this category are limited-risk and guaranteed buyback plans.

• **Mining Shares.** This is a stock market investment. Quite simply, you buy shares in a gold mine or other type of mining company. There are thousands—in the United States, Canada, Australia, South America, South Africa, and elsewhere. They include tiny pick-and-shovel mines and huge multinational corporations.

• **Precious Metals Mutual Funds** offer a quick, low-risk, low-cost way to stake a claim in the precious metals market. You buy shares in a fund that already owns lots of precious metals assets, usually gold mining shares. Professional managers do all the work for you. Mutual funds are a great way to get started. They offer "Gold for the Not So Bold."

• **Precious Metals Options.** It was a long time coming, but they finally thought up a way to invest in a commodity (such as gold or silver) and make big profits *even when the price is going down.* Called an option contract, it's a wonderful investment device—if you're the gambling type and are prepared to take the extra risk. If you win, the rewards can be handsome indeed. If you lose, you can lose it all.

• **Precious Metals Futures.** This is the realm of professional traders and sophisticated, monied investors who can afford to risk tens, if not hundreds of thousands of dollars on overnight price changes. The odds are heavily against you here.

CHAPTER 6

Risk:
The Precious Metals
Wild Card

- **How Much to Invest**
- **Different Precious Metals Risks**
- **Three Ways to Adjust Your Personal Risk Rheostat**

Risk is relative. A high-risk investment for you might be a moderate risk for your neighbor. All investments have a degree of risk, and investors have different risk tolerances.

Some precious metals investments are riskier than others, especially short term. The most adamant backers of gold investing would argue the point, saying that gold is one of the few really *safe* places to put your assets over the long term. Other forms of wealth, they say, especially cash, will ultimately deteriorate, but not gold. And that makes other investments far riskier, in this view.

Nevertheless, between its $800 peak in 1980 and its sub-$300 bottom in 1982 . . . back up to $500, then below $300 again in 1985, gold was no bedrock investment. Many investors made money during those years in precious metals and many others lost. There is precious little solace in being told prices are "bound to increase over the long term" when the gold you own is worth 20 percent less than when you bought it.

HOW MUCH TO INVEST

Whether you have a few thousand dollars in savings and investments or much more, only a small part of what you have should ever be invested in precious metals. The amount is not so important, but how much you have invested in metals in relation to your overall personal wealth is.

The figure you get depends on whom you talk to, how high interest rates are at the time, how other investment markets are doing, and other factors. Risk tolerance toward precious metals, or any investment for that matter, is a highly individual affair. It depends on your own ability to feel comfortable with risking money. It depends on your age; whether or not you have a family or plan to have one; your plans for the future; your other financial responsibilities and commitments. Few generalizations will be adequate. You must determine your own personal risk profile.

Many investors put far too large a portion of their personal savings in gold, silver, platinum, and palladium. Some people just get too wrapped up in the idea, or they get talked into making larger investments by aggressive brokers. There are so many different ways to invest in precious metals, as you'll soon see, that you could select six or eight seemingly different investments and before you know it you'd have tied up way too much of your money.

Financial planners suggest that individual investors hold anywhere from 5 to 20 percent of assets in precious metals. You will rarely see anyone recommend a higher level. It's simply too risky.

People approaching retirement should generally have less of their assets invested in precious metals than, say, a thirty-five-year-old couple with two incomes and a high total net worth. Younger investors have time to recover from a loss. And since metals do best over the long term, individuals beyond retirement age should stick with income-producing investments for the most part.

Other questions you should ask yourself are: How secure is your present income? Are you and your property well insured? Secure coverage may be able to free you to assume greater investment risk. Poor coverage can force you to be more liquid—better able to meet a sudden expense. You don't want to have your money sunk into a gold options contract if it's needed to cover an unexpected medical bill.

Taxes also play a role. Ironically, if you are more highly taxed, you may be able to take more investment risks. Since certain losses are tax deductible, a loss might mean less to an individual in a higher tax bracket than for a person in a lower bracket.

DIFFERENT PRECIOUS METALS RISKS

Risk wears many masks. Here are some of the main types that you should consider before making any investment in precious metals—plus what you can do to avoid and deal with those risks:

Opportunity Costs

Gold, silver, and other metals are "nonproductive" assets. They just sit there. Put the money in a money market account and you get interest every day. Stocks can pay dividends; bonds produce a yield. Gold, well, it actually *costs* you money to own it: insurance, storage charges. You make a profit (on physical holdings) only if the world price of this commodity rises.

You should figure your "opportunity cost" of owning a precious metal. Opportunity cost refers to a situation in which the price of gold drops steadily for six months after you bought it, and you complain to your friend, "See, if only I had put that money in the bank instead, I *could have* been earning 10 or 12 percent (or whatever) interest all this time."

That forgone income is your opportunity cost. It's what you paid for the "opportunity" to invest in gold instead, or put another way, it's what you must pay to forgo the opportunity to invest that money elsewhere.

Opportunity costs can be devastating in precious metals at times of falling prices and rising interest rates.

Falling Prices

The most obvious type of risk in precious metals is that prices will fall. Dealers and assorted metals pundits call this market volatility. They mean that Murphy's Law applies here as often as anywhere else. If something can go wrong it will.

The good thing about rapidly rising and falling prices when you own physical bullion is that you can hang on and ride out the storm. Many investors have bought one day and kicked themselves for weeks, months, or years to come as the price drifted steadily south. But experienced investors also know that what goes down usually comes back up. Not always, but with enough frequency to spawn an entire investment movement called contrarian investing. Contrarians invest only in things that are out of favor, while prices are depressed.

If you buy and the price drops, don't panic. In a volatile market such as this, it will be headed up again, sooner or later. You should recognize that prices invariably will dip, and you should be prepared to ride out these storms.

Lowering Risk by Diversifying

While precious metals investments as a group are risky, some choices within the group are riskier than others. Diversification is the key to lowering your risk. Just as you should consider precious metals a way to diversify, or round out your overall financial profile, you can also diversify *within* the precious metals field to get the most from your investment.

For example, investing only in gold is more risky than including silver and platinum. How can that be, you ask, since silver is a more volatile commodity, which makes it a slightly riskier investment than gold? It's because of the magic of diversification. By taking many *different* risks, you end up with less, not more risk. While the prices of the different precious metals follow one another closely *in general,* and usually follow in the same direction, there are times when one metal will move much more than its brethren.

Investing in different metals is only one way to diversify your holdings and lower your risk.

With mining shares, for example, your risk is modified if the stock you buy pays a dividend. Since the company may derive income from other sources, there is some protection if gold prices drop. But there is the risk the company will go out of business entirely, wiping out your investment. If you own physical metals, you avoid that type of risk.

Also with mining shares, you are betting on the ability of management to make the firm profitable. The best way to radically lower the risk of investing in mining stocks is to buy shares in a precious metals mutual fund. That way you automatically own an interest in a broadly diversified group of holdings through the fund.

If you buy physical gold or silver but store it through one of the many metals storage plans, you have the risk that the firm storing it for you will go out of business and take your gold with it. (Chapter 10 explains how you can lower this risk by choosing a fully segregated storage plan where your metals are kept separately.)

Rare or numismatic coins offer still more risk variations. *Semi-numismatic* coins are valued both for their gold or silver content *and* their value as historical/artistic rarities. This gives you two ways to profit—and two ways to lose as well. Many investors like to own at least a few rare coins as a type of insurance. Even when gold bullion prices are steady or falling slightly, for example, prices for U.S. $20 Double Eagle coins can actually *go up*. Rare coins that have numismatic value as collectibles and also a precious metals value can add diversity to your holdings.

Highest Risk

Precious metals options and futures stand in a risk class by themselves. With an option, you can easily lose every penny you invested. With a futures contract it's even worse. You can lose that, plus a lot more if you don't act fast. But because options and futures are so much riskier, the potential rewards are far greater as well—often at least ten times greater than if you invested a similar amount in other types of precious metals products. With options, at least you can never lose any more than your original investment (although that's quite enough, thank you). You will need an extraordinarily high-risk tolerance to play with options and futures.

Liquidity Risks

If an investment is "liquid," you can sell it fast, just about any time you want, and get the top price at that time. In *most* cases, precious metals investments are highly liquid. But sometimes they are not. Platinum and palladium, for example, are not traded as actively as gold and silver. Since the market is not as active, these metals are not as liquid. You might not be able to sell and get the best price anytime you want.

Some forms of gold and silver are also more liquid than others. Most

liquid are the internationally recognized bullion bars and coins. Least
liquid are the small bars and ingots, as well as privately minted coins.

Risk of Confiscation

Risk of confiscation is a lesser risk, but something that cannot be ignored totally. It has happened before. Precious metals—especially
silver, platinum, and palladium, which are also classified as strategic
metals vital to the nation's defense—could, under *extreme* circumstances, be confiscated by the federal government. For this reason, the
most cautious metals holders store a portion of what they own outside
the United States. To justify this move, all they have to do is point to
the 1930s when the government called in all the gold, and the forty
years up to 1975 when gold ownership was illegal in the United States.
Even today some countries still restrict gold ownership by their cit-
izens. The rule here is to do what makes you feel the most comfortable
about your investment, even though the possibility of confiscation
seems remote.

THREE WAYS TO ADJUST YOUR PERSONAL RISK RHEOSTAT

At times you may feel comfortable taking more risk. If so, here are
three basic ways to temporarily adjust your investment risk level up or
down:

• You can step up or slow down your buying. For example, if you
are purchasing silver on a regular basis through an accumulation plan,
you could purchase larger amounts when you feel the opportunity is
right or open an account for gold as well. Accelerating your investment
activity increases risk, but it does so cautiously.

• You can move a step up or down on the risk ladder. For example,
if you feel strongly that the market is headed up, you could consider
purchasing a "call option" to put some leverage muscle behind the
bullion holdings you already have. (You'll see how options work in
Chapter 16.) But don't give up any of your core holdings to do this. It

should come out of the funds you have set aside for speculation. Move into bullion holdings or mutual funds to lower your investment risk.

• During a prolonged period of market weakness you may want to "house-clean" your precious metals portfolio. If you own mining shares that have already appreciated substantially, consider selling and taking those profits after you've checked the tax consequences of the move. If you own rare coins, consider replacing items that have gone up in value and may be "fully priced" with others that have yet to move.

Recognizing what constitutes risk in precious metals investing, and what doesn't, is important. Some people, however, seem always to be looking over their shoulders. That indicates they are not comfortable with what they are doing. If you keep a sensible portion of your assets in precious metals, keep track of what's going on, and take advantage of opportunities when they arise, gold, silver, platinum, and palladium can have a place in almost anyone's financial future.

CHAPTER 7

Investing in the Bullion Supermarket

- **The Gold Bullion Menu**
- **Bullion Buying Pros and Cons**
- **The Silver Bullion Menu**
- **The Platinum and Palladium Bullion Menus**
- **Getting the Most for Your Money**
- **The More You Buy the More You Save**

The most obvious way to invest in a precious metal is to buy a chunk of it and stash it away. This is the stuff of legend . . . of TV shows and motion pictures. You've seen movies in which uniformed guards laboriously cart huge bars of gold in and out of vaults. Those are the brick-sized bars that governments swap among themselves.

Forget about those images. To meet the needs of individual investors, the metals bullion supermarket has gone modern. It's now more like a sleek suburban food mart with eighty-five varieties of every conceivable item.

THE GOLD BULLION MENU

For example, the following list shows the sizes of bullion bars, wafers, and ingots offered by major international precious metals dealers. The list includes each item's approximate value with gold selling at $450 per ounce. Remember, that's *troy* ounces. All precious metals weights are measured in troy ounces, a unit of measurement based on a troy pound containing twelve of these ounces. A troy ounce is actually a tiny bit larger than the type of ounce you're used to. One troy ounce is the same as 1.09711 standard U.S. ounces (which is called an avoirdupois ounce). Prices listed do *not* include premiums and commissions.

In Europe, and sometimes in the United States as well, precious metals are sold by the gram and kilo. For those of you who've gone metric, a troy ounce equals 31.1035 grams.

The Gold Bullion Menu

Size	*Value at $450/oz.*
400 ounce	$180,000
100 ounce	$45,000
50 ounce	$22,500
20 ounce	$9,000
10 ounce	$4,500
5 ounce	$2,250
2 ounce	$900
1 ounce	$450
½ ounce	$225
¼ ounce	$113
1 kilo (32.15 ounces)	$14,468
½ kilo (16.075 ounces)	$7,234
100 gram (3.216 ounces)	$1,447
50 gram (1.608 ounces)	$724
20 gram (0.6430 ounce)	$290
10 gram (0.3215 ounce)	$145
5 gram (0.1608 ounce)	$72
2½ gram (0.0804 ounce)	$36
1 gram (0.0322 gram)	$15

That's nineteen different sizes to choose from. Not all are popular choices, however, and you might have to check several dealers to find what you want. The prices reflect only the actual value of the gold content and don't take into account commissions or the higher markup (premium) you'd pay on smaller bars.

If you're like most people, you also associate gold with karats. But that's a jewelry, not an investment metals, term. Gold purity for investors varies little and is stated in numbers such as 999.9, which represents parts of pure gold per 1,000. Twenty-four-karat gold, pure gold or close to it, is the only type considered for investing. For example, 18-karat gold is only 75 percent pure, and that's not good in this market.

$$
\begin{array}{rcl}
24 \text{ karat} &=& .9999 \text{ pure} \\
22 \text{ karat} &=& .9165 \text{ pure} \\
18 \text{ karat} &=& .7500 \text{ pure} \\
14 \text{ karat} &=& .5833 \text{ pure} \\
10 \text{ karat} &=& .4167 \text{ pure}
\end{array}
$$

The 400-ounce bar doesn't see much traffic among individual investors. This is what national governments trade back and forth. In fact, many foreign governments keep a supply of gold at the Federal Reserve Bank vaults in New York City. When one country pays another country in gold, bank officials simply pick up the bars at one end of the vault, carry them to another end, and plop them on the stack owned by the other country.

Because of their odd sizes, the 100- and 50-gram wafers also see little activity in the United States.

Each bullion bar is stamped with the name of the company that refined and fabricated the gold. That's the hallmark. Some of the big international names include Johnson Matthey, Engelhard, and Crédit Suisse. Each bar also includes a registration or serial number, the number of ounces or grams, and the degree of purity of the gold. The minimum fineness for top investment grade gold is .995. That's how pure the metal is—99.5 percent pure gold. That's the *minimum*.

Bullion in sizes of 10 ounces and up sold by the international precious metals dealers, for example, is usually guaranteed to be .995 fineness or better, which is stated as .995 + . Smaller bullion bars are usually .999 fineness (99.9 percent pure gold). That purity is also called "triple nine" gold. "Four Nines" gold is even more pure.

Don't let this arithmetic trip you up. Grades of fineness in the mainstream market have become standard. You'll soon become familiar enough with the names of the major refiners and reputable dealers so you won't have to fret when the gold you bought was only .995 while your Aunt Charlotte's bar was stamped .999 purity.

In larger quantities, the price may even reflect this minute difference in the amount of pure gold you're getting. The difference will amount to only a dollar or less per ounce, so it's nothing to get worked up about. You're paying for the gold, not the 0.5 percent of other mysterious elements lurking within the bar.

The metals makers also can't seem to agree on a simple little thing like decimal points. Some write it like this (.9995), a competitor might call that same purity (99.95), and another firm might not use a decimal point at all (9995). They are exactly the same, albeit a bit confusing to the rest of us.

BULLION BUYING PROS AND CONS

Precious metals are commodities. And like consumer products (commodities) on the shelves of your favorite store, gold, silver, platinum, and palladium are packaged and sold in many different ways by many different companies. If you buy bullion in small amounts, you pay a little more, ounce for ounce, just as you do when you buy a small can of peas instead of a big one. It costs money to form your gold (or silver) into a bar and transport it to the "store." Such charges over and above the value of the metal itself are called premiums. This covers the cost of fabricating the gold, or molding it into bars.

The premium is usually figured right into the cost of the gold. Commissions are different, so don't get them mixed up. You'll pay a broker or dealer a commission to buy gold for you, and that's usually on top of the premium you pay for the gold.

You get a better deal if you buy bulk. An investor who wants to acquire 10 ounces of gold, for example, will get more for his or her money with a single 10-ounce bar than with ten separate one-ounce ingots or coins. The difference isn't huge, but it can add up.

Back to the grocery store for a moment. Most people who buy whole milk would recognize no difference between brands. It's all pretty much the same no matter where you buy it, even though each distributor slaps its own name on the carton. Firms that deal in precious metals do the same thing. They stamp their own trademark into the metal and send it out into the world as a traveling advertisement for their company.

In precious metals the right trademark can be a decidedly good thing when it's time to sell. A few of the big names in gold, silver, platinum, and palladium manufacturing include Engelhard, Handy & Harman, Crédit Suisse, Mocatta Metals Corporation, AMAX, ASARCO, Sharps & Wilkins, and N. M. Rothschild's.

Such a stamp doesn't harm the bullion in any way. But small "private label" trademarks could make the gold or other metal more difficult to sell to anyone other than the firm you bought it from or that made it. If you plan to sell back to the same firm, that's not a problem. If you plan to take delivery and might have to sell it to somebody else later, avoid the off-brand bullion bars.

But firms such as Engelhard are, for the most part, not retail outlets. Engelhard Corporation, for example, is a world leader in refining and fabricating gold, silver, platinum, and palladium. This firm is one of a select group of metals refiners whose precious metals bars are accepted and recognized around the world. Each Engelhard bar has the purity stamped on it and comes with an assay certificate. Bars are stamped with a serial number, and in this case carry the ENGELHARD trademark.

Engelhard manufactures a dozen gold bar sizes, all 999.9 fine. The firm also offers a gold medallion, which looks like a coin, in ⅒-, ¼-, ½-, and one-ounce sizes. Like most such private mint medallions, it has a name—American Prospector—and its design shows just that. (The firm also offers this medallion in silver.)

With Engelhard, as well as with most other major manufacturers, you don't buy directly from them. They distribute their bars to retail dealers who mark up the product slightly and sell it to you.

More Brand-Name Competitors

With the popularity of precious metals investments on the rise, more and more fabricators have started hawking their brands to investors. Royal Canadian Mint, a crown corporation of the Canadian government, for example, is a relative newcomer to the field. Royal Mint launched a new series of silver bars in 1984, in one-, 10-, and 100-ounce sizes—the only silver bullion bar backed by a national government. To try to set its bar apart from all the others, the Canadian mint added a special brilliant finish and encased the metal in a kind of plastic body stocking to keep it shiny and looking pretty for investors.

The trap you're trying to avoid when choosing a brand name of bullion to purchase is an *assay*—a chemical test to prove the gold is real and pure. The major names are usually accepted as genuine without question; the minor ones are not. Not only would you have to pay for the assay ($75 to $100 per bar or more), but you would face a delay in completing the deal. If prices are moving rapidly, that could really hurt.

One advantage to owning gold in small sizes is its divisibility. Come time to sell, you may not want to part with all your metal. If your holdings are all stuck together in a single bar, you cannot simply lop off 3 or 4 ounces to sell like so much cheese from a wheel. You would have to sell the entire bar and buy back the amount you wanted to keep.

But *too* small isn't good either. Tiny gold wafers of less than half an ounce aren't in much demand among investors. These are novelty items, not investments, and you're paying much more than the gold's value. They are nice gifts, but if you're serious about investing, avoid them.

THE SILVER BULLION MENU

Silver is much less expensive than gold, ounce for ounce, so it doesn't come in quite as many sizes. But in recent years silver has gained tremendously in popularity among investors, especially among small investors who have adopted it as poor man's gold.

The list on page 84 shows standard silver bullion sizes most dealers offer and the approximate value of each item, with silver selling at $12.00 per ounce (prices do *not* include premiums or commissions).

Each of these silver selections is likely to come in .999 fineness and that's the purity you should look for in your silver bullion investments.

Most of gold's pros and cons also apply to silver, with a few differences. Silver bullion coins, for example, don't enjoy the same tremendous popularity as their gold cousins. As a percentage of the price of your total investment, the premiums on such small size silver bullion will be considerably greater than for gold. It costs just as much to fabricate a silver coin as it does a gold coin, even though the gold is thirty or forty times more valuable. You also face the same storage, insurance, and potential assay costs with silver bullion.

Again, you'll end up paying more in premiums and commissions if you buy only small bars of silver. You get the most for your money with the big bars.

The Silver Bullion Menu

Size	Value at $12/oz.
1,000 ounce	$12,000
100 ounce	$1,200
50 ounce	$600
20 ounce	$240
10 ounce	$120
5 ounce	$60
2 ounce	$24
1 ounce	$12
½ ounce	$6
1 kilo (32.15 ounces)	$386
½ kilo (16.075 ounces)	$193
10 gram (0.3215 ounce)	$4
5 gram (0.1608 ounce)	$2

THE PLATINUM AND PALLADIUM BULLION MENUS

The choices narrow considerably with platinum, and even more so with palladium. No matter. There's still plenty to choose from, and the list of available platinum and palladium choices has been growing with the popularity of these sister elements.

Here are the basic bullion sizes for platinum, and what they'd be worth with the "noble metal" selling at $420 per troy ounce (prices do *not* include premiums or commissions):

The Platinum and Palladium Bullion Menus

Size	Value at $420/oz.
50 ounce	$21,000
10 ounce	$4,200
5 ounce (155.516 grams)	$2,100
1 ounce (31.1033 grams)	$420
½ ounce (15.551 grams)	$210
¼ ounce (7.775 grams)	$105
1 kilo (32.15 ounces)	$13,500
50 gram (1.608 ounces)	$724
10 gram (0.3215 ounce)	$135
5 gram (0.1608 ounce)	$68
2½ gram (0.0804 ounce)	$34
1 gram (0.0322 ounce)	$14

You won't find that many choices for palladium, which has yet to gain as much popularity as its sister metal, platinum. Few Americans have even heard of this substance; fewer still have been sufficiently convinced of its potential to plunk down $15,000 for a 100-ounce bar of palladium bullion.

Palladium bullion will be harder to find. Few precious metals dealers sell it. Commercial banks are limited to selling only silver and gold, so you won't find it there either. Dealers that do offer palladium—Deak-Perera is a leader in the United States—are able to offer bullion in only a few sizes because that's what the refiners are making. Choices typically include the following:

100-ounce bars
1-kilo bars
10-ounce bars
1-ounce bars

With upstart palladium outperforming its more illustrious colleagues in recent years, you may see more palladium choices before long.

GETTING THE MOST FOR YOUR MONEY

Compare the price of eggs at half a dozen different stores on a given day and you'll probably find a substantial spread. It works the same with the precious metals commodities. The prices may be set on the world market, but there is still room for differences from dealer to dealer. It's a rapidly changing and highly competitive market that encourages subtle differences.

With the exception of the lucky investor who happens upon the best price with the first telephone call, most individuals will do best by shopping around. Just as banks pay different interest rates on savings accounts and stockbrokers charge different commissions, precious metals stores have different prices too. Some have higher markups, some higher overheads; some have high volume, some low. It all adds up to opportunities for you.

First keep in mind that the price you're quoted by a dealer over the telephone won't exactly match the market prices reported daily by such stalwarts of the business as Handy & Harman (for silver), Engelhard, Mocatta Metals, or a major commodities exchange such as COMEX in New York, or the Chicago Board of Trade. Nor will it match the London Fix. The price you hear will be *based* on those benchmarks and will reflect how anxious or indifferent your particular dealer is toward buying or selling the metal in question.

Investors who don't check around are throwing money away. Differences can easily reach 5 or 6 percent or more. That's a potential savings of $200–$300 on a $5,000 investment. Even the $100 difference on an investment half that size pays for your commission and first year's storage charges.

When prices are slumping, differences among dealers will be most pronounced. That's simple supply and demand economics. Dealers get hungry and put their wares on sale (although they rarely call it that).

Derby Winners Changing

I can't tell you here which dealers will offer the best prices. They're constantly changing. You'll get a more accurate picture conducting your own mini-survey. Investment advisory newsletters can also offer tips, although most such services in the precious metals field seem to shy away from that kind of pragmatic guidance, preferring to guess at prices.

There are exceptions. The best ongoing advice on this topic I've come across is the investment advisory newsletter *Silver & Gold Report* (SGR), from Bethel, Connecticut. (*Note:* Chapter 21 lists the addresses of this and other investment newsletters and organizations of interest.) SGR runs periodic price checks of major U.S. and Canadian dealers and publishes the results in special reports (many smaller firms aren't covered). Its editors do the kind of nitty-gritty comparisons of dealer prices and service that are useful to investors.

Where you find the best deal will also depend on whether you are buying or selling. Dealers who offer you the best price to *buy* your gold or silver could very well be the worst firms to buy *from*, and vice versa. If they offer you a good price when you want to buy, they're probably making it back on the other end.

Know what you want before you shop. One dealer might have the best price on small amounts of Krugerrands and another might offer the best price on Canadian Maple Leaf coins. Still another could save you hundreds of dollars on your purchase of a larger volume and three others could offer superior prices on bullion bars. And for heaven's sake, use the toll-free 800 numbers that most dealers offer. (Chapter 11 gives dealer listings. The telephone numbers tend to change regularly, however, so you may have to do some updating on your own.)

Ask About Commissions

Asking about the price isn't enough. You'll also have to inquire about commissions *and any other charges that you must pay to take delivery of or store your gold, silver, platinum, or palladium.* Dealer Jones's price might be lowest, but if his commission and storage charges are twice as high as Smith's down the street, your out-of-pocket expense could actually end up higher. Beware of the deal that seems to be an incredible bargain. When somebody's price is way out of line with everyone else's, it's a tip-off that something is wrong. Stay away.

There are also some non-price considerations. If the firm's representative is pressuring you, wants too many details about your personal finances, and won't let you get off the phone, move on. If you call lots of dealers you can expect to encounter some salesmanship. They'll try to feel you out about how serious an investor you are. Don't get hooked into a commitment you're not ready for, and don't give out information about yourself (including your telephone number if that makes you uncomfortable). If that angers the person at the other end of the line, tough. You can take your business elsewhere.

A Cautious Investor's Tip: Many of the most reputable precious metals dealers in North America and elsewhere in the world are listed in this book. Conditions can change rapidly, however, and a listing here is not a guarantee of any kind. These firms have weathered the market's ups and downs and lived to tell about it. That's *something*. A few have been in business for *centuries*. But even the government-regulated banks that sell precious metals offer no federal insurance on your investment.

Remember: Just because a company runs ads in big-name publications doesn't mean everything is hunky-dory. Thousands of investors have lost millions of dollars to companies that ran such ads and later folded. When considering an investment in gold, silver, platinum, or palladium, it's better to ignore the ad come-ons.

Lower-Risk Bullion Buying

There are always risks, and a large part of investing wisely in precious metals is knowing how to minimize those risks. One way you can do that is through a little-known device called a sight draft. Not all dealers offer sight drafts, and those that do certainly don't advertise them. This draft is a surefire way to make certain the company doesn't go bankrupt between the time it cashes your check and the date your gold (or silver or platinum or palladium) is supposed to be shipped.

It works like the standard barroom wager. A third party holds the money until the issue is decided. In this case, a bank (your bank) serves as middleman for the transaction. The sight draft is an agreement under which the dealer ships your purchase to a bank. Once the metal has arrived, you are free to inspect it before the same bank releases your funds to the precious metals dealer.

If you've changed your mind by this time, the sight draft arrangement should place no obligation on you to go through with the deal and accept the delivery, even though the price was locked in at your original phone call.

Sight drafts are one device that especially cautious investors insist on—and which most dealers discourage or begrudgingly provide. Some major dealers don't offer sight drafts at all. Those most receptive to the idea are the larger regional dealers. In any case, there may be added conditions attached to a sight draft sale (or purchase), depending on individual dealer policy. Some ask for a partial deposit, say 20 to 25 percent, and some charge a fee of $20 to $50 or perhaps one percent of the transaction.

Minimum purchases are also common with sight drafts. Although some firms require no minimum, others range from $1,000 to $10,000, or a certain number of ounces or coins that puts the dollar amount in the same range.

THE MORE YOU BUY, THE MORE YOU SAVE

When you buy a product by the case you get a better deal. Wine . . . motor oil . . . and precious metals too. With precious metals, the amount of money involved can be huge.

Typically, when you buy a one-ounce piece of gold, the manufacturing charge, above the price of the metal, might be $4 to $6. On a 5-ounce bar the charge would be around $15, and on a 10-ounce bar this fabrication premium could run perhaps $20 to $30. Look at what that comes out to as an average charge *per ounce*. Five dollars for the littlest bar . . . $3 for the next size . . . and $2 to $2.50 for the 10-ounce bar of gold bullion. You double premiums to buy the smaller bar.

You'll find even larger increments for the other metals. With silver, the cheapest of the bunch, the manufacturing cost for small coins, bars, or ingots can be particularly onerous. A $10 fabrication charge on a 10-ounce silver bar, with silver selling at $10 per ounce, raises your cost per ounce by *10 percent*. That's too much to pay. And it's a good argument for purchasing silver through certificate programs or in larger-size bars.

The price of platinum normally tracks gold closely, but because the metal is more scarce, and not as heavily traded, the fabrication costs are higher—more than double in some cases. As a percentage of your total investment—in larger amounts at least—these charges are still small. With platinum at $500, for example, the manufacturing charge on a 10-ounce bar would amount to only about one percent of your investment.

Buying Wholesale: The American Tradition

Another way to save if you are planning a particularly large purchase is to use a tried method—avoid the middleman and buy wholesale. Wholesalers, such as Mocatta Metals Corporation, J. Aron & Company (a division of the investment banking firm Goldman, Sachs), A-Mark Precious Metals, Johnson Matthey, and Engelhard, don't usually deal directly with individual investors. There's too much paperwork, too many headaches, and they don't have that type of sales and marketing staff. But if you're talking a sizable purchase (how that is defined will vary, but say at least $25,000), they might just take the business if you ask. If you have such a sizable purchase in mind, you can find out by writing or calling the wholesale firms listed in Chapter 11's Dealer Directory.

CHAPTER 8

Dollar Cost Averaging: A Low-Cost, High-Profit Way to Beat the Market Any Investor Can Use

- **A Way to Reduce Your Risk**
- **The Commission Factor**

Dollar cost averaging is a trustworthy (though a bit threadbare) technique that investors have used successfully for many years. A cost-averaging strategy works like this. You invest a *fixed* amount of money in the metal of your choice, on a *fixed* schedule (every week, month, quarter, etc.). Then stick to it. Forget about the price. There's no guesswork involved when you let the averaging concept work for you.

It's one of those dull financial techniques that work. It's a way to build a precious metals stake slowly and steadily, either in small steps or in big ones over a period of years.

Over time, dollar cost averaging puts price swings to work *in your favor*. Consider silver as an example. When the price of silver is low, your fixed monthly (or whatever) investment buys you more ounces every time you purchase. Since you are investing a fixed sum of dollars, when the price is high you are buying less silver. The result is a significantly lower average cost per ounce on your total holdings of silver, even though you buy more ounces when the market is falling than you do when it's rising.

The accompanying table shows you how a hypothetical cost-averaging program for silver might work over a three-year period. It shows a variety of different prices, and includes changes in the time period used and the amount invested to show you the differences. These prices don't reflect commissions or actual silver prices over any particular year, but they are representative of what can happen in the market.

Dollar Cost Averaging at Work in a Changing Silver Market

A hypothetical example

YEAR ONE/MONTHLY INVESTMENTS

Date Invested	Amount	Price	Ounces Bought
January 1	$1,000	$11.96	83.612
February 1	$100	$11.57	8.643
March 1	$100	$11.04	9.057
April 1	$100	$12.10	8.264
May 1	$100	$12.79	7.186
June 1	$100	$13.20	7.575
July 1	$100	$13.04	7.668
August 1	$100	$13.57	7.369
September 1	$100	$14.18	7.052
October 1	$100	$13.90	7.194
November 1	$100	$14.28	7.002
December 1	$100	$14.86	6.729

Year One Totals
Amount invested: $2,100
Average market price/ounce: $13.04
Ounces bought: 167.351
Your **average cost/ounce:** $12.55
"Free" (extra) silver due to cost averaging: 6.3 ounces

YEAR TWO/QUARTERLY INVESTMENTS

Date Invested	Amount	Price	Ounces Bought
January 1	$1,000	$15.06	66.401
April 1	$1,000	$11.65	85.836
July 1	$1,000	$9.44	105.932
October 1	$1,000	$9.12	109.649

Year Two Totals
Amount invested: $4,000
Average market price/ounce: $11.32
Ounces bought: 367.818
Your **average cost/ounce:** $10.87
"Free" (extra) silver due to cost averaging: 14.2 ounces

YEAR THREE/BIMONTHLY INVESTMENTS

Date Invested	Amount	Price	Ounces Bought
January 1	$2,500	$8.55	292.397
March 1	$2,500	$6.90	362.318
May 1	$2,500	$9.06	275.938
July 1	$2,500	$11.12	224.820
September 1	$2,500	$12.40	201.612
November 1	$2,500	$15.60	160.256

Year Three Totals
Amount invested: $15,000
Average market price/ounce: $10.61
Ounces bought: 1,517.341
Your **average cost/ounce:** $9.89
"Free" (extra) silver due to cost averaging: 103.6 ounces

COMBINED RESULTS OF THREE-YEAR PROGRAM

Amount invested: $21,100
Average market price/ounce: $12.06
Ounces bought: 2,052.5
Your **average cost/ounce:** $10.28
"Free" (extra) silver due to cost averaging: 124.1 ounces

A WAY TO REDUCE YOUR RISK

Dollar cost averaging can also lower your risks. You will buy some gold when the price is high, but your disciplined schedule of monthly or quarterly investments assures that if there are ups and downs you will buy *greater* amounts of gold when the price is lowest.

In year two of the example, a $1,000 investment bought 66 ounces of silver when the price was the highest and 110 ounces when the price was lowest. Cost averaging automatically does what so many investors have trouble doing—it buys you the most when prices are low, the least when prices are high.

In these hypothetical examples, the average market price on the days purchases were made in year one was $13.04. But the actual average cost per ounce *to the investor* would have been $12.55. In year two, the average market price was $11.32, but the investor paid only $10.87 per ounce for the silver. In year three, the average market price was $10.61, but the cost to the investor was $9.89, due to the effects of dollar cost averaging.

Over this entire three-year period (which is actually short for a cost-averaging plan), the average market price was $12.06 while the *investor's* average cost per ounce of silver was only $10.28. That brought in a bonus of 124 ounces of silver.

This doesn't mean that over *any* period of time you use cost averaging you will make a profit. No matter how well it works, if the price on the day you decide to sell is lower than your average price over the years you've been accumulating the metal, you will lose money. But studies show that the more patient you are, the longer you stick to a plan (preferably five years or more) the greater your chances of making a profit and the greater those profits will be.

Programs extending beyond four or five years hold the best odds for you. But remember also, this is a program that you set up yourself. *You* decide how much to invest and when. *You* are the one who must stick to it. If, after a few years, you've already compiled a tidy stack of gold at an equally tidy profit, nothing says you can't get out.

THE COMMISSION FACTOR

Dollar-cost-averaging programs work best when there is no commission to pay. That's why it is such a popular strategy for people who invest in no-load (no commission) precious metals mutual funds. In a no-load fund, you can invest as often as you like, and as little as you like (subject to the fund's minimum) without paying a dime in commissions. Sadly, the same is not true with physical metals.

Keep an eye on commissions and other charges. Before you embark on a precious metals buying program, be certain you know what commission you will pay *for the amount you intend to invest,* as well as any storage, insurance, or other fees. Those charges have a nasty habit of eating away your holdings.

This is especially true for small investors. Some purchase plans that offer small minimum investments also charge higher commissions. The big guys seem to get all the breaks. Commissions on large purchases can run between one and 2 percent, but they go as high as 6 percent for those who can afford to invest only $100 at a crack.

There's no sense digging yourself a hole before you start. While the programs offering investments as small as $100 or so might get you started sooner, it could be more advantageous to invest less frequently (perhaps quarterly instead of monthly) in a program that has a lower commission. What seem to be small savings at the time could become thousands of dollars years later if that money goes to purchase precious metals instead of in the broker's pocket.

If you are like most investors, and especially newcomers to the precious metals, you may even have fun watching the ounces grow, and your average cost drop, while the market goes its merry way.

CHAPTER 9

Bullion Coins: Grass-Roots Gold

- **What's a Bullion Coin?**
- **The Gold Coin Menu**
- **Bullion Coin Premiums**
- **Fractional Coins**
- **Silver Bullion Coins**
- **Private Mint Silver Coins**
- **"Junk Silver" Coins**
- **And Now . . . Platinum Bullion Coins Too**
- **Private Storage: Stashing Your Metals Cache**

In 1975, when gold prohibition ended in the United States, few people had ever heard of gold and silver bullion coins. Platinum bullion coins didn't even exist. When prices soared, small investors everywhere discovered they could invest easily in gold by purchasing bullion coins—grass-roots gold. At that time Krugerrands were the rage.

The 1980s erupted with new gold and silver bullion coin offerings to investors. Literally hundreds are minted all over the world. Most aren't worth considering as an investment, however, even if you could find a dealer who carries them. For investors, the action centers around a select dozen or so coins.

WHAT'S A BULLION COIN?

A bullion coin is like a bullion bar except it has been molded into a circle instead of a rectangle. A bullion "coin" is not regular money—at least not in the traditional sense. Even though some countries mint their gold coins with a face value and call them legal tender coins, the real value of the coin is attached to the ever-changing price of gold.

This sets *bullion* coins apart from *numismatic* gold and silver coins that were minted in years past as regular money and now sell as high-priced rarities. Bullion coins were never meant to be used this way. They are made for investment reasons, not to spend at the store. It's simply gold or silver minted with a government hallmark. Although there are private mint bullion coins, most of the popular gold coins are issued by national governments.

The value of a numismatic coin made of gold or silver will depend in part on the price of gold, but even more so on its rarity, condition, and demand among collectors. The same goes for other precious metals items that have historical or artistic value. But bullion coins are bought for their gold content . . . period. Ditto for silver and platinum bullion coins.

Now to confuse you a bit. There are also semi-numismatic coins. As their name implies, they fall somewhere in between a straight bullion coin and a rare (numismatic) coin. Semi-numismatic coins are also rare coins—old money minted as the real thing long ago. But they are not quite as rare as many others, and thus the extra value attached to rarity isn't as great.

So what happens to these coins? Their prices go up and down more in relation to market prices of gold and silver; less according to their value as antiques. Still they command prices higher than what the simple bullion content would dictate. But it can get even more complicated when you consider the tax implications of buying bullion (non–legal tender gold or silver), which might be taxed . . . or semi-numismatic and numismatic coins that tax authorities in their wisdom have granted a different tax status. A complete explanation of the difference can be found in Chapter 18: Tax Tips for Precious Metals Investors.

Gold bullion coins have become so popular that governments now spend millions of dollars promoting their own brands. They have their own marketing agencies, their own public relations firms. PR giant Burson Marsteller, for example, has been behind promotional efforts for the Canadian Maple Leaf gold coin in the United States. Arch rival South Africa created its own agency, Intergold, to boost the image of the South African gold Krugerrand around the world.

As simple as buying a bullion coin would seem to be, alas, this investment option also has its bewildering array of choices and pitfalls. Here's what it looks like:

THE GOLD COIN MENU

The following list shows you the major gold bullion coins available in the United States, with the amount of pure gold contained in each coin in troy ounces. There are many other minor coins. The list could go on ad infinitum. But even among the majors, only a few are well-accepted investment coins. Those are covered in greater detail in this chapter.

Major Gold Bullion Coins

Bullion Coin	Troy Ounces Gold
Canadian Maple Leaf	1.00
South African Krugerrand	1.00
Mexican Onza	1.00
U.S. Gold 1 Ounce	1.00
Mexican 50 Peso	1.2057
Austrian Gold 100 Corona	0.9802
Hungarian 100 Korona	0.9802
Russian Chervonetz	0.2488
English Sovereign	0.2354
Chinese 1 Panda	1.00
Gold Standard Corporation 1 Ounce	1.00

The sales leader of this pack, by a long shot, is the South African Krugerrand. The South Africans pioneered the idea of a bullion coin for the average citizen back in the 1960s. As the world's leading gold-producing country, South Africa has a big stake in keeping gold alive.

But in spite of being the number-one gold investment coin, the Krugerrand has its problems. Worldwide boycotts against investment in South Africa have taken their toll. Many people don't want a coin produced by a racist regime. Because of South Africa's apartheid policies, there have even been attempts in Congress to ban imports of the coin to the United States. With millions of investors still wanting Krugerrands, however, and a thousand different ways to buy them around the world, a ban on the coin would have little chance of taking hold. But the efforts could make trouble in the market. Several major financial firms with precious metals departments have already said they won't deal in Krugerrands.

The Maple Leaf

The Canadians have tried to capitalize on the Krugerrand's woes. Canada introduced the Maple Leaf in 1979, and the coin has gained tremendous popularity among investors, for several reasons.

The Canadian coin is pure gold, of .9999 fineness. The Krugerrand, on the other hand, is not a pure gold coin. It contains exactly one troy ounce of gold just like the Maple Leaf. But it also contains a small amount of copper to make the coin harder and more wear resistant. Overall, the Krugerrand weighs slightly more—total weight 1.0909 troy ounces—because of the hardener.

When you look at the coins, you will notice a slight difference in the color as well. The Krugerrand has a slight copperish tint to it, while the Maple Leaf is a more brilliant gold.

Which is better? Everyone seems to feel differently. If your political sensibilities are offended by owning a South African product, then certainly the Canadian coin is the choice. Other considerations are a matter of personal preference.

The Krugerrand undoubtedly remains the most widely recognized gold coin worldwide, and that means it's the most liquid to own. In other words, the theory is that in a crisis others would be more inclined to accept your Krugerrands without giving you a hassle. But that's a mighty slim argument. The Maple Leaf has become just as well recognized in the United States and around the world. Most dealers that sell the Krugerrand also handle the Maple Leaf. The Canadians have captured more than 20 percent of the world gold coin market, much more in the United States. More and more investors seem to think the Maple Leaf is the new coin of preference—and the coin of the future.

That leaves the issue of purity. Here again, the gold investment market today favors the pure gold coin. Sure it is softer and easier to damage. But few investors carry these coins around in their pockets. The Maple Leaf people claim the manufacturing process makes their coin durable enough for its intended use, thank you. As one of their representatives wrote to me, ". . . they require no protective casings or other special conserving measures. If you were to mistreat a Krugerrand, Maple Leaf or any other precious metal coin, they would incur an equal measure of damage, as precious metals must be treated with care."

A coin that is 99.99 percent pure might arguably be more liquid than one that is 91.67 percent pure (the Krugerrand) since 98 percent of the world's gold trades at a purity of 99.5 percent or better. Neither side will win the argument, and both coins seem equally liquid for all practical investment purposes.

Here are a few other facts about the Maple Leaf:

• Global sales surpass one million ounces yearly, which means more than 50 percent of Canada's gold mine output every year is being used to mint these coins.

• The Maple Leaf is also made in ¼- and ⅒-ounce sizes. The Canadian government backs these coins and has placed a nominal face value on each—$50 for the one-ounce, $10 for the ¼-ounce, and $5 for the ⅒-ounce coin. That's not terribly significant, but should some disaster hit the gold market, and the price collapse, these coins would supposedly still be worth at least the face value declared by the Canadian government.

The Krugerrand

Three-fourths of all the gold bullion coins sold in the world are Krugerrands. South Africa mints them in unlimited quantities and says they are legal tender in that country. The Krugerrand became the leader because it was the first to be made as a new coin specifically for investors, and also because South Africa has more gold than any other country on earth.

Since the Krugerrand contains exactly one troy ounce of pure gold—not an odd amount as do some other coins—people who own it can easily look at yesterday's price in the newspaper and figure out exactly how much their gold is worth. Remember, the coin itself actually weighs more than one troy ounce because of the small amount of copper added to make the coin more durable. The exact amount of gold in the coin is still one troy ounce. The result is a 22-karat coin with a fineness of .91666.

BULLION COIN PREMIUMS

All bullion coins are sold at a price slightly higher than the market price of gold. The difference is the premium. But different coins carry different premiums, and the premium may also vary from dealer to dealer just as it does with bullion bars and ingots.

Premiums can range from less than one percent up to about 10 percent. The less popular gold coins, such as the Austrian 100 Corona and Hungarian 100 Korona, often sell at a *lower* premium, which means you would get more gold for your money. But these coins may no longer be a bargain when it comes time to sell. The price you are offered might be lower than what you could get for a Maple Leaf or Krugerrand. With most dealers, however, you'll get significantly more gold for your money by choosing the Austrian coins, especially if you are buying in large quantities.

Here are the prices and premiums for ten major gold bullion coins bought from a major national dealer as they appeared on a day when gold was selling at $337.50:

Bullion Coin Premiums

Bullion Coin	Price	Melt Value	Premium	Oz. Gold
Maple Leaf	$361.50	$337.50	7.1%	1.00
Krugerrand	$361.50	$337.50	7.1%	1.00
U.S. Gold 1 oz.	$360.00	$337.50	6.7%	1.00
Mexican Onza	$357.00	$337.50	5.8%	1.00
Mexican 50 Pesos	$434.42	$406.92	6.8%	1.2057
Austrian Corona	$342.66	$330.82	3.6%	0.9802
Hungarian Korona	$342.66	$330.82	3.6%	0.9802
British Sovereign	$85.95	$79.45	8.2%	0.2568
China 1 oz. Panda	$370.31	$337.50	9.7%	1.00
U.S. Olympic Gold	$348.00	$163.28	53.1%	0.4838

If your preference runs toward foreign gold coins, minted in France, Switzerland, England, Italy, Australia, Belgium, the Netherlands, West Germany, Chile, and Colombia, among other nations, you may not be able to find them easily at most precious metals dealers. Several U.S. firms that offer a broader than usual array of foreign coins are Manfra, Tordella & Brookes, Inc. (New York); James U. Blanchard & Co. (New Orleans); Deak-Perera (New York and many other cities); and Security Pacific Brokers (Los Angeles). Crédit Suisse, one of the "big three" Swiss banks and also a large international precious metals refiner and fabricator with offices in the United States, also carries a wide assortment of gold coins from around the world.

A Cautious Investor's Tip: Crédit Suisse (CS) publishes a handsome full-color text, the *Gold Handbook* ($13; 25 Swiss francs if you're over there). It includes color photos of many foreign gold coins plus, of course, photos of Crédit Suisse gold bars and ingots. For ordering information, contact a Crédit Suisse office in the United States. There's one in New York at 100 Wall Street, 10005; and also in Los Angeles, Miami, Atlanta, Chicago, Houston, and San Francisco. Crédit Suisse headquarters is at Paradeplatz 8, 8021 Zurich, Switzerland.

For an even more extensive "encyclopedia" of gold coins minted around the world, The Gold Institute in Washington, DC has a publication, *Modern Gold Coinage,* priced at $7. This booklet offers details of all the gold coins issued throughout the world each year (a new volume is issued each year). The address is 1001 Connecticut Avenue N.W., Washington, DC 20036.

FRACTIONAL COINS

The investor love affair with grown-up bullion coins naturally led to baby bullion coins, called fractional coins. Smaller versions of their big brothers and sisters, they come in 1/10-, 1/4-, and 1/2-ounce sizes.

South African, Mexican, Canadian, and U.S. gold coins all come in fractional sizes.

Avoid them if you can. They simply cost too much for the amount of gold you get. They will water down your investment. For example, here is a comparison of a 5-ounce gold purchase done three different ways, with a gold price of $400:

five 1-ounce Krugerrands
ten ½-ounce Krugerrands
twenty ¼-ounce Krugerrands

The Added Cost of Fractional Coins

	Total Cost	*Added Cost*
1-ounce coins:	$2,142.00	——
½-ounce coins:	$2,167.00	+ $25
¼-ounce coins:	$2,266.00	+$124

The difference will magnify even more with the tiny ¹⁄₁₀-ounce coin, and the premiums will also vary from dealer to dealer. In this case, the price for the fractional coins was actually less than if you had bought only a few coins because many dealers offer a price reduction when you buy ten or more coins at the same time. When you buy twenty-five or more the price will drop even further.

In the example above, the premium on the ½-ounce coins was more than 8 percent; it was over 13 percent for the ¼-ounce coins. For ¹⁄₁₀-ounce Krugerrands, at the particular dealer these prices came from, the premium would have been a whopping *20 percent over the actual value of the bullion in the coins.* Unless you have a pressing need to have gold coins in small increments, it doesn't make sense to pay more.

But if you must, a firm that specializes in small gold coins ("No order too small") is Auric United Corporation, in San Antonio, Texas. Auric offers an unusually wide range of fractional gold coins.

A Sampling of Fractional Gold Coins

Coin	*Troy Ounces Gold*
Chinese ½ Panda	.5000
Mexican ½ Onza	.5000
South African ½ Rand	.5000
Mexican 20-Peso	.4823

Coin	Troy Ounces Gold
Austrian 4-Ducat	.4430
Canadian ¼ Maple Leaf	.2500
Chinese ¼ Panda	.2500
Mexican ¼ Onza	.2500
South African ¼ Rand	.2500
Mexican 10-Peso	.2411
South African 2 Rand	.2354
English New Sovereign	.2354
Austrian 20 Corona	.1960
Swiss 20 Franc	.1867
French 20 Franc	.1867
Mexican 5 Peso	.1205
Austrian 1 Ducat	.1107
¹⁄₁₀ Maple Leaf, Rand, Panda	.1000
Mexican 2½ Peso	.0603
Mexican 2 Peso	.0482

U.S. Gold Coins

The U.S. government was a Johnny-come-lately to the bullion coin derby. Between 1978 and 1983 Americans spent about $5 billion on foreign-made gold bullion coins. The United States decided it wanted in on that action. But America's bullion coin program has never been well thought out, and as a result the coins have not been popular among investors.

For one, they really aren't standard coins like the Maple Leaf, Krugerrand, or Mexican Peso. Rather, they are officially called American Arts Gold Medallions. They carry the likenesses of American artists, writers, and performers: Louis Armstrong, Robert Frost, Frank Lloyd Wright, Alexander Calder, Willa Cather, Mark Twain, Marian Anderson, Grant Wood, Helen Hayes, and John Steinbeck. They are best known simply as U.S. Gold.

The total weight of this one-ounce coin (there is also a ½-ounce size) is 1.111 troy ounces, which includes a small amount of copper and silver for hardness. This makes the U.S. Gold coin 0.900 fine, or 21.6-karat gold, slightly less pure than the Krugerrand, although it contains exactly the same amount of gold.

When the program was launched in the early 1980s, these gold medallions were sold at post offices—not exactly surroundings that instill great confidence in investors. Letting people buy directly from the U.S. mint also failed miserably because of the cumbersome red tape. It often took two months for an investor to receive the gold.

When those efforts failed, the Feds signed up J. Aron & Company, a big U.S. metals wholesaler, to market and distribute the coins. That didn't work either.

The problem was the coin itself. The many different designs were confusing. And on top of that, Congress kept everybody guessing whether the program to mint and sell the coins would be extended beyond the mid-1980s. U.S. Gold couldn't compete in a gold bullion coin market full of other more attractive choices.

Other American Gold Coins

The U.S. government once minted a selection of spendable gold coins. Today these rare coins are bought and sold at incredibly high prices by coin collectors and investors. These rare U.S. gold coins from the past include the $20 Double Eagle, also known as the St. Gaudens (after the man who designed the coin); $20 Double Eagle/Liberty type; $10 Eagle Liberty and Indian Head types; $5 Half Eagle Liberty and Indian Head types; the $3 Princess; and the $2.50 Quarter Eagle (Indian Head and Liberty types).

These are not bullion coins but numismatic or semi-numismatic coins. Their prices per ounce of gold are vastly higher than for the bullion coins. The St. Gaudens, for example, is one of the most popular collector coins around. But to buy it in uncirculated condition —which, incidentally, is one of the lesser conditions in numismatics —you would pay a "premium" of over 100 percent above the actual value of the gold. Rare coins are covered in greater detail in Chapter 13.

Gold Coins of Mexico

Mexico's 50 Peso "Centenario" coin, weighing in at a hefty 1.34 troy ounces, with 1.2057 troy ounces of pure gold, is one of the world's largest gold coins. It was first issued in 1921 to commemorate the 100th anniversary of Mexico's independence from Spain.

Some investors and coin experts consider it the most beautifully designed of all the gold bullion coins. But its odd size made it a wall-flower. So in 1980, Mexico created a series of even-weight coins—the Mexican "Onza" in one-, ½-, and ¼-troy ounce sizes. These coins are .990 fine gold. The one-ounce size has a total weight of 1.111 ounces. It would seem to answer the critics of the odd-sized 50 peso coin, but for some reason it has never made it big among investors. Still, this is a legal tender bullion coin that offers a middle ground between the politically offensive Krugerrand, the "soft" 24-karat gold Maple Leaf, and the hard-to-figure Austrian coin that looks cheap on the surface but can burn you on the spread when it comes time to sell.

Restrike Coins

Many gold bullion coins minted around the world today are officially called restrike coins. These coins were minted many years ago as real money, before gold coins were taken out of general circulation. Later, when it became profitable for governments to mint and sell gold coins, these same designs were brought back and restruck as investment coins. The British Sovereign, Austrian Corona, Russian Chervonetz, and many other bullion coins are official government restrikes.

If pure bulk is what you are after in a coin, the Chinese can oblige. China now mints a Grand Gold Panda that weighs an astounding 12 troy ounces (a troy pound) of 99.9 percent pure gold. The coin is 2¾ inches in diameter and joins China's other Gold Panda coins.

SILVER BULLION COINS

Although gold bullion coins abound, silver buffs once had to satisfy themselves with "junk silver" coins and semi-numismatic silver money—the real silver dimes, quarters, and halves we carried around before silver prices headed skyward.

A one-ounce silver bullion coin—the silver equivalent of the gold Maple Leaf—never appeared. There were plenty of numismatic silver coins, and the ubiquitous commemorative silver items celebrating athletic events or other festivities. Though governments merrily minted and marketed gold bullion items for many years, they offered no similar deal for silver.

But no more. Silver bullion coins from private and government mints have made a splash in the precious metals investment waters.

Mexico, a leading silver producer, was long expected to be a leader in silver bullion coins. Finally, that nation created and produced a one-ounce .999 fine silver bullion coin starting with the 1982 mint date. But it took Mexico almost until 1985 to release the coin, called the Libertad Onza. It is, in a mouthful, an "annually dated, non-restrike, one-ounce, legal tender silver coin." The company marketing it in the United States is A-Mark Precious Metals, a Beverly Hills wholesale metals firm.

Since silver has become so popular among small investors, millions of ounces in small bars and coins are snapped up monthly, especially when prices are low and the market is flat. As the first legal tender pure silver coin to become available, the Libertad should easily become the leader in this category, although copycat coins will undoubtedly follow. Libertad coins are sold at over 1,000 coin dealers, banks, and brokerage firms nationwide.

The problem with this and many other one-ounce silver coins is the premium you pay over the actual value of the silver. It costs money to mint, ship, and market these coins, for which you pay in the premium over "melt value." That premium, as a percentage of your investment, can look mighty high on these coins, compared to buying silver in 100-ounce bars or through certificate programs. Beware of the slick sales pitch about all of the advantages these coins offer, and the possibility they will carry additional numismatic value (value for their rarity, in addition to silver content). The bottom line is how much money you are paying *per ounce of silver that you get.*

PRIVATE MINT SILVER COINS

Because the Mexican government was a little slow on the draw, private firms stepped forward with silver bullion coins designed specifically for investors. Here's a sampling:

• Monex International (Newport Beach, California), one of the largest metals dealers in the United States, has its own silver coin called the Silver Eagle. This coin sells at the prevailing market price of silver, plus a premium of 75 cents per coin. It is sold only through Monex, in lots of 500, which rules out small investors. The premium can look attractive, or expensive, depending on the price of silver. With poor man's gold selling at $7.50, that's a 10 percent fee. With silver at $11 or $15, however, it can make the Silver Eagle more competitive with other forms of silver.

The Silver Eagle is minted for Monex by the Royal Canadian Mint, a hallmark that enhances the coin's appeal. But don't confuse it with another Monex product, the Trade Eagle, an entirely different coin.

• Sunshine Bullion Company, part of the big silver mining concern Sunshine Mining (Dallas), has a .999 pure silver one-ounce coin named—appropriately enough—the Sunshine. It usually carries a hefty premium over its silver value, however—often over $1 per ounce. Each Sunshine is dated, carries a serial number, and is guaranteed by Sunshine Bullion Company. One advantage is that you can buy one coin at a time.

• A-Mark, the Beverly Hills wholesale firm, produces Liberty Silver—another one-ounce bullion "round" of .999 pure silver. The Liberty Silver medallion is about the size of a silver dollar but is made with a high-gloss finish so it's more eye-catching. Each coin is guaranteed by A-Mark Precious Metals.

• Gold Standard Corporation, which makes the only privately minted gold bullion coins, also has a silver entrant called the Edward C. Harwood ounce. This .900 fine coin contains exactly one ounce of silver, but actually weighs 1.11 ounces, including the alloys. Gold Standard's lineup includes ½- and ¼-ounce silver coins.

A Slew o' Silver: The Rest of the Silver Coin World

Each year about eighty nations issue silver coins. Most of them commemorate some type of athletic event. The United States minted a silver coin for the 1984 Olympics. Canada did it for the 1983 World University Games in Edmonton. China, Ethiopia, Cuba, Hungary, Poland, and Turkey have all done silver coins commemorating World Cup Soccer championships. France has one depicting the Panthéon in Paris. Italy helped celebrate the 2,000th birthday of poet/philosopher Virgil with a silver coin.

The Silver Institute, in Washington, DC, publishes a booklet, *Modern Silver Coinage*, with detailed information on all silver coins issued around the world each year. It lists coins that depict everything from dictators past and present to the liberation of Venezuela by Simón Bolívar and births of nations such as Israel, the Dominican Republic, and Brunei (the sultanate that occupies the northern coast of the island of Borneo . . . of course!). For the $7 price tag, The Silver Institute includes the names and addresses of the mints from which these silver gems can be purchased. Write: The Silver Institute, 1001 Connecticut Avenue N.W., Suite 1138, Washington, DC 20036.

"JUNK SILVER" COINS

Until 1965, the United States minted coins that were 90 percent silver. Today those coins sell in big canvas bags—called, appropriately enough, bagged silver—as one of the popular ways to invest in this commodity. These old (though *not* numismatic or rare) coins come in bags containing $1,000 worth of coins as measured by their original face value. That means a bag of junk silver contains either 10,000 dimes, 4,000 quarters, or 2,000 half-dollars.

The value of these big bags of coins has nothing to do with their age. The price is linked strictly to the market price of silver. Each bag of junk coins contains 723 ounces of silver. So, with the price of silver at $10, you would have to pay $7,230 plus a small premium to lug one home.

Although bullion bars and coins are more popular, trading in bagged coins is surprisingly active. One attraction is that these coins still are *real money*. Even if silver were to become totally worthless, your $1,000 face value bag of coins would still be worth $1,000 at the grocery store. Uncle Sam guarantees it. Of course, for a bag that cost $7,200 that's not much consolation.

Although $1,000 face value bags are the *main* way to trade junk silver coins, they aren't the *only* way. Coins also trade in partial bags, by the roll and individually—especially old silver dollars. If you read financial publications, you've probably seen the ads hawking Morgan and Peace silver dollars. The rarest specimens of these coins, and the ones in *top* investment grades, sell for prices vastly higher than their bullion value. Most of the remainder are semi-numismatic coins.

The well-worn, circulated silver dollars are little more than junk silver coins. These coins, minted between 1878 and 1935, each contain 0.773 ounce of pure silver, and they too can trade in bags of $1,000 face value.

The Kennedy Clads

Kennedy half-dollars minted from 1965 to 1970 were made of 40 percent silver. These too are bought and sold by the bagful. Each $1,000 face value bag contains 2,000 coins and 296 ounces of silver. Kennedy half-dollars minted from 1971 on might look the same, but they contain no silver.

Since there is less silver in these coins (0.148 ounce), the difference between the face value and the price they sell for on the open market is not as great. Thus the price *floor* on the Kennedy clads is slightly more significant. The coin itself is worth 50 cents face value, which means that *an ounce of Kennedy clad silver can never fall below $3.38.* Buying silver this way has a built-in limit on risk.

But junk coins have their drawbacks as a method of investing in silver. When prices are moving swiftly in either direction, dealers may shun junk silver. It's more difficult to handle. You might be forced to sell for a lower price during such periods. (On the other hand, you might be able to pick up bagged coins at a bargain from somebody else.)

Another drawback is the erratic price. Experts point out that the price relationship between silver clad coins and pure silver bullion can be unpredictable, especially when the market is hot.

The bottom line is: Junk silver can look better when the price of silver is low; but if there is a dramatic increase in prices (a common event with this volatile commodity) your Kennedy clads might not be able to keep up.

Profiting from Coin/Bar Premiums

A little-known way to boost your silver profits is to "play" the difference in premiums between silver coins and 100-ounce silver bars. When prices are low, premiums calculated as a percentage of the total value are proportionately higher on all silver. Overhead costs just as much when the price is $7.50 as when it is $12.

But when the price jumps, the pendulum can swing. Some investors use these shifts to trade back and forth between silver coins and silver bullion bars to pick up "free" bonus ounces of silver that they add to their holdings. If dealers are willing to buy back silver coins at a high premium, and you already own some, you can trade in that silver for larger bars and come away with more metal. When the balance shifts back in the other direction, you can trade again. This is one way to slowly build your holdings without spending any more money. (More in Chapter 19 on strategies.)

AND NOW . . .
PLATINUM BULLION COINS TOO

It was inevitable. Gold was first . . . then silver. Individual investors gobbled up the bullion investment coins by the millions worldwide. Bullion coins made precious metals investing accessible to everyone.

By the mid-1980s, however, gold and silver had stubbed their toes and platinum was gaining recognition. As more investors discovered platinum, more dealers started selling it.

Along came the first platinum bullion coin for investors—the first platinum coin of any kind since the Russians made them in the early 1800s. The coin is the one-ounce platinum Noble, a legal tender British coin (face value 10 British pounds) with exactly one troy ounce of platinum. Since platinum is a harder metal than gold, coins need not contain alloys for toughness.

The Noble was first launched in Great Britain, West Germany, and Switzerland to a rousing welcome from investors. More than 100,000 coins (some $40 million worth) were sold in the first year they were available. Later a ¹⁄₁₀-troy ounce size was introduced.

But here's the catch. The platinum Noble is not yet widely available in the United States, although some dealers have now added it to their bullion menus.

If you wish, you can buy the coins, directly from the firm that has exclusive marketing rights—Ayrton Metals Ltd., in London, an international dealer with a link to a South African platinum producer. To encourage smaller investors, the London dealer will sell one coin at a time. What's more, if you don't want to take possession of the platinum, a certificate program is available for storing your coins overseas.

The Noble is actually minted by the government of the Isle of Man, a British territory. These are the coin's specifications:

Platinum Noble Specifications

Platinum content:	1.0 troy ounce (31.103 grams)
Minimum fineness:	99.95 percent
Diameter:	32.70 millimeters

According to Ayrton Metals, the premium on the coin (the price above the actual value of the metal) will be in line with premiums on gold bullion coins. Purchases of from one to nine coins will be charged a premium of about 6 percent. That drops to 4 percent on larger orders.

If the Noble proves half as popular as the predictions claim, it should become widely available through precious metals dealers in the United States. Meanwhile, if you are in London, you might stop in at The Platinum Shop on New Bond Street, where the platinum Noble coin is also sold over the counter. For more information on this coin contact:

Ayrton Metals Ltd.
30 Ely Place
London, EC1N 6RT
England
Telephone: 01-404-0970

Other Platinum Coins

South Africa and the Soviet Union are the world's two largest platinum-producing nations. They won't be far behind with their own platinum coins if there's a dollar (or rand or ruble) to be made. The Soviets have a 150-ruble platinum coin, and the South Africans toyed with the platinum coin idea for years before taking some tentative steps into the world market. Unless there is a dramatic reversal in platinum's popularity, you should see more platinum coins in years to come.

In the United States, Gold Standard Corporation has its finger in this pie as well. Gold Standard makes and sells its own one-ounce platinum coin, as well as fractional platinum coins in ½-, ¼-, and ⅒-ounce sizes.

PRIVATE STORAGE:
STASHING YOUR METALS CACHE

For investors who want to take possession of their gold, silver, platinum, or palladium, there is the perennial $64,000 question: Where to put it?

Nothing short of physical possession will satisfy the qualms of many Americans today. They've read too many stories about bankrupt dealers, banks, storage facilities, and all manner of supposedly "safe" places to keep precious metals investments. Other individuals remain fearful that the federal government will someday confiscate all privately held gold, as it once did in the 1930s. While that's about as likely today as the Soviet Union or the United States unilaterally disarming, the fear seems to be chronic.

The risk of temporary "confiscation" of assets held at savings institutions has also been dramatically demonstrated in recent years. In 1985, when the State of Ohio forced seventy-one privately insured savings banks to close their doors for several days to prevent a "run," people with safe-deposit boxes were unable to retrieve their holdings. They were, quite literally, left out in the cold.

One thing is certain. Storing your precious metals at home is definitely *not* a good idea. In fact, that is about the worst place of all. Yet some people insist on doing just that, believing their homeowner's insurance will cover any loss should a burglar visit or the entire place go up in smoke, turning those valuable coins into a metallic blob. In most cases, homeowner's insurance policies would pay only a fraction of the actual loss. And don't forget that if you keep valuable items such as gold coins at home, the premium on that policy could be astronomical.

Nevertheless, precious metals dealers tell tales of strange things people do with their metals. One California firm, for example, reports buying back a 1,000-ounce bar of silver that the owner had painted black and was using as a $10,000 doorstop!

Bank Safe-Deposit Boxes

A better alternative, and one that most sensible individuals have chosen in the past, is a safe-deposit box at the local bank or savings and loan association. It's relatively convenient if you do your regular banking there, but there are drawbacks to bank safe-deposit boxes.

Many banks have long waiting lists of depositors wanting safe-deposit boxes. Even if you want one, a safe-deposit might not be available at the bank of your choice. Most banks permit access to safe-deposit boxes only during regular banking hours, which may be inconvenient for you. And for secrecy buffs, handing over your social security number and other information as required by a bank makes this a less than totally private choice.

The Private Vault Phenomenon

Enter the storage phenomenon of the 1980s—the privately owned and operated security vault. As the decade began, such a thing scarcely existed. Now there are more than a hundred private safe-deposit firms all over the country—largely because of demand from millions of precious metals and rare-coin investors.

But private vaults have their problems too. They offer security that is usually as good and often better than banks, but they are not immune to break-ins. And there was such a rush of new companies into the market (the vast majority have been in business only a few years) that many went bankrupt—hardly a reassuring thought for their security-seeking patrons.

The best private storage vaults, though few in number, offer some attractive lures:

• Most offer access 365 days a year, twenty-four hours a day. At some facilities, getting into your box at 3:00 A.M. on Christmas morning might take an appointment, but you could do it.

• Private storage vaults have state-of-the-art security, which usually nets them a *higher* security rating than a standard bank vault. Measures include twenty-four-hour armed guards, special double identification numbers, heat and noise sensors, and television surveillance. All of this does you little good, of course, if the company goes out of business.

• Private storage vaults offer a wider range of box sizes—from letter-size to room-size.

• A few private vaults also offer anonymous storage, something like a Swiss bank account. This has pros and cons, however, since anyone who has your key and knows your personal identification number can loot your box.

• Short-term storage is available through many private firms—handy if you go away for the summer or move.

If price is a top consideration for you, however, the banks would win hands down, at least for the time being. Most private security vault rentals are much more expensive than banks. Private rentals range from $100 for a small box, to thousands per year for the largest.

Yearly rates at a bank can range from as low as $25 to perhaps $150 or so. But that too is changing. Now that financial institutions have been deregulated, some have "discovered" their safe-deposit boxes and have been raising rents to generate income. Others are adding space to meet the demand from consumers.

Insurance Savings

You can even save money by storing your precious metals and rare coins in a bank or private security vault. If the vault has top security measures and a good reputation, you may be able to eliminate this part of your homeowner's insurance coverage.

Instead, take out a separate policy of your own covering the contents of your bank safe-deposit box or private vault box. Several major insurance companies are now offering this type of policy, generally at bargain rates since a vault with armed guards and high-tech detection devices is a much better bet than the security of your home. The price difference between homeowner's coverage and private vault coverage can be as large as 90 percent. It's also a good idea to protect yourself against possible loss at a private firm that runs into financial trouble. Don't count on their promises or on the insurance policy they say they have. It might not be enough.

Use caution in choosing a private security vault. Like most new trends that take off rapidly, there will be a painful shakeout period in the private vault business. Check credentials, check the Better Business Bureau, check the backers of the venture, and inquire into the vault company's financial stability. Don't be shy. It's your gold.

CHAPTER 10

Easy Street: Fast, Simple Ways to Own Precious Metals

- **Certificate Plans**
- **Accumulation Plans**
- **Plans Outside the United States**
- **Certificate Plans: What to Look For**
- **To Segregate or Not to Segregate**
- **Program Profiles**
- **A "Stock Market" for Certificates**

Investments in general can be a big hassle—too time consuming, too much "shopping around," and too many traps to avoid. In the rough-and-tumble world of precious metals, those headaches can become migraines.

There's a way—actually several ways—to own all four metals without many of the common annoyances of direct bullion or coin ownership.

There are lots of variations, but these plans fall into two basic categories:

- precious metals certificates
- precious metals accumulation programs.

They also go by these names:

- warehouse receipts (certificates)
- delivery orders (certificates)
- passbook accounts (accumulation plans)
- storage accounts (accumulation plans).

Don't let all the different names confuse you. They can christen it a certificate, an accumulation plan, a passbook, a storage account, or a dozen other aliases. Whatever the name, most have a similar result—you own the gold, silver, platinum, or palladium, but you don't take physical possession of it. They make owning precious metals simple—a badge that has won the hearts of many investors.

CERTIFICATE PLANS

Some precious metals certificates are offered exclusively by individual firms. Others, such as Mocatta, Brooks, and Bank of Delaware certificates, are offered both through the issuer and through other independent dealers. These are some of the better-known plans:

- Deak-Perera offers a certificate plan that doubles as an accumulation program, for *all four* metals. It's available only through Deak offices.
- Dreyfus Gold Deposits, Inc., part of the huge Dreyfus funds and financial services organization, has a certificate plan all its own.
- Citibank, the huge New York City banking conglomerate, offers a popular gold and silver certificate program, available only through Citibank.
- Bank of Delaware, known primarily as a place where other firms store the metals sold through their certificate programs, offers a certificate plan of its own. It's available directly from the bank or through other precious metals dealers.
- Republic National Bank of New York, one of the country's biggest metals traders, sells bullion and certificates directly to the public through Republic Bullion Corporation (Los Angeles). Republic Na-

tional Bank certificates are also sold through other precious metals dealers.

• Rhode Island Hospital Trust National Bank (RIHT)—despite its rather unusual name—is one of the largest precious metals dealers in the nation. Hospital Trust has gold and silver certificates that are well received in the precious metals field. RIHT certificates are also sold through other precious metals dealers and banks. Those firms may put their own name on the certificate, but the metals are bought and stored by RIHT.

• Prudential-Bache, one of the country's largest brokerage houses, offers a certificate Depository Bullion Program exclusively through its own metals division for gold, silver, and platinum.

• Mocatta Metals Corporation Delivery Orders (certificates) are available from dealers such as International Trading Group, First National Monetary, and C. Rhyne & Associates, among others.

• Brooks, the armored car and courier company, is another firm that markets its own brand of precious metals ownership certificate, although it requires a higher minimum purchase than many others. Monex International handles the Brooks certificate, as does Deak-Perera.

The certificates offered by these firms differ in many ways, even though they have the same basic structure. Minimum amounts required, commissions for purchases and sales, storage methods and charges, and whether or not you can buy by phone are all items that vary.

ACCUMULATION PLANS

An accumulation plan differs only slightly from a precious metals certificate program. While some of the major certificates (Mocatta, RIHT, Republic) are sold by independent dealers, an accumulation plan is unique to the firm that offers it. You may still receive something that looks like a certificate attesting to the amount of metal you own, or simply a periodic statement from the firm with similar information.

The net result is pretty much the same with most plans; you can buy and sell from your account at any time, and the metals are stored in a recognized depository—often the same place that metals for certificates are kept.

Here is an overview of some precious metals accumulation programs:

• Merrill Lynch, the nation's largest brokerage firm, has a precious metals Sharebuilder Plan that lets investors start with $100.
• Shearson Lehman Brothers has a similar plan that you can start with $500.
• Brink's Precious Metals Exchange, Inc., a part of Brink's Incorporated (yes, the armored car company), has one of the newer programs, launched in 1984.
• First National Bank of Chicago offers a precious metals passbook account for gold and silver.
• C. Rhyne & Associates offers a monthly purchase plan.
• Gold Standard Corporation calls its program the 49er Club.
• Dean Witter, the financial services arm of the Sears empire, offers a Precious Metals Portfolio Plan for gold, silver, and platinum through its precious metals group.
• PaineWebber and E. F. Hutton are two other major Wall Street brokerage firms that include precious metals among their offerings.

That's only a small sampling. Most major financial services firms will soon offer investors a way to purchase and store precious metals. (The dealer stores the metals for you.) Even discount stockbrokers are moving into precious metals.

One of the latest and most interesting new arrivals is the discount broker exclusively for precious metals. That's remarkable because precious metals are already sold with rather thin markups and commissions by many dealers. Since 1975 discount stock and bond brokers have revolutionized that field for investors, slashing commissions by as much as 70 percent and offering no-frills, cut-rate service.

The same could happen with precious metals in coming years. Many dealers tend to go heavy on the advice and telephone solicitation. Discounters, on the other hand, don't go out of their way to get business. Their salespeople are on salary, not commission, so there is less pressure for a sale.

Major banks have even stepped in. Security Pacific National Bank, a large Los Angeles–based bank, launched what it called "the first major discount brokerage operation in the United States to offer the sale of precious metals to its customers." Security Pacific Brokers, the bank's affiliate, offers a wide range of precious metals choices, including an accumulation plan.

Benham Certified Metals, in Palo Alto, California, also calls itself a "precious metals discount brokerage firm . . . offering efficient service with none of the costly extras." The muscle behind Benham Certified Metals is the Benham Capital Management Group, which manages more than $2 billion for 150,000 investors. Shareholders in Benham's mutual funds can buy precious metals and pay for them by transferring money directly out of a fund account. Precious metals storage (accumulation) plans are also available through this discounter.

PLANS OUTSIDE THE UNITED STATES

There are many ways to set up a precious metals account outside the United States, if that is your preference. Dealing with some foreign firms, however, can be anything but fast and simple and is not recommended for beginning or small investors. Communications—by mail, telex, or telephone—can be costly or, in the case of the mail, tediously slow. Even though metals prices are quoted worldwide in U.S. dollars, you may have to convert to foreign currencies to purchase gold or other metals in other countries. Other drawbacks: Fees and commissions tend to run higher at foreign outlets; selling is more difficult because of distance; and minimum investments required can be higher than at most U.S. firms.

The following examples are only a small sampling of what you can expect to find if you look beyond U.S. borders.

As you may already suspect, Switzerland is a major center of precious metals trading. All of the major Swiss banks offer precious metals. Remember that banking outside the United States is quite different. Bankers often function as stockbrokers, financial planners, and metals dealers in addition to providing traditional banking services.

Crédit Suisse, for example, offers a full selection of ways to purchase gold, silver, platinum, and palladium. Included is a "metal account" that allows investors to buy free of sales tax and have their gold or other metals stored in Switzerland.

Foreign Commerce Bank (FOCO) and Ueberseebank are two other Swiss banks that have precious metals accumulation plans that are marketed in the United States. Ueberseebank has its Goldplan and Silverplan accumulation accounts, while Foreign Commerce Bank offers precious metals accounts for gold, silver, platinum, and palladium.

The Canadian firm Guardian Trust Company (Toronto) is considered a leader north of the border. Guardian has something called Tele-Trade, which lets you buy or sell gold, silver, platinum, or palladium over the phone, as well as accumulation plans for these metals and managed accounts. Bank of Nova Scotia and Canadian Imperial Bank of Commerce both offer gold and silver certificates, coins, and bullion purchase plans.

CERTIFICATE PLANS: WHAT TO LOOK FOR

A precious metals certificate is a piece of paper that says you own a specified amount of gold, silver, platinum, or palladium stored for you at a designated location. But don't let the word certificate fool you. This is not like a bank deposit certificate that pays interest and expires on a certain date. A precious metals certificate pays no interest and never expires. You can hold it as long as you wish, or sell it the next day.

Think of it more like a receipt for something you have purchased but are having stored elsewhere. The certificate (receipt) absolves you of some of the drawbacks to buying physical gold (or other metals) and offers other attractive advantages. Here are some of the features of precious metals certificates:

• You needn't worry about what size bullion bar or wafer to choose, or which brand will be the most liquid. *With certificate programs, you can invest by dollar volume or by the amount of gold, silver, platinum, or palladium you wish to purchase, depending on the plan.*
• You can take delivery of the metals you buy through a certificate program, but most people don't. After all, that's one of the main attractions of buying this way . . . no questions about how delivery will be made . . . no concerns with where to store it . . . no extra delivery charges tacked on.
• No sales tax. In some states, if you take delivery of your purchases (even if it is actually being stored somewhere else), you will have to pay sales tax. But with most certificate programs, the metals are stored where there is no sales tax (Delaware is the most popular spot).

• If you purchase bullion in small quantities, you could end up paying huge premiums over the actual value of the bullion. Over time, that can add up to thousands of dollars down the drain. With precious metals certificates, you pay a set percentage commission that eliminates this problem.

• Certificate or accumulation programs let you buy precious metals in small amounts on a set schedule to take advantage of a technique called dollar cost averaging. By making purchases of a fixed dollar amount on a set schedule over a period of years, regardless of the price, you will accumulate holdings at a lower *average* cost than the market itself has experienced. That's because you buy a fixed dollar amount, and thus actually purchase more ounces of metal for that amount when the price is low. Over time this works to your advantage.

• Opening a certificate account and making additional purchases couldn't be easier. Fill out a short application form and send a check (or take it in personally). When you want to buy more, just send another personal check. They'll buy the day they receive it and send you a confirmation, or new certificate. Some plans, notably Citibank's, let you buy over the telephone and charge it to a Visa or MasterCard account.

• You may be able to buy by phone and transfer the funds to pay for your purchase directly out of your bank account, money market fund, or other type of investments. When you sell, the proceeds can be automatically deposited to your cash holdings in an interest-bearing account.

A Cautious Investor's Tip: When you lock in any type of precious metals investment over the telephone—a certificate, coins, bullion, options—the dealer will tape-record the telephone conversation. Your verbal agreement and their confirmation will be on tape. The dealer will follow up immediately with a written confirmation of your order. If ten minutes after you hang up the price goes against you, you cannot call back and say, "Never mind!"

• Certificates offer a fast way to shift all or part of your holdings outside the United States *even if you buy through a U.S. dealer.* Check the box requesting storage abroad and presto, you own gold or silver stored in Britain, Switzerland, Canada, or other countries.

• You should be able to buy and sell at attractive prices through certificate plans because you are actually buying in bulk through the facilities of these major institutional traders. Citibank, for example, adds up all the purchases for the day (the cutoff time for buying is 12:30 P.M. New York time), then goes into the market to make those purchases as a big lump, which should mean a better price for you.

• The metal you own will automatically be insured—an expense you will pay for in the annual storage/insurance charge.

• Many firms offering certificates throw in the first year of storage free. At least one (RIHT) has only a small one-time charge and no yearly storage fee. When the market isn't doing so well, other firms may offer to waive storage costs as an incentive for you to invest more.

• A precious metals certificate is *not* negotiable. If somebody steals it, he will not be able to cash it in. If your certificates are lost, they can be replaced easily. That's also crucial if you ever carry one (or many) of these certificates out of the country. Since it's non-negotiable, you don't have to declare it with customs.

But there's another side to this issue. You will have to sell the certificate (and the metals it represents) back to the firm from which you bought it. You can't take your Deak-Perera certificate to Republic Bullion and expect to sell it.

TO SEGREGATE OR NOT TO SEGREGATE

How the certificate issuer stores your gold, silver, platinum, or palladium is a serious matter. There are two basic ways. One is to specifically label the metals in a vault as yours. That means there will actually be a little stack of gold bars (or whatever) in the Bank of Delaware vault that says this metal belongs specifically to you. In trade lingo, that's called non-fungible storage.

The other method, you may have already guessed, is fungible storage. In this case, you still own the metal, but it is *not physically separated* in storage as belonging specifically to you. It doesn't have your name on it.

The metal is still there. You own a recorded, undivided interest. But your holdings are lumped together with metals belonging to other certificate holders.

Why is this important? In most cases it isn't if you are dealing with large, reputable international firms and the metal is stored at a third-party facility where it is separately insured. Still, there is always the chance that the firm you bought from could go bankrupt. No firm is completely safe. Even some of the big names in the business have been caught up in bankruptcies that have shocked investors.

If the firm holding your gold does go bust, there is still a good chance you will get 100 percent of your investment out under either method of storage. But there is a slightly better chance if storage is specifically segregated, or non-fungible.

Investors have lost millions in the past at bogus dealers who did not actually have the metals in the vault, even though buyers believed it was there. When several large precious metals dealers went belly up in the early 1980s it sent a scare through others that offer certificate and storage plans. Investors started calling, wondering if their gold was *really there*.

In response to those worries, Deak-Perera, for one, has a special audit run periodically to assure its certificate customers that the metals are there. Accounts are also insured by Lloyd's of London. That assurance was necessary because Deak's plan, like most others, doesn't separate metals by individual owners. Other dealers take steps to reassure investors. Rhode Island Hospital Trust National Bank, for example, has a Big Eight accounting firm count up the gold and silver every year to help ease any fears.

Who Segregates?

The Mocatta Metals Corporation Delivery Order (same as a certificate) is one of the few that offers non-fungible (segregated) storage of your holdings. They are available from dealers that handle Mocatta's products.

Bank of Delaware depository receipts that represent segregated storage of your metals are available from the bank or through other dealers. Brooks certificates can be set up as non-fungible accounts if you wish, and Brink's Precious Metals Exchange says metals kept in its storage program are "individually segregated and clearly marked with your transaction number . . . they are stored in your name and insured." Republic National Bank certificates can also call for segregating the metal, if so desired.

PROGRAM PROFILES

Here is a closer look at some of the best, most popular, and most interesting precious metals certificate, accumulation, and storage programs. *All minimum purchase amounts, fees, and commissions come from the dealers themselves and are subject to change.*

Certificates

Deak-Perera Certificate/Accumulation Program

This is how Deak describes its own certificate plan: "We take care of everything—purchasing the metal, arranging for shipment, and placing it in insured storage in a precious metals depository. This approach relieves you of any concern over security or the expenses of fabricating, shipment, insurance, assay or sales taxes that can be associated with taking physical delivery."

Here's how it works. You call Deak, talk to one of the firm's salespeople, and lock in a firm price quote for whichever metal you are buying. The order is confirmed right there over the telephone, and you can specify whether you want your gold, silver, platinum, or palladium stored in the United States or abroad. If you want it stored outside the United States, however, a firm price won't be locked in until the next day.

Deak's representative will tell you exactly how much you owe for the purchase. If you are a first-time customer, you may be asked to wire funds for the purchase or send a money order. But a personal check will often suffice, if you insist. Later on, when you add to your account a check will be the simplest way to buy. If you haven't already done so, you will have to fill out an application/order form for the account. If you want, you can authorize Deak to accept your telephone instructions to buy and sell metals for your account. Without that authorization, you'll have to buy and sell in person or by mail. The ability to trade by phone is one benefit of this plan not available through some others.

When they have your money, they will issue a certificate stating exactly how much metal you own (to three decimal points) and where it is stored. To sell, you can call Deak, confirm the sale over the telephone, and send your signed certificate back to them later. After they receive it, they will send out your money.

To get started in a Deak-Perera certificate accumulation program you will need a minimum of $1,000. But after that, purchases can be made for as little as $100.

Commissions and Other Charges

Here are the commissions and other fees Deak charges (others will differ, and these are subject to change):

Size of Your Purchase	Percent Commission
$100 to $1,000	3
$1,000 to $10,000	2½
$10,000 to $50,000	2
More than $50,000	1½

There will also be a one percent commission anytime you take delivery of your metals, sell any portion of them, or transfer ownership to someone else. The minimum charge for any transaction is $10.

Deak offers free storage and insurance for the first calendar year you own the metals through a certificate. If you buy in January, for example, you won't have to pay storage charges for an entire year. But if you buy in December, you'll receive less than a month of free storage and insurance. After that, there is a ½ percent charge per year for storage and insurance. If you redeem your certificate before the yearly storage charge is all used up, that fee is *not* refundable, according to Deak.

The Deak Goldline Account Storage Program

Deak offers virtually the same accumulation/storage program under another name—the Goldline Account. Through it you can buy all four metals; the minimum purchase amounts are the same, commissions are the same (except there is a $15 minimum here), and you can buy and sell basically the same way over the telephone. One difference: Instead of a certificate you get a quarterly account statement.

You can also buy metals in different forms. For example, in addition to bullion bars, you can also invest in gold and silver coins through this account. You can choose domestic storage (at Bank of Delaware) or storage abroad (at Bank Leu, in Zurich, Switzerland). The only items you cannot store abroad through this plan are U.S. Gold medallions and junk silver coins.

You might even be able to shift funds into a Deak statement account directly through a stockbroker you already deal with. If your brokerage firm clears trades through Control Data's BTSI unit, you can sell stocks or bonds and have that money instantly shifted into precious metals in a Deak account.

Yet another variation available through Deak is the Brooks Armored Car storage account. You can purchase gold, silver, platinum, and palladium through Deak and have it stored by Brooks, which is a non-bank depository used by many major banks for safekeeping metals. Its vaults are in Wilmington, Delaware (no sales tax). If you buy this way, you will be issued a "warehouse receipt" for your metals, which will be stored individually in your name, separately from the metals owned by others. Brooks will bill you separately for storage charges. Typical Brooks storage charges are $7.50 per year for a 100-troy ounce silver bar; $18 per year for a bag of junk silver coins; $15 per year for one "unit" of gold coins (twenty coins); $18 per year for a 1,000-troy ounce silver bar; $22 per year for a 100-troy ounce bar of platinum or palladium; and $15 per year for a 10-ounce bar of those metals. (Brooks warehouse receipts are also available through Monex International, in Newport Beach, California.)

Citibank Gold and Silver Certificates

Citibank offers only gold and silver, not platinum or palladium. And its commission is a tad higher on smaller purchases. Here's the rundown (all fees, of course, are subject to change):

Size of Your Purchase	Percent Commission
Under $50,000	3
$50,000 to $100,000	2
$100,000 to $250,000	1¾
$250,000 to $500,000	1½

Citibank offers the first calendar year of storage and insurance free; then the charge is ½ percent yearly. When you sell or take delivery of the gold and silver there will be a one percent commission. With Citibank's certificate, however, *you can transfer ownership at any time without paying a commission.* (Deak charges a one percent commission on transfer.) There's never an assay charge as long as you do not take physical possession of the metals.

The only way to purchase over the telephone through the Citibank program is to charge it on your MasterCard or Visa credit card. You cannot call up and lock a price in on the telephone, then send a check as you can with some other certificate programs.

You can sell all or any part of the gold or silver you own at any time, through the mail or at any one of Citibank's offices in the United States and ninety-six other countries around the world. If you want, you can even walk in and pick up your metal at the depository you've selected, either in Delaware, London, or Zurich. (While it might sound exotic to stroll into a Swiss bank and pick up some gold bullion from your account, you'll get hit with a stiff Swiss "turnover tax" of about 6 percent if you do so.)

The minimum purchase at Citibank is $1,000 to start (which means that after the 3 percent commission, $970 would go to buy your gold or silver), and additions must be $100 or more. Each time you buy more you get another certificate, but only for the amount of additional metals you bought. So if you frequently buy this way in small amounts, you will soon have a fat sheaf of certificates to deal with.

Mocatta Metals Corporation Delivery Orders

The type of certificate issued by Mocatta Metals is called a Delivery Order. But since Mocatta rarely deals directly with the public, it is available mainly through other precious metals brokers and dealers. It doesn't matter from whom you buy it, since the delivery order is backed by Mocatta. The dealer is only an intermediary.

Delivery orders offered by Mocatta—one of the world's leading precious metals firms—work differently than the certificates already covered. Here you must purchase specific amounts (lots) of gold or silver. You cannot purchase by dollar amounts.

The minimum purchase through a Mocatta Delivery Order will be considerably higher. These are the different types/sizes available:

- 20 Krugerrands
- 20 Maple Leaf coins
- 20 Mexican 50 Peso coins

- 20 Austrian 100 Corona coins
- 1,000-ounce silver bar
- $1,000 face value bag of junk silver coins
- 1-kilo gold bar
- 100-ounce gold bar
- 400-ounce gold bar

Each bullion bar or sealed lot of gold coins is given a serial number that also appears on your Delivery Order. The certificate is proof that you legally own that specific numbered and sealed tube of coins, or bullion bar. According to Mocatta, "Ownership of the Delivery Order is identical to ownership of the specific lot of gold to which it refers."

Unless you ask to have the metal stored in Delaware, gold and silver in this program will automatically be stored in Switzerland (at a firm called MAT Securitas Express Ltd., well known in its field). Your gold or silver is insured by Lloyd's of London. You can transfer ownership of a Mocatta Delivery Order as you wish.

Paper Gold Done Right

Mocatta's delivery orders aren't nearly as flexible as some others. But for people who buy in larger amounts and worry about the safety of their investment, Mocatta's program goes the extra mile to ease your mind.

Before any delivery order (I'll also call them certificates for simplicity) is issued, Mocatta plunks a specific numbered bar or sealed tube of coins on the storage shelf in Switzerland. The serial number then goes on the certificate. The outfit that stores the metals (MAT Securitas) must deliver that specific gold or silver to the certificate holder on demand.

This is a totally segregated, or non-fungible, program. If Mocatta Metals Corporation or the storage company were to go bankrupt, your holdings would not be affected. The bill collectors would have no claim against your gold.

Where Can I Sell It?

Legally, this piece of paper is called non-negotiable. But you can assign, or transfer, it to another person or company—for a price. That's one way to sell a delivery order.

You might also sell it back to Mocatta Metals Corporation. The firm's policy "as a convenience to investors" is to buy back your delivery order if you want to sell. But Mocatta is under no *obligation* to buy it back. And remember, the company will buy back only from the original owner.

You can also sell by taking delivery of your gold or silver (you'll have to pay delivery charges if you do), and then sell that back to any other precious metals dealer. Mocatta buys bars made only by the major international refiners, so you should have no trouble.

To take delivery of your metals, you will first have to pay any outstanding storage charges and a small "out charge" of $20 per order. Storage charges at Mocatta are ½ percent per year for the first five years, then 2 percent yearly.

The price you pay for a Mocatta Delivery Order will include these elements:

- Mocatta's "base price" for gold on that day, which includes a profit margin.
- A $100 Delivery Order issuance charge.
- The storage charge due for the remainder of the first calendar year.
- Your dealer's commission, perhaps 3 percent.

A Cautious Investor's Tip: Even though a delivery order is nonnegotiable, getting a replacement for a lost certificate can be a hassle. The storage firm might even require that you post a bond equal to twice the value of your holdings. It's a good idea to keep precious metals certificates in a safe-deposit box or other secure place.

Dreyfus Gold Deposits, Inc.

This branch of the huge Dreyfus mutual funds and financial services group offers a certificate plan only for gold bullion and gold coins. The minimum purchase is $2,500, but you can add to your certificate in amounts as little as $100. Dreyfus isn't very well known as a precious metals dealer, even though it has been selling gold since it became legal to do so in 1975. The commissions on its certificate plan are:

Size of Your Purchase	Percent Commission
$2,500 to $50,000	2
More than $50,000	1

When you sell the gold back to Dreyfus, there is also a 2 percent commission for amounts under $50,000 and a one percent commission for amounts above that.

Storage fees are charged by a different method under the Dreyfus plan. Instead of paying ½ percent per year on the value of the metals, here you pay 15 cents per ounce per month. Under most circumstances this would result in a slightly lower storage charge for your gold. The metal is stored in Delaware in bulk, and your holdings are *not* individually labeled as yours.

You can buy either bullion, subject to the minimum amounts, or gold coins, subject to a ten-coin minimum initial purchase; five coins for add-ons. The four coins offered by Dreyfus are the Krugerrand, Maple Leaf, Austrian Corona, and Mexican Peso. The cost for storing gold coins is also 15 cents per ounce monthly.

Telephone Ordering

One attractive feature offered by Dreyfus is the ability to buy gold by phone. You lock in the price by phone; and they must receive your payment within five business days. But before you can deal by phone (you can sell your gold this way too), you will have to complete a telephone authorization form.

As with other certificate programs, there is no sales tax as long as you have the gold stored in Delaware. If you do take delivery, be prepared to pay any applicable sales taxes, plus a delivery charge, fabrication charge, handling charge, and administration fee.

Benham Certified Metals (BCM)

Benham Capital Management is a mutual fund group that has moved into precious metals. Its affiliate, Benham Certified Metals, is a discount precious metals broker. It doesn't keep an inventory of gold or silver but waits for investors to place an order before buying it on the wholesale market. Employees here work on salary, so you shouldn't be subject to the high-pressure sales pitches you sometimes get elsewhere.

One of the products Benham offers is a Depository Trust Account through the Bank of Delaware. This is a segregated (non-fungible) type account. Your gold and silver is individually labeled in your name and is physically separated from everybody else's.

With Depository Trust Account Storage, you receive a depository receipt (certificate) from the Bank of Delaware. BCM will bill you twice a year for storage costs and include an inventory of your holdings at that time. Storage fees are calculated monthly, at a rate of ¼ of one percent per year of the market value of your gold. For silver the storage charge is ½ of one percent.

If you decide to take delivery, the only additional charge is a $25 handling cost, plus postage and insurance. The big accounting firm Peat Marwick Mitchell audits BCM's holdings at the Bank of Delaware twice a year.

Or you can sidestep the dealer once you've made your purchase and deal directly with the Bank of Delaware. In that case, the bank will issue a certificate in your name for your gold or silver and deal directly with you. The bank will bill you for storage and insurance charges at the same rate. There is a minimum charge of $30. You can have the metal delivered whenever you want, for a $25 handling charge, plus postage and insurance to get it to your doorstep.

BCM's Pricing and Ways to Buy

When you buy, BCM will charge you the wholesale price it pays, plus one percent. When you sell back to Benham, the price is wholesale minus one percent.

One drawback for sellers: BCM will buy back only metals that it has sold, so don't expect to sell all of your previous holdings at top prices through this firm. Minimum purchase amounts are $2,000 for gold and $1,000 for silver.

Part of the attraction in dealing with a mutual fund family such as this is the ability to shift money from a stock or money market fund directly into precious metals. You can do it through BCM by filling out a telephone authorization form. If, for example, you have money invested in the Benham California Tax Free Trust, you can buy $1,000 worth of silver and pay for it by asking Benham to draw the funds from that account, or write a draft on your account. You can also pay by bank wire, certified check, or personal check.

Rhode Island Hospital Trust National Bank (RIHT)

This federally insured commercial bank is a heavy hitter in U.S. gold and silver wholesale markets. RIHT alone accounts for half of the gold and silver traffic in the United States and is the largest single player in the commercial market.

Rhode Island Hospital Trust plays both sides of the precious metals fence. It is a behind-the-scenes firm that provides the gold and silver sold through many of the country's major banks, brokerage firms, insurance companies, and precious metals dealers. If you purchase gold or silver through a program at your corner bank, the firm that actually handles the transaction could be RIHT. It works much like those discount stock brokerage operations you've seen springing up in banks and savings and loan associations all across the United States. They don't actually execute the stock market transactions themselves. Most often they have a deal with a major brokerage firm to provide that service for them. The same idea works with trading gold and silver bullion and certificates.

But you don't have to go through a bank, brokerage firm, or insurance company. You can buy directly from RIHT, as it also sells retail, offering a lesser-known but attractive precious metals certificate program for gold and silver. (*Note:* Federal rules permit commercial banks to sell gold and silver only. You will not find platinum or palladium from this source.)

Key attractions of the RIHT gold and silver certificate program are:

• Low minimum initial investment: only one ounce of gold, 50 ounces of silver.
• No storage charges beyond a one-time ½ percent "administration fee."

Here are the commissions RIHT charges to make a purchase of gold or silver:

Size of Your Purchase	Percent Commission
Up to $10,000	3
$10,001 to $50,000	2
More than $50,000	1½

The minimum charge on all fees and commissions is $10. The commission to sell back to RIHT is one percent on any size transaction.

One feature you will *not* find in a gold or silver certificate issued by Rhode Island Hospital Trust is segregated, or non-fungible, storage. The reason, quite simply, is that it is much cheaper to store in bulk. That's how RIHT can avoid charging any storage or insurance fees. To assuage the inevitable fears of some investors, it has the big accounting firm Coopers & Lybrand audit the gold pile every year to make sure it's all there. The metals are actually stored in the vaults of the bank's Providence, Rhode Island, headquarters.

Although RIHT buys and sells bullion, it is the certificate program that has gained popularity among individual investors. In the early 1980s, RIHT's gold and silver sales were roughly 75 percent bullion and 25 percent certificates. But by 1985 those figures had reversed. Explains an RIHT official: "Why pay three to five percent more for Krugerrand coins from a coin dealer . . . plus sales tax on top of that? Then you have to go out and rent a safe deposit box to keep them in."

In its letters to potential gold and silver investors, RIHT makes an important point. Gold and silver bought through a bank is *not* insured by the Federal Deposit Insurance Corporation (FDIC), as are cash deposits. That doesn't mean you would lose your investment if the bank goes under. It should still be safe, since it is separately insured (which you pay for) and stored at a separate location if you request it.

Republic National Bank
Gold and Silver Safekeeping Certificates

Republic National Bank (New York) is another heavy hitter behind the U.S. precious metals scene. RNB markets gold and silver bullion with its own hallmark, and also has a respected gold and silver certificate program.

If you plan to deal with Republic, however, it is best to work through the bank's precious metals retail arm—Republic Bullion Corporation, in Los Angeles. Although individual investors can buy and sell metals through the bank in New York, extracting information and help out of the metals division in New York can be exasperating for the individual investor. The metals division in New York, geared for institutional trading, doesn't seem interested in the individual. And without the right telephone number, trying to find your way from a large bank's switchboard to the department you want makes a chess match with Bobby Fischer seem like a cakewalk. Dealing through Republic Bullion Corporation should be easier.

Both gold and silver certificates from Republic can be purchased over the telephone. Republic will give you a fixed price over the phone for your purchase. You then must send a bank check, certified check, or money order postmarked within twenty-four hours.

The confirmed price you receive over the phone is fixed. If the price goes up after you put down the phone, so much the better for you. If it goes down, get used to it. You'll never be able to get each little blip on the price radar to go in your favor. Part of the fun in making a purchase is watching prices in the days preceding your purchase, as well as later on.

A Key Difference: By the Ounce, Not the Dollar

With Republic's certificates, you purchase metals by the ounce, not by dollar amount as you do with many other popular programs. The minimum gold purchase for a Republic Safekeeping Certificate is 5 ounces, which, at $450 for gold, would mean a minimum outlay of about $2,250. That puts it higher than some other certificates. You must also spend a little more to add to your Republic certificate. Subsequent orders must be for *full ounce amounts only*. So for investors looking for maximum flexibility in a gold certificate, this might not be the right choice.

For silver the situation is different. A first-time purchase must be for at least 100 ounces. Depending on the price of the white metal, you might be able to get started here for less. But add-on purchases for silver must be in 100-ounce increments. Other key points:

• The storage/insurance fee for gold is 10 cents per month per ounce of metal; 2 cents per month per ounce of silver.
• There is no service charge to have a Republic gold or silver certificate registered, transferred, or exchanged.
• Gold and silver can be stored in the United States (Bank of Delaware) or in Geneva, Switzerland.
• The certificate can be redeemed at any time, and Republic says you will receive your gold or silver within fifteen days. The delivery fee depends on the size of the bars or ingots. It ranges from 3 percent for one-ounce bars to one percent for 50-ounce.

Republic's certificates are sold at the prevailing market prices of gold and silver (Republic's "base price," which should be one of the lowest), plus these commissions.

Size of Your Purchase	Percent Commission
$1,000 to $50,000	2¾
$50,000 to $100,000	1¾
$100,000 to $250,000	1¼

The commission to sell metals from a Republic Certificate, no matter what the amount, is 0.75 percent.

First National Bank of Chicago:
Precious Metals Passbook Account

First National Bank of Chicago's program works much like a regular gold or silver certificate, except they've dubbed it a Precious Metals Passbook instead. Don't confuse it with a regular savings passbook account. This type of passbook pays you *no* interest.

This is another bank program where you must buy by the ounce instead of in dollar amounts. The minimum purchase is 5 ounces of gold, 100 ounces of silver. You can add to your precious metals passbook account at First National in one-ounce increments for gold, 50-ounce for silver.

You can buy or sell as often as you like, as long as you pay these commissions:

Size of Your Purchase or Sale	Percent Commission
Gold	
1 to 25 ounces	2
26 to 100 ounces	1½
More than 100 ounces	1
Silver	
50 to 400 ounces	2
401 to 1,000 ounces	1½
More than 1,000 ounces	1

Also of interest: First National Bank of Chicago offers a gold coin storage account. Coins available are Canadian Maple Leaf, Mexican Peso, Austrian 100 Corona, and U.S. Gold one-ounce. The minimum purchase to open a coin storage/accumulation account is five coins.

Accumulation, Depository, and Other Storage Plans

Brink's Precious Metals Exchange

Brink's Incorporated's armored cars move $5 billion worth of valuables door-to-door every day. Now Brink's is banking on its name to drum up business for the firm's latest project—Brink's Precious Metals Exchange, a new entry to the precious metals dealer derby. Brink's foray into precious metals got off to a rocky start, but the firm's recognized name and good selection of services should attract a following.

Brink's sells Krugerrands; Maple Leafs; gold, silver, and platinum bars; U.S. junk silver coins (including circulated silver dollars); and gold, silver, and platinum "rounds" (from Engelhard).

Although the main focus is on cash and delivery, Brink's also offers an individually segregated storage plan. The minimum purchase requirements are:

- Gold: 5 ounces, in any denomination or combination of bars or coins.
- Silver: 100 ounces of bullion in any combination of bars or rounds, 1/10 of a bag of junk silver, or 20 junk silver dollars.
- Platinum: 5 ounces of bullion in any combination of bars or rounds.

Pricing works differently at Brink's. The firm *will* give you a firm price over the phone, and that price will include *all* fees and commissions. That doesn't mean you're paying more. It's just added up differently. Instead of selling metals at the market price and then adding a percentage commission, Brink's figures those costs into the price it quotes you, *before* it gives it to you.

The storage fee at Brink's is ¾ of one percent yearly figured on the value of the metals you own. There is also a one-time "handling fee" of $15 and a minimum $25 storage fee for any one transaction.

Oh yes, and one other thing. If you decide to take delivery, a Brink's armored truck *does not* pull up to your front door. Like most other dealers, Brink's relies on the good old U.S. Postal Service to ship precious metals (registered and insured of course). As an added "touch" Brink's even sends it wrapped in a plain brown wrapper with the return address marked simply BPME.

Merrill Lynch Sharebuilder Plan

Few precious metals investment plans let you get started with so little ($100), add to your holdings whenever you want in such small amounts ($50), and offer three major metals—gold, silver, and platinum.

Merrill Lynch's Sharebuilder Account is not exclusively for precious metals. Merrill (the nation's largest brokerage firm) also aims this program at beginning stock market investors for an even lower minimum ($25). Once you have funds invested in a Sharebuilder Account, you can switch back and forth among the different metals, and between precious metals and stocks with great ease. By switching around, however, you get hit with fees and commissions that can erase any benefits that prompted your move in the first place.

If you are looking for a convenient place to dabble in precious metals and like the idea of keeping all of your finances under one roof (stocks, bonds, money market funds, etc.), firms like Merrill Lynch can certainly oblige. But if you are looking for a program that offers the widest choice of gold, silver, platinum, and palladium investments, you'd best go to a precious metals specialist. Metals are only a tiny part of a financial giant such as Merrill Lynch.

Sharebuilder Commissions

Here is Merrill Lynch's commission schedule for transactions in the Sharebuilder program.

Size of Your Investment	Commission
$300 or less	6 percent
$301 to $600	2 percent plus $12
$601 to $2,500	1½ percent plus $15
$2,501 to $5,000	1 percent plus $27.50

Unlike most other certificate and accumulation plans, Merrill Lynch sets a maximum amount of $5,000 that you can invest per transaction. If you want to sell, you can do it anytime with a phone call. They'll send you a check within five business days.

You may be wondering how you can buy $25 of any stock you choose, since many cost much more than that for a single share. And what kind of price will you get on your precious metals purchases in such small amounts?

It works like this: Merrill gathers up all the orders for each stock or precious metal made on a given day, then buys in bulk and puts the securities and metals in safekeeping. The gold, silver, and platinum are stored in London and Delaware depositories and are insured by Lloyd's of London. There is no additional fee for the storage. The plan includes a quarterly statement showing the status of your holdings.

Shearson Precious Metals Accumulation

Merrill Lynch rival Shearson Lehman Brothers Inc. (a subsidiary of American Express) lures investors through its own Accumulation Account. The minimum to start in this plan is $500, and there is no maximum amount.

This program caters to investors who already have an account at Shearson. If that's the case, the firm will gladly take the money out of an existing account to buy precious metals on your behalf. Platinum is not available under the Shearson plan, but you can purchase gold and silver bullion, and Krugerrands. If you wish, you can also have regular purchases made *automatically*—either weekly, monthly, or quarterly, always on a Wednesday. The minimum purchase is always $100. The funds would be plucked from another of your accounts at Shearson.

When you purchase gold or silver through Shearson's Accumulation Account, the metal is not segregated in your name. You own an interest in an unspecified block of metal that Shearson owns and stores. If you wish, you can request segregated ownership at Shearson's "bulk segregated account" at the Bank of Delaware *for a price*. For segregated storage you must pay 5 cents per ounce per month for gold; 3 cents for every 10 ounces of silver per month. If you want to avoid these charges, you must go along with unallocated storage.

If you buy metals this way, it is also best not to take delivery. Shearson will send you your gold or silver if you ask, but for anything less than a standard unit (100 ounces for gold; 1,000 ounces for silver; but only one Krugerrand) you will be charged a hefty fabrication fee. On a 108-ounce delivery, the 8 ounces, divided up into eight 1-ounce bars, could carry an extra $10 charge per bar.

You can avoid those charges by having your purchases made in Krugerrands. Better yet, if you intend to take delivery of the metals, buy through a dealer that does not charge these extra fees.

Here are Shearson's commissions:

Size of Your Purchase	Commission
$100 to $200	$6
$201 to $400	$10
$401 to $600	$12
More than $600	2 percent

Prudential-Bache Depository Bullion Program

Prudential-Bache, another financial services giant, has set up its precious metals account so it works just like buying shares of stock. Called the Depository Bullion Program, through it you can invest in gold, silver, and platinum bullion.

Again it works best if you already deal with this firm as your regular broker. In that case, you call up your account representative and place your order. There are no contracts, no delivery instructions. If you have ever purchased stock and let the brokerage firm retain custody of the certificates, this plan works the same way. Prudential-Bache holds the metals (in its name), even though you actually own them. There are no fabrication charges, no delivery charges (since you don't take delivery), and the bullion is insured while in storage.

You receive a written confirmation of each buy or sell order, and a summary of your holdings would appear on each regular account statement from Prudential.

You don't escape storage and insurance charges, however. They are automatically deducted from your account twice a year. Minimum orders are 100 ounces of silver, 5 ounces of gold, 10 ounces of platinum. You pay the spot price for bullion plus Prudential-Bache's markup (or markdown for sales), but no other commissions.

Dean Witter: A Metals Grab Bag from Sears

Dean Witter, part of the Sears financial network, deals precious metals in a variety of ways—from the straightforward to the bizarre. But its programs are not aimed at the small investor. The per order minimum is 10 ounces of gold and 500 ounces of silver, which you can have delivered or put into storage.

The commission to buy gold coins ranges from 1.25 to 1.75 percent, with a $60 minimum per order. If you are buying a kilo bar or larger, the commission ranges from 0.80 to 1.20 percent with a $120 minimum per order. For silver, the commission ranges from 1.25 to 1.75 percent with a $45 minimum.

Storage charges are reasonable: a one-time charge of 4/10ths of one percent of the value of your purchase.

Those are the straightforward ways to invest through Dean Witter. The offbeat plan concocted by this firm is called The Precious Metals Portfolio Plan for gold, silver, and platinum. It works like this:

Dean Witter packages a little of *all three metals* into a "portfolio" and then sells pieces of this marble cake in $1,000 units. So for your $1,000, you get roughly 40 percent in gold, 40 percent in silver, and the other 20 percent in platinum. The firm issues a new series of units each week that investors can continue to purchase, but only in $1,000 lumps.

The big catch is this: Each portfolio unit has a limited life of three years. Exactly three years after you buy it, Dean Witter will automatically liquidate (sell) your investment whether you want to or not. The proceeds, which could reflect a profit or a loss, would go into your Dean Witter account. So much for freedom of choice, let alone investment flexibility.

To buy into this program, you pay a 4 percent commission, plus a one-time one percent storage charge. Out of your $1,000, only $950 actually buys you precious metals. You *can* sell whenever you want, and there is no additional commission, but if you request delivery of your metals threesome you'll be socked with a hefty 4 percent delivery charge per unit, *plus* possible fabrication charges.

There are better ways.

Certificates and Accumulation Plans Outside the United States

Crédit Suisse: Your Own Swiss Bank Account

Some folks insist on protecting part of their assets, especially precious metals, outside the United States. If you are an investor with a burning desire to ''go international,'' even with ample opportunities stateside and added delays from dealing with foreign firms, you have many choices, mostly in Switzerland and Canada.

You may even be surprised how easy some of the banks and precious metals dealers make it for investors in the United States to set up an account. You don't need to be an international wheeler-dealer or a millionaire to own gold, silver, platinum, or palladium in a Swiss bank Metals Account. Here's how one account works.

At Crédit Suisse, a Swiss banking giant, you can open a Silver Metal Account for a mere 5 kilograms (about 160 ounces). With silver at $10 per ounce, that's only a $1,600 initial investment—lower than some certificate plans in the United States. (Just think of how impressed the in-laws will be with your new Swiss bank account, if you tell them.)

Minimum purchases for the other metals, however, are considerably higher. To open a Crédit Suisse Metals Account for gold the minimum is 30 ounces of coins, or one kilo (32.15 ounces) for bullion. Coins available through a Crédit Suisse accumulation account are Mexican 50 Pesos, Austrian 100 Corona (the Swiss call them Crowns), Canadian Maple Leaf, and Krugerrands (they insist on calling them Kruger Rands in Switzerland), including fractional coins. For platinum the minimum purchase is also one kilo (32.15 ounces).

A palladium accumulation account—hard to find from U.S. dealers—is also available at Crédit Suisse, for the standard one kilo (32.15 ounce) minimum purchase.

As with most such plans, you will be free to request delivery of your gold, silver, platinum, or palladium at your leisure—free of any commission—by cable, telephone, or letter. If you want to arrange for delivery in the United States (via New York), you will be charged a fee.

One pitfall is the rate of exchange between the Swiss franc and the dollar. Although Crédit Suisse quotes precious metals prices in dollars to its foreign customers, the transactions are actually settled in francs. Depending on the strength of the dollar against Swiss currency, you could either gain by the conversion or lose. You can get around this by simply asking Crédit Suisse to open a U.S. dollar account for you at the bank and to execute your metals purchases in dollars. But unless you ask, they will automatically convert to Swiss francs.

The storage fee per year for gold and platinum in a Metals Account is $1.50 for each $1,000 in value. The yearly storage fee (or bookkeeping commission) for silver is $3.00 for each $1,000 in value.

According to Crédit Suisse, purchases and sales in and out of a Metals Account are not subject to the Swiss "turnover tax" (recently 6.2 percent). Also, under current rules, any realized profits from a Crédit Suisse Metals Account will not be taxed in Switzerland, although a U.S. resident would have to pay U.S. tax on those profits.

Besides the Metals Account, Crédit Suisse also sells bullion for all four metals, offers to store it for a fee, and handles precious metals futures (forward) contracts.

Foreign Commerce Bank, Switzerland (FOCO)

Foreign Commerce Bank is one of many smaller Swiss banks that offer precious metals investments, in addition to traditional banking services. Although FOCO does not have a formal certificate or accumulation account program, it does offer storage in Zurich for the bullion and coins you can buy through the bank. So, in effect, it works about the same way.

Here's what the bank offers:

Silver Bullion: The minimum initial investment is $5,000, with no minimum on additional amounts—as little as one ounce. The commission on both purchases and sales is one percent, and the storage/insurance charge is 0.4 percent yearly.

Silver Coins: $1,000 face value bags of U.S. junk silver coins (dimes and quarters)—one bag minimum purchase. Storage of the junk silver is in New York, with a yearly cost of $30.

Gold Coins: FOCO sells major gold bullion coins for a minimum initial investment of $5,000. Again, you can add to your holdings in amounts as little as one ounce. There is a ½ percent commission on purchases and sales of gold coins, and a 0.3 percent yearly storage and insurance charge.

Gold Bullion: Minimum initial investment is $5,000—no minimum for add-ons. Same commission and storage charges as for coins.

Platinum: Same as for gold—$5,000 minimum, ½ percent commissions, and 0.3 percent storage charge.

Palladium: Same minimums and conditions as gold and platinum.

Goldplan and Silverplan from Ueberseebank

Ueberseebank, a medium-size Swiss bank, is a subsidiary of American International Group, a U.S.-based insurance company. The Swiss arm has crafted a series of accumulation accounts in gold and silver (platinum and palladium are not available).

This account comes with an unusual twist—check writing against the value of your precious metals. You must have accumulated at least $12,500 worth of gold or silver to qualify, and you're actually borrowing the money so you pay interest, but it's a frill others aren't offering.

The three basic choices:

(1) Start an account with a minimum $5,000 investment and establish a schedule of *monthly* additions of at least $250 for a period of years. The commissions will total 5 percent over the entire term of the plan.

(2) Start an account with a minimum $5,000 investment and make additions only when you feel like it (minimum $2,500). Commission is 3 percent of the invested amount, deducted from your payments.

(3) Send the bank a lump sum (minimum $30,000), which will be used to make monthly gold or silver purchases for you. Commission is 3 percent of the invested amount, deducted from your payments.

In any case, you retain control and can pull out anytime you wish, although there is a fee for doing so.

Here are the other fees and charges:

- A yearly storage fee of 0.325 percent for gold, 0.375 percent for silver.
- If you pull out of the plan before five years, there is a "termination charge" of ½ percent.
- Delivery charges will vary, depending on where, when, and how you want your gold or silver delivered.

Canadian Plans

Deak-Perera Canada

The Canadian branch of Deak-Perera offers the same basic gold, silver, platinum, and palladium menu as its affiliate in the United States. The specifics—including minimum purchases, commissions, and other charges—are similar.

Bank of Nova Scotia (Scotiabank)

Scotiabank claims to be the first dealer in the world to issue gold certificates, dating back to 1958. Today the bank offers gold, silver, and gold coin certificates through a network of 1,000 branch offices in Canada and around the world. The bank is headquartered in Toronto, and that is where gold and silver are stored.

To buy your first Scotiabank gold certificate, you need purchase only *one ounce*; for silver the requirement is 50 ounces, which makes it appealing to smaller investors.

But even though initial purchase minimums are stated in even ounces, you can add to your certificate account in tiny fractions of an ounce, down to three decimal points. That means you can use this plan to buy either by the ounce or by dollar amounts.

The system of storage fees is a little more complicated here. (All amounts are in U.S. dollars.) The fee on gold is 3 cents per 100 ounces per day, with a minimum yearly charge of $5. For silver, the rate is $1 per 1,000 ounces per month, again with a $5 per year minimum charge.

Certificates are available for four major gold bullion coins: the Canadian Maple Leaf, Austrian 100 Corona, Mexican 50 Pesos, and the British Sovereign.

Commissions: ¼ percent on the first $5,000; then ⅛ percent, with a $5 minimum.

Guardian Trust Company

Toronto-based Guardian Trust, among the new precious metals supermarkets, has one of Canada's most extensive metals menus. The Guardian Trust precious metals certificate is available not only at Guardian and its branches but also at major Canadian brokerage firms such as Dominion Securities Ames, McLeod Young Weir, Midland Doherty, Nesbitt Thomson, Pitfield MacKay Ross, and Wood Gundy. This is one of the certificates that now trades on the Montreal Stock Exchange gold and silver certificate market (discussed later in this chapter).

Gold bullion, Maple Leaf, and Krugerrand certificates are available for a 5-ounce minimum, then in one-ounce increments. Silver certificates have a 50-ounce minimum initial purchase. Platinum and palladium certificates are also available. Platinum has a 5-ounce minimum, and palladium is sold only in 10-ounce increments.

An Accumulation Plan

Guardian's accumulation program is called Compu-Trade. It is available for all four metals. Under this plan, you send Guardian a lump sum of cash that is placed in an interest-bearing account, either in Canadian or U.S. dollars. Then you select how often you want the firm to tap those funds and make purchases of your chosen metal. It can be weekly, monthly, or quarterly.

The minimum amount to start is $5,000 (Canadian). After that, you can invest as little as $100 every week, month, or quarter. There are no sales tax, no manufacturing or storage/insurance charges, and no administration fee. The commission is 2 percent when you buy, another 2 percent when you sell—about the same as most other plans. The lack of a storage charge is the attractive feature. You can sell part of your holdings by telephone. Once the plan is set up, however, there is a penalty fee if you cancel.

Trading by Telephone

Another choice available through Guardian is an account called Tele-Trade. With a phone call, investors buy gold, silver, platinum, or palladium, and either have it sent or let Guardian Trust Company place it in a storage account.

To open one of these accounts you need $5,000. Any amount not immediately invested in metals will earn interest. This is Guardian's commission schedule:

Size of Your Purchase	Percent Commission
Up to $4,999	2
$5,000 to $19,999	1¾
$20,000 to $49,999	1½
$50,000 to $99,999	1¼

The minimum buy/sell amounts for Tele-Trade are 5 ounces of gold, 250 ounces of silver, 5 ounces of platinum, and 10 ounces of palladium. Guardian says all transactions are confirmed with a contract statement sent the same day. There are no manufacturing, storage, insurance, or administration fees for buying precious metals this way and having them stored at Guardian. According to this dealer, the metals are insured, held in trust, and separately accounted for—although not individually segregated in your name.

(The range of other precious metals investment choices available through this Canadian dealer includes margin loans, options and futures contracts, managed accounts where they buy and sell for you, numismatic coins, precious metals funds, and gold mining stocks.)

A "STOCK MARKET" FOR CERTIFICATES

If you can trade pieces of paper representing chunks of a corporation (stock), why not do the same thing with pieces of paper that represent shares in a pile of gold or silver? That's what officials at the Montreal Stock Exchange asked themselves. Their answer was to create the Gold and Silver Certificate Market as part of the Montreal Exchange. The new market does for different precious metals certificates what stock exchanges do for stocks—provide an organized place to buy and sell.

Canadian banks and trust companies that offer certificates were excited about this new market. The Montreal Exchange boasted widely about being the first to break ground in this area. But what good does it do you?

Since this is largely a market of Canadian dealers for Canadian investors there, it doesn't have a great deal to offer most Americans. Plenty of certificate plans are available in the United States without having to go through a Canadian brokerage firm (or a U.S. firm that is a member of the Montreal Exchange) to buy gold or silver certificates. But for a still-developing field it is an important addition that offers some advantages.

Under the wing of a major stock exchange, this precious metals certificate trading program provides added assurance to investors who fear buying certificates through firms they know little or nothing about. Investors can buy a certificate through a regular stockbroker and not have to find a precious metals dealer.

All certificates traded on the Montreal Exchange must meet these conditions:

• The certificate must be backed 100 percent by fully insured gold or silver stored at a location approved by the exchange.
• Firms offering certificates must guarantee timely delivery of gold or silver that meets acceptable guidelines for purity.
• There can be *none* of the traditional fees often charged by certificate issuers, either for purchase, sale, or during the period the certificate is held.
• The certificate must offer a minimum investment no greater than 5 ounces for gold, 250 ounces for silver.

It all works much like buying regular shares of stock. An investor calls a broker, asks what the price is, and enters an order. In this case, the order can come in different forms. Instead of buying immediately at the price the broker quotes over the phone, you could enter something called a limit order. That's the type of order that tells the broker to buy or sell *only* if the price hits a certain level.

For example: Assume that you already own a silver certificate that you bought when the price was $9.14. Recently the price has reached as high as $12.50 per ounce and has now begun to drift back. You want to sell and take a profit, but only if the price threatens to drop below $11.50. When you call the broker, you find the price is $11.90. You can place a limit order, instructing the broker to sell your certificate at $11.50. If the price remains steady, you retain the certificate and benefit. If it drops, your holdings are sold before it goes too far, thus protecting the profit that you had. After you've placed the order, you can forget about it.

CHAPTER 11

Metals Merchants: Surviving the Dealer Obstacle Course

- How to Find a Metals Dealer You Can Trust
- Tips on Choosing a Metals Dealer
- Metals Merchants: A Directory of Dealers

HOW TO FIND A METALS DEALER YOU CAN TRUST

At times, the business of buying and selling precious metals in the United States seems like a badly written crime novel. In one recent two-year period a dozen firms that sold precious metals failed. Thousands of investors lost millions of dollars. As the drama unfolded, armed guards turned angry investors away from the doors of a defunct metals dealer. There was murder, suicide, fraud, and international flight to avoid prosecution. There have been lawsuits, endless court

149

proceedings to sort out the shambles of multimillion-dollar bankruptcies, and many broken dreams and bank accounts.

Those were the headline-grabbing debacles. Through it all remains a core of solid, honest dealers. They can offer consumer/investors what passes for worry-free investing in the precious metals field.

The Law of the Jungle

Point number one to remember: The precious metals business is *not* regulated by the federal government. It is *not* like banking. Banks and other financial institutions are highly regulated at several levels, and deposits are insured by Uncle Sam. Not so with gold, silver, platinum, and palladium.

Nor is this like the stock market. People who sell stocks must be specially trained. They must pass exams before they are licensed to deal in securities. The United States Securities and Exchange Commission (SEC) watches over the stock market. Ditto for bonds, mortgage-backed securities, tax shelter partnerships, and so on. Most brokerage firms carry insurance to protect investors in the event the firm gets in financial trouble.

But these rules don't apply for precious metals. Anyone can open an office, give it an impressive-sounding name, and start selling gold. And it seems that just about everyone has done just that. When interest in precious metals investing soared, so too did the number of retail "stores." But again, while there are many reputable firms that have been in business many years and have served clients well, the "Wild West" atmosphere in precious metals trading has spawned more sleazy boiler-room firms than ever before. They advertise in magazines and newspapers. Their junk mail shows up at your front door. They promise, entice, cajole with all manner of come-ons. One firm brags that "no salesman will *visit* you"—but you can be certain one will call since its coupon says any request for further information will not be processed unless you give your telephone number.

Not all dealers are like this. But there is a vocal minority that is often most aggressive in seeking new customers—people like you.

Advice on Giving Out
Telephone Numbers: Don't

Many precious metals dealers follow a formula in their advertising. They offer a free report about all the wonderful profits you can make in metals through their firm. To get it you send in your name, address, and *telephone number*.

They may say that if you don't give them your phone number they won't send you the information. That's no loss on your part. They try to fool you, claiming that "phone number is necessary to verify address" or "computer will not process without phone number" or some other nonsense. As surely as rocks sink, one of their salespeople will be calling your number within hours of receiving it.

The same thing will happen if you call to request information. The dealer will want your phone number. Some will refuse point-blank to send you information without it. But there is only one reason they want that number—to get a salesperson on your trail.

The Only Solution: Don't give out your phone number until you have checked out the firm and decided to use it to buy or sell precious metals. If the account representative (its name for a salesperson) gives you a hard time, try another firm. There is no shortage of dealers that act professionally and will not bother you with phone calls.

Some firms will ask for the phone number but will respect your decision to decline.

Caveat Emptor

To be brutally frank, the path to big profits in precious metals is littered with corpses. Three out of every four precious metals brokerage firms formed in the early 1980s have failed. But there are always three or four more to take their place.

A particularly gruesome period was 1982 and 1983. Among the more infamous failures of that period:

• Bullion Reserve of North America petitioned for bankruptcy in October 1983. Investors got back some of their money, but casualties included some 20,000 individuals who lost nearly $60 million. Alan Saxon, who headed this Beverly Hills-based firm, committed suicide several days before the bankruptcy filing.

• International Gold Bullion Exchange (IGBE) went under in April 1983. Investors were burned to the tune of $72 million. A year later one of the former owners of IGBE was murdered in his Fort Lauderdale home.

• United Precious Metals, Inc., failed and was closed on October 20, 1983, leaving 3,000 investors out an estimated $3.5 million.

• When still another firm, Universal Precious Metals, Inc., closed shop near the end of 1982, about 600 customers lost nearly $6 million.

The list of other trouble spots is long. Premex, a California firm that specialized in selling precious metals by leverage contracts, bit the dust in 1984. It joined the likes of JVF Investment, Inc.; First Guaranty Metals Co.; Empire State Metals, Inc.; and many others. All either failed or were forced out of business by Federal or state watchdogs. (NOTE: Further details about leverage contracts and other pitfalls in Chapter 14.)

Nobody seems immune to the dangers. In 1984, within the span of only a few months, two of the biggest names in the world of precious metals became tarnished—Deak-Perera, long a precious metals leader in the United States, and Johnson Matthey, a world renowned London-based metals firm. In both cases the precious metals divisions of these multi-part firms were not directly involved. The culprits were banking subsidiaries that got stuck with troubled loans and couldn't cope.

In Deak's case it was not the precious metals portion of the family-run financial empire that filed for bankruptcy. Deak-Perera U.S., the best known of the Deak & Company subsidiaries and the one that handles precious metals trading, carried on. It was the holding company, Deak & Company, and two other subsidiaries, Deak-Perera Wall Street and Deak-Perera International Banking Corporation, that filed for protection from creditors under Chapter 11 bankruptcy rules. But the linkage to the units that did go bust raised a caution flag in the minds of precious metals investors.

Johnson Matthey's troubles also came as a shock to many. This was one of the ultra-distinguished members of the most exclusive precious metals "club" in the world—the London Fix. The problems did not directly affect the precious metals operations but centered around the firm's banking unit.

What to Look for in a Precious Metals Dealer

The Dealer Directory at the end of this chapter lists many well-known firms that deal in gold, silver, platinum, and palladium. Use it with caution. The directory is intended to show you a broad cross section of dealers both large and small, including brokerage firms, banks, and independents. It is *not* an endorsement of these firms. That's impossible to do in a book like this because conditions change too rapidly. Even the biggest of the big—firms that "nobody would have expected" to get into financial trouble—can go down. (Firms dealing mainly in rare coins are listed in Chapter 13.)

You can tilt the odds in your favor by shopping among the leaders. This is a risky investment field to start with, made even riskier by its unregulated nature. There is little reason to add yet another hazard by sending money to firms you never heard of and have not thoroughly checked out. It's amazing, but the same people who shop carefully to save nickels and dimes at the grocery store think nothing of sending off thousands of dollars for an investment they've seen advertised, without doing some checking.

A good place to start with is the Better Business Bureau in the dealer's area. If you are able to get through (the BBB's phones are incessantly busy), be prepared to ask about a *specific* firm. Going in blind for general guidance doesn't seem to work. Although the bureau has at times offered pamphlets about selecting a precious metals dealer, it may or may not have such items in stock, or the person you talk to might not know about them.

Nevertheless, be persistent. The Better Business Bureau *does* have a report, "Investor Alert—Gold and Silver," offering advice on choosing a dealer. If your local bureau doesn't have it, check with the Council of Better Business Bureaus (1515 Wilson Boulevard, Arlington, VA 22209) or the North American Securities Administrators Association (100 East 9th, Suite 204, Topeka, KS 66601).

TIPS ON CHOOSING
A METALS DEALER

• Ask questions—lots of questions if you have the time—about commissions, bid/ask spreads, and other fees or charges. Feel that you know exactly what dealing with this firm will cost you.

• Don't be swayed by little perks such as a newsletter or special reports on the metals markets. These are a dime a dozen, and the ones written by precious metals firms for their clients are inevitably slanted.

• Consider how long the dealer has been at its current address. Frequent moves are suspect, as is an emphasis on selling precious metals under leverage, margin, or deferred delivery deals.

• Find out whether the firm is audited regularly by an independent accounting firm, and whether it is bonded or insured.

• Consider whether the firm is willing to answer all of your questions *before* selling you metals. If it wants to sell first and talk later, consider another dealer. Or try a small transaction at several dealers as a test. Then continue with the one you like best.

• Ask for recommendations and references. There are several ways to do this. If you have friends or business associates who have had experience investing in precious metals, ask if they were satisfied. Or, if you have a dealer in mind, call the firm and ask for specific references (not those vague references printed in its advertisements). That might be the firm's auditor, its bank, or a precious metals wholesale firm that supplies the dealer. Get the name of the *individual* to talk to at the bank or auditor so you don't have to waste time being transferred on the phone.

• Don't count on precious metals brokers or dealers for investment advice. They make a living selling precious metals investments and their "advice" is skewed by self-interest. No, you'll either have to make your own decisions here or go elsewhere for independent investment guidance.

• Stay away from odd-sounding investment schemes and firms or salespeople that come on too strong. Any plan touted as a "guarantee" of profits of any kind smells. Nobody can make such guarantees in the precious metals market, and doing so may even be illegal.

• If you get references from a dealer, check them out. Just getting the names is not good enough. What you learn might surprise you.

If the dealer is reluctant to offer references, move on. When you follow up, ask about the firm's net worth; what it does with customer payments between the time they are received and the time the metals are shipped; how long the dealer has been in business; and whether there have been complaints about the company.

• Be especially skeptical of leverage plans, deferred delivery arrangements, "special deals" that claim to offer metals at bargain prices. Yes, dealer prices will differ. But the price of gold is still rather standard around the world at any given moment, and nobody can sell a product for less than it costs them and remain in business for very long. That is precisely what the bankrupt firm International Gold Bullion Exchange was doing, and it was a tip-off for investors who recognized it and pulled out early.

And a Few Others from the Better Business Bureau

• Don't buy precious metals advertised at "below spot prices." Spot prices mean today's prices fixed on major exchanges. Dealers selling below spot are selling below market. This is a danger sign. These dealers often do not buy the ordered metals, hoping that the market will go down. Although they tell customers that gold is going up, the only way dealers selling below spot can make money is if the price drops so they can later buy the ordered metal at a lower price.

• Make sure the dealer segregates funds. Find out if investment funds are kept separate from operating funds of the company in some sort of trust arrangement. If the salesperson won't confirm that funds are segregated or you can't find out some other way, steer clear of the dealer.

• Be careful about offers to invest in "strategic" metals such as cobalt and titanium. Some unscrupulous dealers misrepresent the potential risks and earnings connected with dealing in these metals.

• Ask for written information, and read it. *Do not be rushed.*

One other thing investors can do is to read investment periodicals that regularly keep a close eye on the precious metals dealers. I've already mentioned *Silver & Gold Report,* a newsletter that takes a gloves-off approach to dealers and issues warnings against firms that it feels are suspect. SGR regularly publishes dealer surveys with up-to-date information. It's not cheap ($144 per year for a subscription), but if you are planning a substantial commitment to precious metals, it may be worth it. (Chapter 21 has the address.)

METALS MERCHANTS:
A DIRECTORY OF DEALERS

A Consumer's Guide to Firms That Buy and Sell Gold, Silver, Platinum, and Palladium Investments (Not a Recommendation)

Dealer/Broker/Bank	Comments
A-Mark Precious Metals, Inc. 9696 Wilshire Blvd. Beverly Hills, CA 90212 (213) 550-8861	A precious metals wholesale firm; does *not* deal directly with the public but may suggest dealers that carry its products.
Auric United Corporation P.O. Box 29568 San Antonio, TX 78229 (800) 531-7171 (800) 348-GOLD (in Texas) (512) 696-1234	No investor too small.
Bank of Delaware Precious Metals Division 519 N. Market St. Wilmington, DE 19899 (302) 429-1210	Stores metals for numerous other firms. Also offers its own certificates.
Benham Certified Metals 755 Page Mill Road Palo Alto, CA 94304 (800) 447-GOLD	Discount broker. Linked to Benham Capital Management mutual funds group.
James U. Blanchard & Co. 4425 W. Napoleon Ave. Metairie, LA 70001 (800) 535-7633 (504) 456-9034	Cash and carry. Big on foreign and domestic coins.

Brink's Precious Metals Exchange, Inc.
6 Thorndal Circle, Box 1225
Darien, CT 06820
(800) 243-3575
(203) 655-8781

The armored car company.

Brooks
4200 Governor Printz Blvd.
P.O. Box 1223
Wilmington, DE 19899
(302) 762-5444

Brooks warehouse receipts sold by other dealers.

Citibank, N.A.
Precious Metals Service
399 Park Ave., Level A
New York, NY 10043
(800) 223-1080
(212) 559-6041 (in New York)

Recorded gold and silver prices on: (212) 559-6041, updated several times daily.

Colonial Coins
909 Travis St.
Houston, TX 77002
(800) 231-2392
(713) 654-0910
(800) 231-4739 (in Texas)

Small regional dealer.

Crédit Suisse (U.S. office)
100 Wall St.
New York, NY 10005
(212) 422-1450

The big Swiss bank, world leader in precious metals.

Other U.S. offices:
Crédit Suisse
800 Wilshire Blvd.
Suite 888
Los Angeles, CA 90017
(213) 489-2720

Crédit Suisse
1200 Brickell Ave., 16th fl.
Miami, FL 33131
(305) 374-1144

Deak-Perera
29 Broadway
New York, NY 10006
(800) 221-5700
(212) 635-0540 (in New York)

Oldest and one of the largest
U.S. dealers. Goldline 24-hour
recorded prices: (212)
586-2175.

Other selected Deak offices:
(NEW YORK)
41 E. 42nd St.
New York, NY 10017
(800) 223-6484
(212) 883-0400

630 Fifth Ave.
New York, NY 10111
(800) 223-5510
(212) 757-0100

(LOS ANGELES)
Deak-Perera California, Inc.
Hilton Hotel Center
677 South Figueroa St.
Los Angeles, CA 90017
(800) 421-8391 (out of state)
(800) 252-9324 (in California)
(213) 624-4221

(BEVERLY HILLS)
Deak-Perera California, Inc.
Beverly Wilshire Hotel
9500 Wilshire Blvd.
Beverly Hills, CA 90212
(213) 274-9176

(SAN DIEGO)
531 "C" St.
San Diego, CA 92101
(800) 522-2010 (Southern California only)
(800) 852-2200 (out of state)
(619) 235-0900

(SAN FRANCISCO)
100 Grant Ave.
San Francisco, CA 94108
(800) 792-0825 (Northern
California only)
(800) 227-4076
(415) 362-3452

Goldline price quotes: (415)
362-3382.

(DENVER)
Deak-Perera Colorado, Inc.
918 16th St.
Denver, CO 80202
(800) 332-6357 (in Colorado)
(800) 482-0274
(303) 571-0808

(WASHINGTON, DC)
Deak-Perera Southeast, Inc.
(Retail location)
1800 K St., N.W.
Washington, DC 20006

Recorded precious metals and
foreign currency prices: (202)
872-1630.

Mailing address:
1120 Vermont Ave., N.W.
Suite 902
Washington, DC 20005
(800) 424-1186
(202) 872-1233

(MIAMI)
Deak-Perera Florida, Inc.
One Southeast Third Ave.
Miami, FL 33131
(800) 432-2773 (in Florida)
(800) 327-6172
(305) 372-8888

(CHICAGO)
Deak-Perera Chicago, Inc.
17 North Dearborn
Chicago, IL 60602
(800) 621-1915
(800) 972-2192 (in Illinois)
(312) 236-0042

Recorded gold and silver
prices: (312) 346-7789.

(BOSTON)
Deak-Perera Boston, Inc.
160 Franklin St.
Boston, MA 02110
(800) 882-1147 (in Massachusetts)
(800) 225-1709
(617) 426-0016

(DALLAS)
Deak-Perera Texas, Inc.
Diamond Shamrock Tower
717 North Harwood St.
Suite 111 Lock Box #16
Dallas, TX 75201
(800) 492-4847 (in Texas)
(800) 527-7316
(214) 748-7403

Dean Witter
Precious Metals Division
One World Trade Center
New York, NY 10048
(212) 524-3743

Part of the Sears empire.
Brokerage firm has branches
across U.S.

Dreyfus Gold Deposits, Inc.
666 Old Country Road
Garden City, N.Y. 11530
(800) 544-4424
(718) 895-1330 (in New York)

Part of the Dreyfus financial
services empire.

Engelhard Corporation
Specialty Metals Division
70 Wood Ave. South
Iselin, NJ 08830
(201) 321-5900

A major metals fabricator; does
not deal directly with the
public.

First National Bank of Chicago
Attn: Gold Desk
One First National Plaza
Suite 0221
Chicago, IL 60670
(800) 621-4156
(312) 732-5890 (in Illinois)

Gold and silver passbook
account program.

First National Monetary Corp.
First Center Office Plaza
26913 Northwestern Hwy., 6th fl.
Southfield, MI 48034
(800) 521-2400
(313) 353-9770

Gold Standard Corporation   Mints/sells full range of its
1600 Genessee   own gold, silver, and platinum
Kansas City, MO 64102   coins.
(800) VIA-GOLD
(816) VIA-GOLD (in Missouri)

E. F. Hutton   Good accumulation plan for
Precious Metals Division   cost averaging. Offices
26 Broadway, Suite 1001   throughout U.S.
New York, NY 10004
(212) 742-2719

International Trading Group   Largest seller of Mocatta
60 E. Third Ave.   Metals investment products.
San Mateo, CA 94401
(800) 227-3150
(800) 652-1600 (in California)
(415) 340-8000

Other International Trading Group Offices:
350 California St., Suite 2200
San Francisco, CA 94104
(800) 433-6200
(415) 433-6200

701 B St., Suite 2300
San Diego, CA 92101
(800) 422-4900
(800) 826-4900 (in California)
(619) 239-4900

2600 Douglas Road
Coral Gables, FL 33134
(800) 327-9597
(800) 432-0173 (in Florida)
(305) 446-2400

One Executive Drive
Somerset, NJ 08873
(800) 526-3718
(201) 560-9833

505 N. 3rd St.
Fairfield, IA 52556
(515) 472-8451
(800) 247-2240

Investment Rarities
One Appletree Square
Minneapolis, MN 55420
(800) 328-1860
(612) 853-0700 (in Minnesota)

Rare coin specialist. Pioneered
sight drafts. Lots of consumer
safeguards.

Johnson Matthey & Wallace
One World Trade Center
New York, NY 10048
(212) 488-0600

Major international refiner;
British-based parent.
Recognized around the world.
Not a retail firm.

also:
Johnson Matthey Ltd.
550 S. Hill St. #1635
Los Angeles, CA 90013
(213) 689-1577

Platinum specialist; call for
dealer referral.

Manfra, Tordella & Brookes
59 W. 49th St.
New York, NY 10112
(800) 535-7481
(212) 621-9502 (in New York)

Large national firm: big
selection of U.S. and foreign
coins and bullion.

Merrill Lynch
Sharebuilder Program
P.O. Box 520
Church Street Station
New York, NY 10008
(800) 221-2856

Sharebuilder Plan starts at
$100. Offices throughout U.S.

Mocatta Metals Corporation
4 World Trade Center
New York, NY 10048
(212) 938-9600

Major international
refiner/wholesaler. Certificates,
options offered through retail
dealers/brokers.

Monex International Ltd.
4910 Birch St.
Newport Beach, CA 92660
(800) 854-3361
(800) 432-7013 (in California)
(714) 752-1400

Full range of investment
choices. Large national
clientele. A leverage firm.

PaineWebber
Precious Metals Division
140 Broadway
New York, NY 10005
(212) 437-3800

Major national brokerage firm.
Platinum and palladium
offered. Also offices
throughout U.S.

Prudential-Bache Metal Co.
100 Gold St.
New York, NY 10292

Major national brokerage firm;
offices throughout U.S.
Handles platinum and
palladium.

Republic Bullion Corp.
1605 W. Olympic Blvd. #400
Los Angeles, CA 90015
(800) 762-4653
(213) 381-5578

Retail metals outlet of Republic
National Bank (NY). Quotes:
(213) 380-2770.

**Republic National Bank of
N.Y.**
Fifth Ave. at 40th St.
New York, NY 10018
(212) 930-6338
(800) 223-0840

For daily gold and silver quotes
call: (212) 930-6527
(800) 223-5578.

**Rhode Island Hospital Trust
National Bank**
Precious Metals Division
15 W. Minister St.
Providence, RI 02903
(401) 278-7595
(401) 278-8000

Despite the weird name, is a
major player in U.S. Has
gold/silver certificates.

C. Rhyne & Associates
110 Cherry St.
Seattle, WA 98104
(800) 542-0824 (in Washington)
(800) 426-7835
(206) 623-6900

Regional dealer; choices include Mocatta certificates.

Security Pacific Brokers, Inc.
297 N. Marengo Ave.
P.O. Box 7000
Pasadena, CA 91109-9990
(800) 272-4060 or
(818) 304-3593

New discount broker for precious metals. Linked to Security Pacific Bank.

Shearson Lehman Brothers Inc.
Precious Metals Division
2 World Trade Center
102nd floor
New York, NY 10048
(212) 321-7155

Accumulation Plan starts at $500. Offices throughout U.S.

Sunshine Bullion
Box 214509
Dallas, TX 75221
(800) 527-5769
(214) 922-0162

Retail arm of the big silver mining company. Sells only its own silver.

Western Federal Corporation
8655 E. Via De Ventura, E155
Scottsdale, AZ 85258
(800) 528-3158
(602) 998-1000 (in Arizona)

Midsize regional firm. Choices include options contracts.

Beyond U.S. Borders:
Selected Foreign Firms

Canada

Bank of Nova Scotia
44 King Street West
Toronto, Ontario M5H 1H1
(416) 367-1940

Deak-Perera Canada, Inc.
10 King St.
Toronto, Ontario M5C 1C3
(416) 863-1611
(800) 268-8155 (in Canada)

Other Deak Canada offices:
(MONTREAL)
1155 Sherbrooke St. West
Montreal, Quebec H3A 2N3
(800) 361-8645 (in Canada)
(514) 285-1307

(VANCOUVER)
Pacific Centre
Stock Exchange Tower
617 Granville St.
Vancouver, BC V6C 2A7
(604) 687-6111
(800) 663-9092 (in Canada)

**Canadian Imperial Bank of
Commerce**
Commerce Court Postal Station
Toronto, Ontario M5L 1A2
(416) 862-2211

Guardian Trust Company
74 Victoria St.
Toronto, Ontario M5C 2A5
(416) 863-1100
(800) 268-9556 (good from the
U.S.)

Other Guardian Trust offices:
(MONTREAL)
618 rue St. Jacque
Montreal, Quebec H3C 1E3
(514) 842-8251

(VANCOUVER)
571 Howe St.
Vancouver, BC V6C 2C2
(604) 687-0011

24-hour price quote numbers:
Toronto: (416) 863-6235
Montreal: (514) 282-1393
Vancouver: (604) 687-8383

National Bank of Canada
600 W. De La Gauche Tiere
Montreal, Quebec H3B 4L2
(514) 394-4000

Wood Gundy Ltd.
Box 274
Royal Trust Tower
Toronto Dominion Centre
Toronto, Ontario M5K 1M7
(416) 869-8100

London

Ayrton Metals Ltd.
30 Ely Place
London, EC1N 6RT
Tele: 01-404-0970

The five "London Fix" firms are:
Johnson Matthey Bankers Ltd.
5 Lloyds Ave.
London, EC3N 3DB
Tele: 01-481-3181

Mocatta & Goldsmid Ltd.
Park House
16 Finsbury Circus
London, EC2M 7DA
Tele: 01-638-3636

Samuel Montagu & Co., Ltd.
114 Old Broad St.
London, EC2P 2HY
Tele: 01-588-6464

N. M. Rothschild & Sons Ltd.
New Court
St. Swithin's Lane
London, EC4P 4DU
Tele: 01-626-4356

Sharps, Pixley Ltd.
10 Rood Lane
London, EC3M 8BB
Tele: 01-623-8000

Switzerland

Crédit Suisse
Paradeplatz 8
P.O. Box 590
8021 Zurich
Switzerland
Tele: 01-215-11 11

Foreign Commerce Bank
(FOCO Bank)
Bellariastrasse 82
8038 Zurich
Switzerland
Tele: 01-482-66 88

Mailing address:
P.O. Box 5022
8022 Zurich

Goldplan AG (Ueberseebank)
Volkmarstrasse 10
P.O. Box 213
8033 Zurich
Switzerland
Tele: 01-361-35 50

Or:
Ueberseebank AG
Limmatquai 2
8024 Zurich

Valeurs White Weld, S.A.
1, quai do Mont-Blanc
1211 Geneva
Switzerland

The Valeurs precious metals
option contract is sold through
U.S. dealers.

Bank Julius Bar
Bahnhofstrasse 36
CH-8022 Zurich
Switzerland

Bank Leu
Bahnhofstrasse 32
Ch-8022 Zurich
Switzerland

CHAPTER 12

Precious Metals Mutual Funds

- **Fund Magic: Advantages for Investors**
- **Funds with a Twist**
- **Inside the Gold Funds**
- **Fund Investor's Checklist**
- **Directory of Precious Metals Mutual Funds**

Americans have taken to mutual funds like hungry dogs to a pork chop. These communal-type investments have been around for decades. The money market fund variety was the darling of the 1970s. But equity funds—which include the stock market and precious metals funds—became hot items in the 1980s.

Total assets of precious metals mutual funds were only a few hundred million dollars at the beginning of the 1980s. But by 1985 those assets had bloated to beyond $3 billion.

Mutual funds are an incredible invention for the average guy on the street who wants to put his money in stocks without having to first earn a PhD in economics. Mutual funds make it simple, safe, and accessible to the investor of modest means.

FUND MAGIC: ADVANTAGES FOR INVESTORS

A mutual fund gathers together money from lots of individuals and invests that lump of cash in stocks, bonds, Treasury bills, or in this case gold mines or other precious metals–related assets. Most precious metals funds are linked primarily to gold, with very little invested in silver, platinum, or palladium. (Precious metals funds normally invest most of their money in gold mining stocks, not bullion.)

Individuals looking for a convenient way to link some of their finances to gold needn't look further than the gold funds. These are just a few of the advantages they offer investors:

• Low minimum initial investments. The most common minimum initial investment for a mutual fund is $1,000. But in some funds you can start with as little as $250. And you can usually add funds in increments as small as $100.

• No-load funds charge no commission—no fee of any kind for you to invest. That's right, none. When you invest $1,000 in a no-load precious metals fund, for example, every penny goes to buy you shares in the fund. Many precious metals funds available in the United States are no-load funds, or nearly as good, the new variety low-load funds. Low-loads charge a far lower commission than load (fee-charging) funds. One reason no-load funds are able to operate without a commission is that they don't sell shares through regular brokers. The only way to buy is direct from the fund. There is no middleman—and no middleman markup.

• Professional management. When you buy into a precious metals mutual fund, in most cases you are buying shares in a portfolio of gold mining company stocks. Those mines may be in Canada, the United States, South Africa, Australia, Brazil, or other gold-producing nations. Investing in gold mining shares on your own is a tricky affair. Through a mutual fund, you buy the expertise of the fund's managers, who spend most of their time looking for the best stocks for the fund's portfolio and buying and selling them.

• Leverage. Put simply, when bullion prices are rising, the prices of gold mining stocks will rise even further, and probably faster. Here's why. Assume it costs a mining company $250 to produce an ounce of gold from its mine. If the world price of gold is $350, the mine makes $100 on the ounce. If the price moves to $550, the mine's profit is

$300—*an increase of 200 percent*. The price of the stock should follow. But if you owned the gold bullion at $350 and it rose to $550, that same $200 rise would represent only a *57 percent increase* on your original investment. While the final results don't work out quite so neatly, gold shares do give investors more bang for the buck than bullion.

• Flexibility. Some precious metals funds belong to mutual fund families—a group of different types of funds managed by the same company. Investors can switch their money among different funds with a simple phone call. Fidelity Select–Precious Metals, for example, is a low-load fund that belongs to the gigantic Fidelity group of mutual funds. Investors who own shares in this fund can switch into other funds in the Select Portfolio group, including funds that invest in energy stocks, financial services firms, utilities, high-tech stocks, and entertainment companies, among others.

• No-load mutual funds are another good way to dollar cost average your investment—there is a low minimum investment and no commission.

• Mutual funds make it a snap to start investing. Just call and ask the fund to send a prospectus, the document that by law they must provide before you can invest. Read it. It has all the details about how the fund works. After you've read it, fill out an application form and send a check. To add funds, you tear off a stub from the statement/confirmation you receive on each transaction and send it with another check.

• The price of your fund is easy to follow. For all major funds, look in the newspaper. *The Wall Street Journal* and other major newspapers carry a table of mutual fund prices daily. Some of the larger fund groups—including Fidelity—also have high-tech setups that let you tap into your account via the telephone or a personal computer at home. You can find out the balance in your fund account, keep apprised of current prices, and even shift assets between different funds by punching in numbers on your telephone.

• Cashing in your fund shares—called redemption—requires only a phone call if you have signed up for the fund's telephone redemption service and if the fund offers such a service. If not, you will have to send a written request, with a signature guarantee. Some low-load funds may charge a fee for redemption. Fideltity, for example, charges one percent on redemptions. Other funds charge nothing.

• Less risk. Owning shares in a precious metals mutual fund that has scores of different gold stocks in its portfolio is far less risky than owning only a few of those stocks on your own. The key is diversification. Individual gold shares are risky. The more that risk is spread around, the better off you are. A precious metals mutual fund, which already owns dozens of individual gold stocks, is ideal for providing that kind of diversification.

• Dividends. Precious metals mutual funds can give you something physical metals never could—a dividend. Since the funds own stocks and stocks *sometimes* pay a dividend, that money is divvied up among the shareholders. You will be given the choice of either receiving those dividends in cash or reinvesting the money automatically in more shares of the fund. Unless you're hard up for the cash, opt for reinvestment. It puts even more teeth into a dollar-cost-averaging program, since the money is automatically reinvested on the date dividends are paid. (Franklin Gold Fund even gives you the choice of reinvesting your dividends *in gold coins*. At your request, the fund will automatically send your dividend check to Deak-Perera, which buys the coins in bulk and sends them via registered mail to investors.)

• Retirement accounts. Under current rules for Individual Retirement Accounts (IRAs), you are *not* allowed to invest retirement account money in gold, silver, platinum, or palladium *bullion*. But you *can* invest your IRA cash in a precious metals mutual fund. Most funds now offer special IRA accounts that can be opened for lower minimum initial investment and subsequent investments, and sometimes with no minimum investment at all. You should expect to pay a small yearly fee for an IRA account.

Where else can you get all of those advantages for almost nothing?

You may also wonder about the performance of precious metals mutual funds. As with most precious metals investments, mutual funds should be thought of for the long term. Precious metals funds can also be erratic. In the 1980s alone, for example, the gold funds had years when they were the best performers of all mutual funds in the United States. At other times they've been the doormats of the investment league. It all depends on how the price of gold is doing. When it is headed up, the funds inevitably top the "best-dressed" lists of mutual funds published in all the major financial magazines. That's when investors throw money at them. But just as inevitably, that's when the funds do an about-face, leaving many stunned investors in their wake.

FUNDS WITH A TWIST

Not all precious metals funds are no-load funds; and not all are invested exclusively in gold mining shares. As the popularity of gold funds soared, new twists were added. Some funds are invested more heavily in bullion; some are structured differently as closed-end funds.

The most popular no-load mutual funds are all open-end funds. That means there is no limit on the number of shares they can issue. When a new investor sends in his or her money, the fund grows by that amount and new shares are issued. The more popular the fund, the larger it gets.

A closed-end fund is created with a *fixed* number of shares. These shares are then traded on a stock exchange, just like other stocks, and are bought and sold through stockbrokers. One of the latest developments is a fund that invests in platinum- and palladium-related assets as well as in gold and silver.

There is even a mutual fund devoted specifically to silver, which is most often mined as a by-product of other metals such as zinc, nickel, and copper. Strategic Silver Fund, Inc., was the first fund devoted only to poor man's gold. Some funds own silver mining shares as part of their overall portfolios, but silver generally makes up only a small piece of the whole pie.

INSIDE THE GOLD FUNDS

Here are the details on selected funds. Again, dollar amounts are subject to change.

United Services Gold Shares

This no-load fund, with some $500 million in assets, has been a top performer, and one of the most popular mutual funds of recent years. It's actually part of a small fund family that includes the Prospector Fund, U.S. Treasury Securities Fund, Good and Bad Times Fund, Growth Fund, and Income Fund. The two funds that are specifically for precious metals are U.S. Gold Shares and Prospector Fund. United

Services began as a fund in 1970, but did not become a *gold* fund until 1974.

Clark Aylsworth, president of the parent firm, United Services Advisors, Inc., says of his approach, "We do not consider ourselves to be gold bugs. Nor are we 'greenbackers' or fanatically anti-gold. We do try to view things the way they are, not the way we would like them to be. We believe that the future course of economic events could well be traumatic . . . and that well-selected gold stocks offer the investor a measure of protection and possible profit not available elsewhere."

Aylsworth also points out that since the price of gold shares can and does fluctuate with sometimes breathtaking speed, it can be emotionally upsetting unless you are prepared to take the long-term view.

United Services Gold Shares is popular among beginning investors because of its low minimum investment ($500) as well as a low minimum requirement for additions ($50). You can switch money into any of the other funds in this group, as long as that move is for $1,500 or more. If you have registered for the telephone exchange feature, you can make a switch by phone.

That works only if you have *not* requested that the fund issue certificates for your shares. When you invest in shares of a mutual fund, you receive a confirmation and regular statements, but you do not receive an actual stock certificate. It's simply too much paperwork, and funds hate having to issue certificates, even though you can get them if you ask.

Unless you have a special reason for needing those extra pieces of paper, there is little reason to do so. For simplicity's sake, don't mess with the certificates. If you hold them yourself, you will have to worry about storing them in a safe place (you'll pay a fee to have them replaced if they are lost or stolen). And when you want to sell, having the certificates in your possession will only cause hassles. They will have to be signed and sent to the fund's "transfer agent" before your shares can be liquidated. For maximum convenience, *don't* ask the fund to issue certificates.

United Services Gold is one of many funds that offer an automatic purchase program. The minimum amount required to start is the same ($500), but additions can be as little as $20. The plan works like this: You designate a checking account at your bank, and the fund will automatically withdraw a set amount from that account each month and invest it for you. You can choose to have it done either on the first of the month or on the 15th, or both.

You can open an IRA account at United Services Gold Shares with *no minimum initial investment.* There is a $5 startup fee and a $10 annual fee for IRA accounts.

United Services also offers a way to systematically *withdraw* your money. If you have at least $5,000 invested, the fund will send you a monthly or quarterly check for a specific amount of money of your choosing.

What the Fund Invests In

United Services Gold Shares is largely invested in South African mining shares. In the past, about 80 percent of the fund's assets were invested in that gold-producing nation. Since South Africa is the world's largest single producer of gold, that's not surprising. Many of the world's most financially stable mining companies are there. Political uncertainty is the key drawback. Some believe it is only a matter of time before the minority white government comes crashing down, with potentially devastating results for these mining shares. Even if you were right about investing in gold, and the price shoots up, you could get hurt if something goes wrong in South Africa. Ironically, such an event could send world gold prices and thus mining shares soaring elsewhere.

Prospector Fund: Staying Out of South Africa

Growing numbers of investors have joined the boycott against South Africa or feel the political situation there is just too shaky. An investment in gold and other precious metals *should* provide added financial insurance, diversification, and protection against unforeseen economic moves. It doesn't make sense to gamble on uncertain politics when there are so many other ways to link a portion of your finances to gold. And South Africa's racist policies are simply too repugnant for many people.

An alternative is one of the new kids on the block, the United Services Prospector Fund. This precious metals mutual fund invests *only* in mining firms located outside South Africa. That means in Canada, the United States, and a few other gold-producing nations.

The trade-off is this: Prices of mining shares outside South Africa are considered more risky, more volatile. As this fund's managers themselves caution: "Prospector Fund is not for an investor who is faint of heart. The nature of these stocks and the markets that control them can cause wide fluctuations in price on a daily basis during a volatile market."

Because this fund is still an adolescent, and tiny by comparison to its cousins in the field, United Services initially was charging a 2 percent redemption fee to get out. That means when you want to sell shares, you are charged 2 percent of the value. It was meant to discourage investors from pulling their money out of the fund too quickly. Such withdrawals can force a small fund to sell stocks in its portfolio, and that's bad for all investors in the fund.

Prospector Fund is still a no-load (no sales charge) fund going in, however, and has the same $500 minimum ($50 add-on) requirements as the other funds in this group.

Two documents will give you basic information about any mutual fund—the prospectus and the most recent annual or quarterly report. They are both excruciatingly boring documents. But the prospectus will answer those inevitable questions that crop up. (For example, How much do the professional managers of these funds get paid to play with your money? Answer: The fee for managing the Prospector Fund is one percent of the fund's average net assets for the year, for the first $250 million assets, then ½ percent.)

The prospectus will warn you of the risks involved. (The government says it must do so.) Here, for example, are the special risks listed for the Prospector Fund:

• Gold and silver by themselves are risky and subject to large price swings. Since mining shares tend to move even more dramatically than bullion prices, they are considered even riskier (though the payoff will be greater too).

• Investing in foreign corporations injects still other variables. Those include changing currency values and difficulties in trying to sell some foreign stocks if the market turns sour.

• Prospector Fund will buy shares in some of the smaller gold mines, shares that more conservative fund managers wouldn't touch. In some cases, they are simply guessing about the firm's future prospects or are going by a "seat-of-the-pants" feeling. Some of the stocks the fund buys might end up as worthless paper.

> *A Cautious Investor's Tip:* Any gold fund's most recent quarterly report will include a complete list of mining stocks that it owns, including the number of shares. You might use it for ideas if you are buying gold shares on your own.

Golconda Investors: Heavier Stake in Bullion

Golconda Investors Ltd. is the gold fund member in the Bull & Bear group of mutual funds. This is one of the funds that invest a larger portion of their holdings in gold *bullion*. Golconda's stake in bullion has been around 30 percent. (For an even larger stake in bullion, check into Lexington Goldfund, which has at times held nearly 45 percent of its assets in gold bars.) The rest is often split among North American mining companies (about 30 percent), South African mining companies (about 28 percent), and other precious metals trading and refining companies.

Some features of this fund and the Bull & Bear Group:

• No sales charge or redemption fee.

• You can make additional purchases by phone and switch into other funds in this group. However, redemptions by telephone are not allowed.

• An automatic purchase plan is available; plus a systematic withdrawal plan and IRA and Keogh retirement plans are offered.

Fidelity: One of the Giants

With some $22 *billion* under management, the Fidelity group of mutual funds can legitimately be called a giant in the investment field. This is the same firm that runs a discount brokerage operation and has lately opened up retail Fidelity Investment Centers in some thirty cities around the United States.

Fidelity's horse in the precious metals race is the Fidelity Precious Metals and Minerals fund. This fund is part of a unique little group called the Fidelity Select Portfolio, which stands apart from the rest of the Fidelity fund empire.

Fidelity pioneered the sector fund concept with this group. Sector funds invest exclusively in very narrow industries, in this case energy, utilities, high technology, financial services, health care, leisure and entertainment, defense/aerospace, and precious metals. It has been one of the most popular and successful groups in fund history. The precious metals fund was established in 1981.

Sector funds were actually too popular, and Fidelity slapped on a sales charge a few years later to slow the stampede. (These funds started out as no-load and are now classified as low-load.) The sales charge to invest in the Precious Metals and Minerals fund is 2 percent. There is a one percent redemption fee, for a total in-and-out charge of 3 percent—not huge. Fidelity claims its superior performance and long list of perks make it worthwhile, but that's for you to decide. Other funds that don't charge a penny to invest in or redeem shares have also done well.

The perks? You can freely switch between funds within the Select Portfolio group *without paying a sales charge or redemption fee*. There are limits on this, however. You can make only four free exchanges per year within the group. After that, there's a $50 charge per switch. If you're into switching (one of the hottest mutual fund investing trends of the 1980s), this flexibility is handy. And if you like push-button electronic features available through your telephone, you'll love Fidelity's Automated Service Telephone. With it, you can move money between Fidelity funds, get updates on your account balance, and even open new accounts.

The minimum initial investment for Fidelity Precious Metals is $1,000, and additions to your account must be at least $250.

Fidelity also lets you buy more shares by telephone (they must receive your payment within seven calendar days). Telephone purchases must always be for $1,000 or more. With this fund, and most other funds that accept telephone orders, your conversation will be recorded.

To give you an idea of what an actual precious metals fund portfolio looks like, here is a snapshot of the Fidelity Precious Metals and Minerals fund portfolio, including its areas of heaviest concentration and fifteen largest individual holdings at a point where it was 87 percent invested in common stocks (the portfolio will have since changed):

Fidelity Precious Metals: What Stocks Has It Owned?

PRECIOUS METALS AND MINERALS

PORTFOLIO CONCENTRATIONS:
COMMON STOCKS—86.9%
UNITED STATES—11.1%

Diversified Metals	7.1%
Gold	1.3
Silver	2.1
Miscellaneous	0.6

CANADA—11.8%

Diversified Metals	1.9
Gold	8.1
Miscellaneous	1.8

SOUTH AFRICA—64.0%

Diversified Mining Finance	13.4
Long-Term Gold Mines	22.7
Medium-Term Gold Mines	21.6
Short-Term Gold Mines	4.2
Miscellaneous	2.1

SHORT-TERM OBLIGATION—13.1%

FIFTEEN LARGEST HOLDINGS

1.	Vaal Reefs Exploration & Mining Ltd. ADR*	5.2%
2.	Hartebeestfontein Gold Mining ADR	4.0
3.	Kloof Gold Mining Ltd. ADR	3.9
4.	Driefontein Consolidated Ltd. ADR	3.8
5.	Western Deep Levels Ltd. ADR	3.6
6.	President Steyn Gold Mining ADR	3.6
7.	Anglo American Gold Investment Co., Ltd. ADR	3.3
8.	Randfontein Estates Gold Mining Co.	2.9
9.	Southvaal Holdings Ltd. ADR	2.8
10.	ASA Ltd.	2.7
11.	Harmony Gold Mining Ltd.	2.6
12.	Newmont Mining Corp.	2.5
13.	Agnico Eagle Mines Ltd.	2.4
14.	Impala Platinum Holdings Ltd. ADR	2.2
15.	De Beers Consolidated Mines Ltd.	2.1

*ADR stands for American Depository Receipt, a method of owning foreign stocks in the United States.

Fidelity Precious Metals and Minerals Portfolio

Investments

COMMON STOCKS—88.6%

UNITED STATES—5.0%

	Shares	Value
Diversified Metals—3.9%		
Bethlehem Steel Corp.	45,000	$ 742,500
Engelhard Corp.	73,700	1,695,100
Handy & Harman	134,300	2,115,225
Newmont Mining Corp.	26,200	844,950
		5,397,775
Gold—0.5%		
Alhambra Atlanta Gold Mines & Properties, Inc.	50,200	31,375
Bull Run Gold Mines Ltd.	35,000	124,687
Klondex Mines Ltd.	9,100	6,916
Sonora Gold Corp.	100,000	466,000
		628,978
Silver—0.6%		
ASARCO, Inc.	29,900	583,050
Hecla Mining Co.	20,000	287,500
		870,550
TOTAL UNITED STATES (Average Cost $9,985,233)		6,897,303

CANADA—13.0%

	Shares	Value
Diversified Metals—3.7%		
Dome Mines, Ltd.	200,000	1,775,000
Lacana Mining Corp.	125,100	915,732
Placer Development Ltd.	89,000	1,227,310
Teck Corp. Class B.	124,600	716,450
United Hearne Resources, Ltd.	225,000	379,688
		5,014,180
Gold—9.3%		
Agnico Eagle Mines Ltd.	385,000	3,946,250
Bachelor Lake Gold Mines Inc.	95,900	299,208
Breakwater Resources Ltd.	30,000	136,875
Coniagas Mines Ltd.	100,000	390,000
Dickenson Mines Ltd.	20,000	60,000
Dumagami Mines Ltd.	92,500	341,325
Echo Bay Mines Ltd.	210,000	1,496,250
Giant Yellowknife Mines Ltd.	47,500	552,187
Kiena Gold Mines Ltd.	94,900	1,534,533
Lac Minerals Ltd.	120,400	2,336,964
Muscocho Explorations Ltd.	75,000	98,438
Pamour Porcupine Mines Ltd.	108,000	646,920
Quebec Sturgeon River Mines Ltd.	118,000	413,000
St. Andrews Goldfields Ltd.	100,000	266,000
		12,517,950

SOUTH AFRICA—70.6%

	Shares	Value
Diversified Mining Finance—13.2%		
ASA Ltd.	100,700	$ 4,795,838
Anglo American Corp. of South Africa ADR	195,000	2,461,875
Anglo American Gold Investment Co., Ltd. ADR	57,600	5,083,200
Gold Fields South Africa Ltd. ADR	196,500	2,677,313
Impala Platinum Holdings Ltd. ADR	178,00	1,980,250
Lydenburg Platinum Ltd. ADR	27,500	178,750
Rustenburg Platinum Holdings ADR	93,00	767,250
		17,944,476
Long-Term Gold Mines—25.6%		
Driefontein Consolidated Ltd. ADR	220,000	6,215,000
Kloof Gold Mining Ltd. ADR	158,800	6,014,550
Libanon Gold Mining Ltd.	27,500	598,125
Randfontein Estates Gold Mining Co.	46,000	4,370,000
Southvaal Holdings Ltd. ADR	95,000	3,895,000
Vaal Reefs Exploration & Mining Ltd. ADR	85,400	7,920,850
Western Deep Levels Ltd. ADR	147,600	5,682,600
		34,696,125
Medium-Term Gold Mines—26.0%		
Buffelsfontein Gold Mining Co. Ltd.	53,600	2,144,000
Doornfontein Gold Mining ADR	87,000	1,435,500
Free State Geduld Mines Ltd. ADR	82,000	2,326,750
Harmony Gold Mining Ltd.	281,500	4,433,625
Hartebeestfontein Gold Mining ADR	1,000,000	5,375,000
Kinross Mines Ltd.	41,000	666,250
President Brand Gold Mining ADR	113,900	3,644,800
President Steyn Gold Mining ADR	147,700	5,723,375
St. Helena Gold Mines Ltd. ADR	100,100	2,464,962
Unisel Gold Mines Ltd.	135,000	1,164,375
Unisel Gold Mines Ltd. ADR	47,000	405,375
Western Holdings ADR	96,500	3,570,500
Winkelhaak Mines Ltd. ADR	66,400	2,025,200
		35,379,712
Short-Term Gold Mines—3.5%		
Consolidated Modderfontein ADR	162,000	789,750
Deelkraal Gold Mining Ltd. ADR	60,000	180,000
East Daggafontein Mines ADR	235,000	646,250
East Rand Gold Uranium	217,000	1,274,875
Grootvlei Proprietary Mines	200,900	1,757,875
		4,648,750
Miscellaneous—2.3%		
De Beers Consolidated Mines Ltd.	625,000	3,144,562
TOTAL SOUTH AFRICA (Average Cost $137,351,521)		95,813,625
TOTAL COMMON STOCKS (Average Cost $172,309,174)		120,243,058

Financial Group Portfolios, Inc.

Of the three major sector fund groups that include a precious metals fund (Fidelity, Financial Programs, Inc., and Vanguard), Financial Programs is the only 100 percent no-load group. This group of six funds is called Financial Group Portfolios. GOLD Portfolio is the precious metals member.

Financial Group permits unlimited switching between funds in this group. There is no sales charge and no redemption fee. The fund has only a short track record, however (it was formed in 1983), and is one of the smallest in the precious metals field. The minimum initial investment is $1,000. Additions must be $100 or more; $500 if you are purchasing by telephone. Other funds in the group are Energy, Health Sciences, Leisure, Pacific Basin, and Technology.

Vanguard Gold and Precious Metals

The Vanguard Group is another of the giant mutual fund organizations in the United States with billions of dollars under its wing. In 1984 it too jumped on the precious metals bandwagon with its Gold and Precious Metals Fund. Vanguard's gold fund is part of a group called Vanguard Specialized Portfolios.

There is a minimum investment of $1,500 in this fund; additions must be $100 or more. There is no sales charge but there is a one percent redemption fee when you sell. You can switch without charge into other funds in the Specialized Portfolios group. But if you switch out of the group and into any of Vanguard's other assortment of funds, you will be charged the one percent redemption fee.

Other Funds to Choose From

As you will see from the Directory of Precious Metals Mutual Funds at the end of this chapter, there are many more choices. No two funds are exactly the same. They all offer something slightly different.

Sales charges—where they exist—range from 2 to 8½ percent; redemption fees, where they are charged, are one to 5 percent. Minimum initial investments range from a low of $100 (at Franklin Gold Fund) to $1,500 at several funds. And the minimum for additions to an account ranges from zero to $250. Check the directory for the specifics of each fund.

Don't Forget the Canadians

Closed-end funds offer one advantage that their open-end cousins cannot. Under certain market conditions, the closed-end funds that own gold bullion may actually sell at a *discount* to the market value (net asset value) of the fund's holdings.

For example, that happened when gold was slumming along in the low $300 range. The market seemed disenchanted with anything that had "gold" in its name, and shares of the Canadian closed-end gold funds were driven down. They plunged so far that they began selling at *discounts* of 20 percent or more. BGR fund (see the Directory for details on Canadian funds as well) was selling at $7½ per share while the net asset value of the fund's shares was $9.79. At the same time Guardian Morton Shulman fund hit $7¼, its net asset value was $10.00. Goldcorp had a net asset value of $9.33 at the time, but was selling in the stock market (Toronto Exchange) for $7⅛.

Goldcorp Investments Ltd., with assets of about $175 million, is the largest of this group of Canadian closed-end gold funds. It holds a higher percentage of gold bullion than most gold funds in the United States—at one point about 65 percent. The rest of the fund's assets were in gold mining shares (about 28 percent) and a small amount in cash and other short-term investments.

Following the Funds

Many major daily newspapers, and some smaller ones as well, now carry mutual fund listings. You can easily follow the day-to-day changes in prices by looking at those listings. If your paper doesn't carry mutual fund prices, pick up *The Wall Street Journal* or *USA Today*. Both carry complete listings daily.

For in-depth historical information on all no-load mutual funds, one of the best publications around is *The No-Load Fund Investor* (monthly, $32 per year). Each year it also publishes *The Handbook for No-Load Fund Investors,* which includes information on many precious metals funds and costs $32, or if you also want the quarterly updates, $49. (It is available from The No-Load Fund Investor, Box 283, Hastings-on-Hudson, NY 10706.)

Another helpful fund newsletter is *Mutual Fund Forecaster* published by The Institute for Econometric Research (3471 North Federal Highway, Fort Lauderdale, FL 33306). It's a monthly and the annual subscription price is $49.

When you invest in a fund, you will receive regular reports (quarterly and annually) of how the fund has been doing, including a breakdown of stocks owned by the fund. There is usually a substantial lag time before you receive this material, however, and you should be keeping closer tabs on your fund on your own.

FUND INVESTOR'S CHECKLIST

Considering a precious metals fund? Here are some tips and important questions to ask yourself:

• Are you planning to invest short- or long-term? Precious metals funds are designed for the long haul—don't expect to buy in and turn a quick profit in a few months, although it could happen. Investing directly in mining shares is the best way to hit those quick speculative profits, but you'll face much greater risk.

• Think twice about the load funds—those that have a sales charge. An 8½ percent load costs even more in real terms. Calculated as a percentage of the amount you actually invest (after subtracting the load), the charge comes to 9.3 percent. Why start from a hole?

• Should you own shares in more than one precious metals fund? Since performance of most precious metals funds is linked to the same thing—the price of gold—investing in more than one makes little sense. The exception: If you want the choice of switching into a certain fund family's other offerings, you might want to spread your funds around. If you stick with the no-loads, at least it won't cost you anything to try.

• For funds that invest in foreign mining shares, currency movements (the strength or weakness of the dollar) will play a role in how your investment performs. If your fund is heavily invested in foreign stocks, it will perform better when the other country's currency rises in relation to the dollar (falling dollar). A muscular dollar can hinder performance of a precious metals fund with international holdings.

• Gold funds may give you more bang for the buck than bullion in a rising gold market. But they will ride that roller coaster just as fast *down* the other side.

• Prices for mutual fund shares are set only once daily, at the close of business. That differs from regular stocks where prices change minute to minute throughout the trading day. No matter what time the fund receives your buy order, you get the end-of-the-day price. But that's an advantage for investors. If you intend to trade by telephone, you can follow the price during the day to see what direction it is going before making a decision on whether or not to buy or sell.

• If your precious metals fund offers you a choice of receiving capital gains and dividends in cash or having them automatically reinvested in shares of the fund, opt for reinvestment. It's a great way to accumulate shares at a low average cost. You'll be surprised at how it helps your money grow.

• Do you own gold or silver mining shares on your own? If you do, buying a precious metals mutual fund might be redundant. Check the fund's specific holdings. It may own the same shares that you do. The overlap would work against you. Instead, look for a precious metals investment that will extend your diversification.

• Unless you have a special reason (loan collateral, for instance), don't request certificates for your mutual fund shares. It will only cost you time and money to safeguard them, and cause you delays when you want to sell.

• If you want to link part of your Individual Retirement Account (IRA) or Keogh Plan to precious metals, mutual funds are the way to do it. Most of the funds listed in this chapter offer special IRA setups for individual investors.

• No-load mutual funds are the brokerless way to invest in precious metals mining shares. So if you don't have a stockbroker, or have one but don't like dealing with brokers, this is the way you can do it.

• Gold funds offer instant diversification. For individual investors there is no better or cheaper way to buy into a broad, professionally managed portfolio of gold mining shares. How else could you own pieces of the world's major gold mining companies for as little as $500? That diversity also means greater safety. Precious metals mutual funds carry no guarantees, but they let you ride in a much larger, sturdier ship than if you were sailing the investment seas on your own.

> *A Cautious Investor's Tip:* Mutual funds (and all investment salespeople for that matter) love to point out past performance results—if they are good. But *past performance is never a guarantee of future results.* Few funds can consistently stay on top, and frequently the ones that do best one year stumble the next. Good performance figures make enticing advertising copy, but today's basement dwellers might well be tomorrow's stars.

DIRECTORY OF PRECIOUS METALS MUTUAL FUNDS

A Consumer's Guide to Mutual Funds That Invest in Gold, Silver, Platinum, Palladium, and Related Assets

This list of exclusively precious metals–related funds includes funds that are 100 percent invested in precious metals, some that invest only a portion of assets in metals, and some that move in and out of gold as conditions warrant. You will find open-end, no-load funds as well as low-load, load, closed-end, and some Canadian precious metals funds. Use the toll-free numbers where they are provided to request information on a fund. To help in your shopping, this fund directory includes information on the minimum investment required by each fund for the initial purchase and later additions (the second figure after the slash). Sales and redemption charges are also listed, along with other comments. All details come from the funds but are subject to change. Mutual funds are also notorious for changing their phone numbers, so you may have to do some updating later on.

Open-End Funds

Comments

Colonial Advanced Strategies Gold Trust
Colonial Investment Services, Inc.
75 Federal St.
Boston, MA 02110
(800) 225-2365
(617) 426-3750 (in Massachusetts)
Offers two unique features: will not invest in South Africa; large portion invested in gold-denominated bonds.

Minimum investment: $250/$25

Sales charge: 6¾%
No IRA plan offered.

Fidelity Select Portfolios: Precious Metals and Minerals
Fidelity Investments
P.O. Box 832
82 Devonshire St.
Boston, MA 02103
(800) 544-6666
(617) 523-1919

Minimum investment: $1,000/$250

Sales charge: 2%
Redemption fee: 1%

Full range of other services available.

Financial Group Portfolios, Inc. GOLD Portfolio
P.O. Box 2040
Denver, CO 80201
(800) 525-9831
(800) 332-9145 (in Colorado)

Minimum investment: $1,000/$100

Sales charge: none

Telephone exchange: $500 minimum

Franklin Gold Fund
(formerly Research Capital)
155 Bovet Road
San Mateo, CA 94402
(800) 632-2180
(415) 570-3000
Fund invests about 60% in South Africa; 40% North American mines.

Minimum investment: $100/$25

Sales charge: 7¼%, included in asking price.

Freedom Gold and Government Trust
Tucker Anthony Management Co.
3 Center Plaza
Boston, MA 02108
(800) 225-6713
(800) 392-6021 (in Massachusetts)
This fund is run by a subsidiary of John Hancock Mutual Life Insurance Co.

Minimum investment: $1,500/$200

Sales charge: 5%
Redemption fee: none

Golconda Investors, Inc.
Bull and Bear Group
11 Hanover Square
New York, NY 10005
(800) 431-6060
(212) 785-0900

Minimum investment: $1,000/$100 ($500 by telephone)

Sales charge: none

E. F. Hutton Investment Series
Precious Metals Series
One Battery Park Plaza
New York, NY 10004
(212) 742-5000

Minimum investment: $500/$250

Redemption fee: 5% first year, drops to zero in 7th year

Can buy only through E. F. Hutton account representatives.

IDS Precious Metals Fund
IDS Financial Services
P.O. Box 534
Minneapolis, MN 55440
(612) 372-3733

Minimum investment: $2,000/$100

Sales charge: 5%

Keystone Precious Metals Holdings
99 High Street
Boston, MA 02110
(617) 956-1300
(800) 343-2898

Minimum investment: $250/none

Sales charge: none
Redemption fee: 4% first year, drops to zero after 4 years

Lexington Goldfund
Park 80 W. Plaza 2
Saddlebrook, NJ 07662
(800) 932-0838 (in New Jersey)
(201) 845-7300 or
(800) 526-4791

Minimum investment:
$1,000/$50

Sales charge: none

No telephone switches.

Oppenheimer Gold Fund
c/o Shareholder Services
P.O. Box 300
Denver, CO 80201
(800) 525-7048
(303) 671-3200

Minimum investment:
$1,000/$25

Sales charge: 8½%

Permanent Portfolio Fund
P.O. Box 5847
Austin, TX 78763
(800) 531-5142
(512) 453-7558
This fund invests only about 25%
in gold and silver.

Minimum investment:
$1,000/$100

Sales charge: none
Startup fee: $35

Monthly fee: $2

Research Capital
(Name changed to Franklin Gold
Fund)

Sherman, Dean Fund Inc.
120 Broadway
New York, NY 10271
(212) 577-3850
This fund is mainly an aggressive
growth fund in the natural
resources area; but happens to
have about 40% in gold shares.

Minimum investment:
$1,000/$100

Sales charge: none

Strategic Investments
Strategic Silver Fund
The Strategic Building
2030 Royal Lane
Dallas, TX 75229
(800) 527-5027
(214) 484-1326 (in Texas)

Minimum investment:
$500/$100

Sales charge: 8½%

United Services Gold Shares
P.O. Box 29467
San Antonio, TX 78229
(800) 824-4653
(512) 696-1234

Minimum investment:
$500/$50

Sales charge: none

United Services Prospector Fund
P.O. Box 29467
San Antonio, TX 78229
(800) 824-4653
(512) 696-1234

Minimum investment:
$500/$50

Redemption fee: 2%
Fund does not invest in South Africa.

Vanguard Specialized Portfolios
Gold and Precious Metals
Vanguard Group
P.O. Box 2600
Valley Forge, PA 19482
(800) 662-SHIP
(215) 648-6000
This is one of the newest gold funds, and a new addition to the vast Vanguard fund empire.

Minimum investment:
$1,500/$100

Sales charge: none

Redemption fee: 1% if leaving group

Other Selected Funds, Including Closed-End and Funds Outside the United States

American Precious Metals Fund
707 Westchester Ave.
White Plains, NY 10604
(914) 681-4412

At this writing, American Precious Metals was still in formation. It was to be the first closed-end precious metals fund to invest in all four metals—gold, silver, platinum, and palladium, and related assets.

Dynamic-Guardian Gold Fund
Dynamic Funds Management Ltd.
74 Victoria St., Suite 300
Toronto, Ontario M5C-2H5
Canada

(416) 363-5621
(800) 268-8186 (in Canada)

This flexible fund is designed so its managers are allowed to invest in all of the precious metals, and it can hold bullion as well as mining shares. There are no commissions or brokerage charges to purchase or sell shares.

The Sound Monetary Fund
(Central Fund of Canada Ltd.)

This closed-end fund holds mostly gold and silver bullion, with smaller amounts in shares and cash. Shares trade on the Toronto and Vancouver stock exchanges, and are available through brokers.

Goldcorp Investments Ltd.

Managed by CSA Management Ltd., this Canadian closed-end fund invests at least 75% of its assets in gold-related investments. Often that's mostly bullion. Listed on the Toronto Stock Exchange.

BGR Precious Metals Inc.

This is another Canadian closed-end gold fund. It is managed by Beutel, Goodman & Co., N. M. Rothschild, and Guardian Trustco. Invests 95% of its assets in precious metals–related areas. Trades on Toronto Exchange.

Guardian Morton Shulman Precious Metals Inc.

A Canadian closed-end fund managed by Guardian Investment Management Services Inc. Also trades on Toronto Exchange.

These Canadian closed-end funds can be bought through any U.S. stockbroker that handles shares listed on the Toronto Stock Exchange, or through Canadian brokerage firms.

International Gold Fund Inc.
P.O. Box 1044
Grand Cayman, Cayman Islands
British West Indies

This is technically called an "off shore" fund because it is located in the tax haven Cayman Islands. 70% of the fund must be in gold investments. It owns mostly South African shares. The minimum investment is $10,000 and there is a 5% sales charge.

CHAPTER 13

Rare (Numismatic) Coins: Back Door to Precious Metals

- **Coin Performance Review**
- **The Rare Coin/Precious Metals Double Play**
- **Grading Is Everything**
- **Silver Dollar Quicksand**
- **Essentials of Coin Grading**
- **"Coin Speak": The Language of Numismatics**
- **Coin Dealers: A Short List**

Rare coins have been star investment performers over the last forty years. This is a specialized field with its own curious nooks and crannies to navigate. But rare coins and precious metals do overlap. Numismatic investments offer a back door entrance to gold and silver—an entrance with unique benefits and pitfalls.

COIN PERFORMANCE REVIEW

Rare or numismatic coins are not the same as gold and silver *bullion* coins. A numismatic coin is an old coin, once minted as real money, that has become a high-priced collector's item. That price is greater than the market value of the gold or silver in the coin—sometimes a little higher, sometimes by a factor of hundreds.

Bullion coins—Krugerrands, U.S. Gold medallions, Canadian Maple Leaf one-ounce coins—are not rare. They are minted currently in unlimited quantity. Numismatic coins are rare—really rare. The more scarce the coin, the better its condition, and the more the demand among collectors and investors, the higher the price. The higher the price of the coin due to its rarity, the less of a straight precious metals investment it will be. Super rare coins, where only a few exist, are an exception. They're valuable regardless of condition.

Semi-numismatic coins fall somewhere between rare coins and bullion coins. The "semis" are no longer being minted, but they are not particularly scarce. Some numismatic experts arbitrarily pick World War II as a cutoff point. Coins made before that time, they say, are more likely to be considered numismatic items, even in lesser condition. Still, there are many investment grade coins minted after the war that are legitimate numismatic items, commanding top prices in today's market.

Contrary to some rare coin advertising, however, just because a coin is old does *not* make it valuable. Beware. The rare coin market is small enough and volatile enough that prices for a certain type of coin can be manipulated by a few dealers who decide to promote a coin heavily.

Back in 1980, when coin prices peaked, rare coin barons were flying high. Then came a slow-motion crash. Over the next few years, many coin values tumbled 50 percent or more. But in the years that followed, coin prices rebounded nicely, while gold and silver remained flat or dropped. That, to many observers, is evidence that rare coins—as a combination precious metals/collectible investment—offer *better* profit potential than the precious metals alone.

For example, in January 1981 the world price of gold was about $585 per ounce. At the same time a good investment grade U.S. $20 rare gold coin fetched about $1,665 in the coin market. A year later gold had dropped to below $390 per ounce, but the rare gold coin had *increased* slightly in value to about $1,725. By the end of 1983, gold had climbed back to about $415 per ounce, but the value of the numismatic gold coin in top condition jumped to nearly $2,100.

One advantage rare coins have that precious metals don't is a strong base of support from collectors—some 12 million of them in the United States alone. The collectors are always there, in good times as well as bad. While their pocketbooks feel a recessionary pinch as much as the next guy's, the continuous demand from such a large body of eager traders forms a floor below which rare coin prices are unlikely to drop.

Most rare coin charts and graphs you'll see are misleading. They show prices going up, up, and further up. Granted, rare coins have had some good times. But, like most other investments, rare coins run in cycles. That's what investors need to understand most about this market. It is not the express lane to big profits it's sometimes cracked up to be.

The following table, based on an index of rare coin prices compiled by the Chicago firm Numisco Rare Coins, shows some of the ups and downs of investment coins between 1971 and 1985, separated into three bull market periods and two bear market periods.

Index of Rare Coin Performance

BULL MARKET #1

Date	4-Month Change	Cumulative Change This Cycle
January 1971	——base/starting point——	
April 1971	+2.0%	+2%
August 1971	+2.9	+5
December 1971	+16.2	+22
April 1972	+11.5	+36
August 1972	+25.0	+70
December 1972	+24.7	+112
April 1973	+45.3	+208
August 1973	+17.2	+261
December 1973	+9.4	+295
April 1974	+8.1	+327
August 1974	+5.4	+350
December 1974	+8.0	+386
April 1975	+5.6	+413
August 1975	+1.2	+419
December 1975	+8.5	+463
April 1976	+43.5	+708

BEAR MARKET #1

Date	4-Month Change	Cumulative Change This Cycle
August 1976	−1.1%	−1.1%
December 1976	−0.1	−1.2
April 1977	no change	−1.2

BULL MARKET #2

Date	4-Month Change	Cumulative Change This Cycle
August 1977	+0.4%	+0.4%
December 1977	+12.5	+12.9
April 1978	+5.5	+19.2
August 1978	+0.5	+19.8
December 1978	+2.1	+22.3
April 1979	+23.6	+51.1
August 1979	+40.1	+111.8
December 1979	+84.9	+291.5
April 1980	+97.1	+671.7

BEAR MARKET #2

Date	4-Month Change	Cumulative Change This Cycle
August 1980	−12.2%	−12.2%
December 1980	+0.8	−11.5
April 1981	−4.9	−15.8
August 1981	−13.3	−27.1
December 1981	+0.1	−26.6
April 1982	−14.7	−37.8
September 1982	−17.8	−48.5

BULL MARKET #3

Date	4-Month Change	Cumulative Change This Cycle
December 1982	+3.1%	+3.1%
April 1983	+26.6	+30.5
August 1983	+23.4	+61.1
December 1983	−2.9	+56.5
April 1984	+7.0	+67.4

Date	4-Month Change	Cumulative Change This Cycle
August 1984	−5.5	+58.2
December 1984	+14.3	+80.2
April 1985	+8.7	+95.9

SOURCE: Numisco Rare Coins, Ltd., Chicago

The net result of this fourteen-year history of coin prices is that based on the particular group of coins in Numisco's index, one dollar invested in 1971 would have been worth over $50 by 1985.

THE RARE COIN/PRECIOUS METALS DOUBLE PLAY

Precious metals investors who already own a stake in other gold assets—such as gold bullion, certificates, mining shares, or mutual funds—often branch into numismatic gold coins. Rare gold coins offer a way to "double dip" into two markets—gold bullion and collector coins. If you hit it right, you could turn it into a double play.

The most popular numismatic gold coins are the U.S. legal tender gold coins struck before gold coinage was abandoned in 1933. The choices include different types of $1, $2.50, $3, $5, $10, and $20 U.S. gold pieces. Over the last decade or more, they have outpaced gold bullion when the direction was up—and you can usually count on numismatic gold to drop less when the gold market turns around.

Says numismatic expert Donald H. Kagin, "No matter what happens in the coin market, [numismatic gold coins] will always be worth at least the value of their gold content. On the other hand, if gold prices decline, the numismatic value of these pieces assures that they will have a market among collectors.

"The less rare a numismatic gold coin is, the more likely it will be to fluctuate in value with the price of bullion. The U.S. $20 St. Gaudens coin is an example of such a *semi-bullion* [same as semi-numismatic] coin. Even among semi-bullion pieces, the higher the grade of the coin, the less it will be tied to the spot price of gold."

For example, notes Kagin, who is president of his own coin firm based in San Francisco, "From mid-January 1980 to the end of September 1983, spot gold prices declined 41 percent. But the semi-bullion $20 St. Gaudens coin in extremely fine condition fell in price only 17 percent. The same coin in a much higher grade [MS-65, investment grade] *rose* in value by 74 percent over the same period."

Here are a few other reasons this expert says numismatic gold coins can at times be a better investment than strictly bullion-related gold coins:

- **Double Demand:** If gold values rise, rare U.S. gold coins will also rise by at least the same rate. In addition, demand will continue to increase from coin collectors and investors.
- **Limited Supply:** Unlike bullion coins, the last numismatic gold coins were made over half a century ago. Supplies are limited and can only decrease.
- **Better Tax Treatment:** Court decisions have confirmed that semi-bullion coins such as the U.S. $20 gold piece—in uncirculated (MS-60) or better condition—are numismatic coins and not bullion. That's important for tax reasons. When they are traded for other rare coins, the deal is considered a "like kind" exchange and is not taxable.

GRADING IS EVERYTHING

If you plan to invest in rare coins, remember this: Grading is everything. If you get stuck with an overgraded coin by a firm that won't guarantee its merchandise, you could be out 70 percent or more on your investment. Learning coin grading basics is essential even for the casual investor.

Start by purging yourself of the idea that "uncirculated" is top shelf. It's not so simple. Some uncirculated coins are nearly perfect; others are of poor quality. Tiny scratches barely visible to the naked eye can make hundred-dollar differences in a coin's price. With that kind of money riding on a subjective judgment, you can bet there is chicanery in the coin-grading business.

A perfect uncirculated coin (some say it doesn't exist) would be an MS-70 grade. The "MS" stands for mint state. A typical uncirculated coin is MS-60. Investment grade coins are usually considered to be

MS-63, MS-65, and MS-67. Price differences within those three grade alone can be tremendous.

Grading rare coins is an inexact task. Here are the stakes for investors:

Assuming a U.S. $20 gold piece sells for $1,500 to $1,700 in MS-65 grade, knock it down a notch or two in grade and the price plummets to between $500 and $700. Another example: A silver 1826 half-dollar, worth $5,200 in MS-65 grade, drops to $1,700 in MS-63; $800 in MS-60, and $300 in AU (about uncirculated) condition.

Combine dramatic price spreads with widespread controversy over coin grading, throw in a dash of human greed with the temptation to deliberately misgrade a coin, and you have a mess—and a bright red flag for investors.

David Hall, a leading rare coin expert, agrees that improperly graded coins are the biggest problem facing investors in this field. In an interview with an industry newsletter, he claimed that ". . . 90 percent of all coins sold are overgraded by at least half a grade."

Since the subtle art of coin grading could take years to master, Hall and most other coin experts say you should look closely at the terms you get from a coin dealer. Is there a guarantee on the grade of the coin? Will the dealer buy back the coin at that grade? What assurance do you have that the coin is what that dealer says it is?

To avoid getting stuck with overgraded coins, demand an *unconditional* guarantee from the dealer, of both the authenticity and the grade of your purchase. Many dealers will offer a buyback policy, but they won't tell you at what *price*. Make certain the guarantee has some teeth in it. Many dealers will balk at the suggestion, but the largest, most reputable firms are willing to stand behind what they sell. Those are the firms you should seek out.

Shady dealers try to make money by purchasing coins a grade below their true grade and then selling them for a grade above the actual condition. Even if you obtain a "guarantee" from the dealer that the coin is correctly graded, few such guarantees are ironclad. Best is an unqualified guarantee that you can get your money back—all of it—or exchange the coins if other experts do not agree with your dealer's grading.

The American Numismatic Association (ANA, 818 N. Cascade, Colorado Springs, CO 80903) is the national organization of coin enthusiasts that finally developed a uniform system for grading and certifying coins. Through the ANA Certification Service, anyone can (for a fee) send in a coin and have it independently graded and certified by the ANA.

Sounds great, but the service has been under fire since it was launched in the early 1980s. Coin dealers are constantly sniping at the ANA's grading standards, complaining of inconsistency. The system for grading coins, as precise as it might sound to the layperson, still leaves room for "creative interpretation" by dealers. MS-60 coins are called Select Uncirculated. MS-63 to MS-65 coins carry the Choice Uncirculated label, and MS-65+ coins are known as Gem Uncirculated.

Predictably, some dealers have invented new terms: Choice Borderline Uncirculated, Almost Gem, and Virtually Uncirculated. That's like being Virtually Pregnant.

In defense of the chaps who attempt to grade coins, it is a complex task. With silver dollars alone, there are hundreds of millions of individual coins, each with its own slight variations, produced at five different mints (Philadelphia, Denver, New Orleans, Carson City, and San Francisco). That comes to over 100 different mint mark and date combinations. Strictly speaking each coin should be judged only in comparison to others of the same year and mint mark.

If you are serious about investing in rare coins and want to check the prices, there's a way to do it. Read the same published wholesale price lists that the dealers read. The font of all knowledge in coin pricing is *Coin Dealer Newsletter*, a weekly publication that dealers call The Gray Sheet. The newsletter's address is P.O. Box 11099, Torrance, CA 90510. A subscription costs $89 per year.

Three other handy publications are: *Numismatic News* (Krause Publications), 700 East State St., Iola, WI 54990, at $21.50 per year; *Coin World* (Amos Press), 911 Vandemark Rd., P.O. Box 150, Sidney, OH 45365, at $24 per year; and *Rare Coin Market Report*, P.O. Box 16637, Irvine, CA 92713, at $19 per year.

Coin Grading Lessons by Video

The lastest innovation is a videocassette that offers a quickie course in rare coin grading, called *Collecting and Grading U.S. Coins*. It is endorsed by the American Numismatic Association. As the title implies, it's not just for grading. This is a beginner's guide to investing in rare coins.

There's also a book on coin grading that comes with the video tape called *Basics of Coin Grading*. The book/tape combination sells for $79.95 and is carried by some dealers, or can be ordered from Educational Video, 31800 Plymouth Rd., Livonia, MI 48150.

New Guaranteed Coin Packets

The coin-grading imbroglio has hatched new products to ease investor fears. One of the most interesting is a plastic-sealed rare gold coin that comes with a guarantee of authenticity and grade. The coins being sold this way are the most popular of the gold numismatic coins—the $20 Double Eagle, also known as the St. Gaudens, and the $20 Liberty. The firm behind the program is A-Mark Precious Metals, Inc., a Beverly Hills–based wholesaler. The guaranteed-grade coins are sold only through retail firms such as: James U. Blanchard & Co. (Metairie, Louisiana); Deak-Perera (Los Angeles offices); and Security Pacific National Bank (throughout California).

The A-Mark guaranteed gold coins are aimed at people who have avoided this precious metals "double play" investment fearing they will be stuck with overgraded or downright counterfeit coins. Each coin comes with a written guarantee. The coin itself is placed right on the certificate, which is then sealed in a tamper-resistant packet. If the package is ever tampered with (it can easily be done with tools), the guarantee is no good.

Bet on Quality

Coins are like other things you buy. You get what you pay for. In numismatics, the experts suggest that you buy the best grade coins you can find and afford. High-grade (MS-65 or better) coins have the best chance to appreciate. That has often been proven. According to coin expert David Hall, high-grade coins can outperform their inferior cousins by 100 to 400 percent when prices are on the rise.

SILVER DOLLAR QUICKSAND

No other numismatic coin is as popular—or as potentially poisonous to your pocketbook—as the silver dollar. It is beloved for its beauty, its affordability, and as a double-play investment in silver.

But silver dollars are also a favorite of rare coin hucksters. You've probably seen their ads running in major financial publications. They'll offer "BIG DISCOUNTS" on a "newly acquired" batch of silver dollars. They'll tell you the coins are worth, say, $30 or $40, which to most people doesn't sound unreasonable, and that their $20 half-price offer is for "a limited time only."

Nice of them, isn't it? If you took the time to check the price of the goods being offered with other coin dealers (few people do), you might find it's all a scam. Most such coins are semi-numismatic items, if not outright junk silver, and should sell for a low premium over their silver value.

Three groups you can contact if you have a question about a dealer are: Professional Numismatists' Guild, P.O. Box 430, Van Nuys, CA 91408; ANA, 818 N. Cascade, Colorado Springs, CO 80903; and the American Numismatic Society, Broadway at 155th St., New York, NY 10032.

Does that mean you should stay away from silver dollars? No, but be on your toes. The silver dollar you buy will be a good investment only if you get a good deal in the first place. Again, buy the best-quality coins you can afford. A common mistake is buying lower-priced coins only because they are cheaper. Lesser-quality coins are rarely a real "bargain," and don't even consider those special silver dollar "deals" you see hyped in print.

Another potential pitfall is the mixed-grade roll of silver dollars. Coin rolls should be one grade only, unless you know exactly how many coins of each grade are in the roll. A mixed MS-63/65 roll might have one or two top-grade coins, even though the price of the roll would reflect a fifty-fifty mix. Beware. Again, the value of a coin jumps dramatically from one grade to the next. An MS-63 Morgan silver dollar, with full mint luster and a few bag marks, might sell for $75–$100. The same coin in MS-65 condition could easily sell for *three to four times that much, or about $275 to $350.*

Of the two silver dollar types minted between 1878 and 1935— Morgan dollars (named for the designer of the coin) and Peace dollars (so called because of the design on the coin)—Morgans are the older and more popular investment coins. They were minted for circulation between 1878 and 1904, when a silver shortage hit, then started again in 1921, which is the most common date for the Morgan dollar. Peace dollars were made from 1921 to 1935 (except for 1929–33).

Silver dollars are not pure silver. That would be too soft. They are 90 percent silver and 10 percent copper. The copper makes the coin tougher. A silver dollar contains about 0.7734 ounce of pure silver. A $1,000 face value bag of "junk silver" dollars has about 773 troy ounces of silver. Bagged coins bang against one another all the time, producing "bag marks" so they can never be the top-grade investment pieces that command the top prices.

They are also traded in partial bags or tubes of twenty coins. Coins in a tube don't rub against one another (each coin rests on its neighbor's rim), so they should stay in good condition if they are packed properly.

A word of caution about storing silver dollars. *Never* keep them in plastic holders that are made with PVC—polyvinylchloride. The chemicals in this substance react with silver and can leave a rather disgusting green slime on the coin.

Toning, incidentally, is a nice word for tarnish. It is the natural discoloration of the coin's surface that occurs over time (when it's not jangling around in somebody's pocket). Coin collectors *like* this stuff, and it can actually make the coin more valuable. In some cases, toning occurred because canvas bags used to hold coins were treated with sulfur to make them last longer. The coins that touched the canvas were exposed to the sulfur, which over time caused the coin to "tone" where it had come in contact with the bag. Numismatic experts talk themselves blue in the face warning neophytes *never* to try to clean a silver dollar, or any other coin for that matter. You could literally "clean" away hundreds of dollars of value.

ESSENTIALS OF COIN GRADING

"Proof" coins are at the top of the coin heap. They aren't the same as uncirculated coins. In fact, the term "proof" refers to how the coin was made, not its condition. Proofs are specially struck, using the best dies (the "mold" for the coin) under the best conditions, to obtain the most nearly perfect specimens.

The terms "mint state" and "uncirculated" are used interchangeably. Perfect Uncirculated is MS-70. Gem Uncirculated is MS-67, Choice Uncirculated MS-65, Select Uncirculated MS-63, and Typical Uncirculated MS-60.

Choice About Uncirculated (AU) coins show the barest traces of wear and carry the AU-55 grade. Next steps down are About Uncirculated (AU-50), Choice Extremely Fine (EF-45), Extremely Fine (EF-40), Choice Very Fine (VF-30), Very Fine (VF-20), Fine (F-12), Very Good (VG-8), Good (G-4), and About Good (AG-3).

Everything sounds as if it's in great condition. It's like trying to buy olives in the grocery store—where "giant" size means the little ones. You have to find Super Colossal before you can really call it a big olive. For investment coins, Gem Uncirculated is a big olive; Extremely Fine is the pits.

"COIN SPEAK":
THE LANGUAGE OF NUMISMATICS

Here's a little rare-coin terminology to help you along.

• **Bag Marks:** Most common on large silver and gold coins, bag marks are the minor nicks or scratches caused by the jostling of the coins against each other while still in the canvas mint bags.

• **Brilliant Uncirculated (BU):** Means the same as "mint state" but is not used as an official grading term by the American Numismatic Association.

• **Business Strike:** A business strike coin is a coin made for general, or "business," circulation.

• **Cull:** The term for a worthless or inferior numismatic specimen.

• **Current Coins:** Gold coins that were legal tender in the period of circulating gold currency. More commonly used in the bullion field.

• **Exergue:** The area of the coin near its bottom edge, usually where the date and face value are placed.

• **Face Value:** The value of the coin as it was originally intended, stated on the face of the coin.

• **Fantasy:** A numismatic specimen that looks like a coin but was not issued by official authorities.

• **Fields:** The blank areas of a coin, between the design.

• **Grade:** The condition of the coin as defined by exacting standards. The grade of a coin will make a huge difference in what it is worth.

• **Mintage:** The number of coins originally struck. In the case of silver and gold coins, the number struck does not necessarily reflect the number that have actually *survived*. Many were later melted down.

• **Mint Mark:** A small letter or symbol that indicates where the coin was made. With the exception of the Philadelphia mint, which uses no mint mark, you will see S for San Francisco, D for Denver, O for New Orleans, and CC for Carson City.

- **Mint Set:** A family of select, uncirculated coins, sold by the mint to collectors.
- **Mint State (MS):** Another term used interchangeably with uncirculated coins. Standard grading uses this designation for the top-grade coins.
- **Obverse:** The front of the coin, or face side. Better known by all coin flippers as heads. It's usually the side that has the date and the principal design.
- **Proof Strike:** Proof coins were specially made for collectors. They were never intended for circulation and were struck with greater state-of-the-art care. They are the most perfectly struck examples of most coins.
- **Rarity:** An important part of what determines a coin's value. It recognizes not only how many coins were originally minted but how many have survived in top condition.
- **Reverse:** This is tails. It's the back side of the coin, the side that carries the secondary design. The opposite of obverse.
- **Strike:** A measure of quality; how well the coin's design was imprinted in the metal. A well-struck coin is superior—the design is more well defined. A good strike will increase a coin's value. Likewise, a weak strike will make a coin worth less.
- **Toning:** Otherwise known as tarnish. It is the natural discoloration of a coin's surface. Toning should not be disturbed and can enhance a coin's value.
- **Uncirculated:** Same as mint state. It means the coin is fresh, regardless of age, and was never placed into circulation, and thus shows only the wear of bag marks. Remember, there are many grades of uncirculated, from average to perfect.

COIN DEALERS: A SHORT LIST

The United States is bulging with coin dealers. A list could quickly grow to Manhattan telephone directory proportions. This much abbreviated list is not an endorsement or recommendation of any dealer but includes many of the major firms. Use it as a convenient starting point for your own window shopping.

Asset Services, Inc.
1414 Avenue of the Americas
New York, NY 10019
(212) 319-1818

James U. Blanchard & Co.
4425 W. Napoleon Ave.
Metairie, LA 70001
(800) 535-7633
(504) 456-9034

Bowers & Merena
P.O. Box 1224
Wolfeboro, NH 03894
(603) 569-5095

Cumberland Investment Corp.
225 Franklin St.
Boston, MA 02110
(800) 556-7550, 7551
(617) 542-6669

**(David) Hall's Numismatic
Investment Group**
P.O. Box 16637
Irvine, CA 92713
(714) 553-0110

Heritage Rare Coin Galleries
The Heritage Building
311 Market St.
Dallas, TX 75202
(214) 742-2200 (in Texas)
(800) 872-6467

**International Coins &
Currency**
11 E. State St. Box 218
Montpelier, VT 05602
(800) 451-4463
(802) 223-6331

Investment Rarities, Inc.
One Appletree Square
Minneapolis, MN 55420
(800) 328-1860
(612) 853-0700

**Kagin's Numismatic
Investment Corp.**
One Market Plaza
Steuart Tower, 26th floor
San Francisco, CA 94105
(800) 227-5676
(415) 777-5529

Kurt R. Krueger
160 N. Washington St.
Iola, WI 54945
(715) 445-3845

Lee Numismatics, Inc.
Box 1045
Merrimack, NH 03054
(800) 842-3000 (in New
England)
(800) 835-6000
(603) 429-0869

Littleton Rare Coins
253 Union St.
Littleton, NH 03561
(603) 444-6770
(800) 258-4645

Manfra, Tordella & Brookes
59 W. 49th St.
New York, NY 10112
(800) 535-7481
(212) 621-9502

Medlar's Coins
220 Alamo Plaza
San Antonio, TX 78205
(512) 226-2311

New England Rare Coin Galleries
89 Devonshire St.
Boston, MA 02109
(800) 225-6794
(617) 227-8800 (in Massachusetts)

Numisco Rare Coins, Ltd.
1423 West Fullerton Ave.
Chicago, IL 60614
(800) 621-1339
(312) 528-8800

Numismatic Professionals, Inc.
33 Boston Post Rd. West
Suite 320
Marlborough, MA 01752
(617) 235-2030 (in Massachusetts)
(800) 343-4926

Paramount International Coin Corp.
Doral Executive Office Park

3785 Northwest 82nd Ave. Suite 315
Miami, FL 33166
(305) 594-4919
(800) 327-9853

C. Rhyne & Associates
110 Cherry St.
Seattle, WA 98104
(800) 542-0824 (in Washington)
(800) 426-7835
(206) 623-6900

Stack's
123 W. 57th St.
New York, NY 10019
(212) 582-2580
(One of the oldest and most prestigious in the country.)

Superior Stamp & Coin Co.
9301 Wilshire Blvd.
Beverly Hills, CA 90201
(213) 272-0851
(800) 421-0754
(800) 874-3230 (in California)

CHAPTER 14

Precious Metals Pitfalls: The Soft Underbelly of Hard Assets

- **Defining Leverage Contracts**
- **Avoiding Leverage Contract and Other Margin Deals**
- **Ersatz Metals: Spotting and Avoiding Counterfeit Coins**
- **What's Safe?**
- **Double Trouble with Double Eagles**
- **Authenticating Your Coins**

One of the largest, longest-running, officially overlooked investment bunco games ever perpetrated upon the American public is alive and flourishing today. It goes by several names: leverage contract, deferred delivery plan, margin buying, and others. Not all precious metals leverage contracts are bogus. And not all firms that sell them are operating outside the law.

But most precious metals frauds that have been uncovered in recent years have used this concept to hook investors. And even where legitimate firms are involved, leverage contracts are considered tainted merchandise by many respected voices in the field.

Strong words . . . but well worth heeding. In some cases of out-and-out swindle, the victims have included widows and retirees who have

207

lost their life savings. Horror stories abound, but dealers are loath to raise the issue.

During the first half of the 1980s, tens of thousands of precious metals investors were defrauded of hundreds of millions of dollars by commodity "bucket shops." Most such shops operate with high-pressure telephone sales tactics. Some of these operations look legitimate . . . sound legitimate . . . advertise in legitimate publications and even on radio and television. They can be tough to spot.

Government agents have busted dealer after dealer. They've hauled major precious metals firms into court, charging them with peddling illegal precious metals investment contracts. But it still goes on. The shady operators number in the thousands, according to government investigators, and operate largely in the open, even though what they are doing violates federal regulations. There simply is little chance they will get caught.

Government agencies responsible for tracking down fraudulent precious metals operations are woefully undermanned. State officials in Florida—a hotbed of commodities fraud in the past—say it's far more difficult to get a license to sell liquor or to become a barber or hairdresser than it is to set up a precious metals bucket shop. An official from California once complained to a Senate investigating committee that dozens of fraudulent operators only laughed at her agency's subpoenas and restraining orders. And the chief enforcer for the federal Securities and Exchange Commission (SEC) told the same Senate committee that individual investors should expect no help from the SEC since most precious metals fraud falls outside that agency's jurisdiction.

Aside from several sensational bankruptcies that rated national headlines, little has been written about the dangers of leverage contracts and similar deferred delivery deals. As a result, unsuspecting investors, who understand little about the extreme risks, are being flimflammed by slick ads and fast-talking salespeople. Government files are bulging with complaints. Lawsuits have stretched on for years as the firms selling the contracts argue successfully over definitions of what is legal, what is not, and what can or cannot be sold without clearance of the federal government.

DEFINING LEVERAGE CONTRACTS

The principle of leverage contracts is not as complicated as all the variations make it. For a relatively small initial outlay, of perhaps $5,000, an investor is told he or she can control perhaps ten times that amount of gold. That's the "leverage." You are allowed to do so because you also agree to purchase the rest of the metals at some future date for a set price. The leverage firm can, in effect, lend you money to "buy" (for future delivery) much more metal than you would otherwise be able to afford. Then they've got you. Leverage contracts are similar to futures contracts, except they are traded on no organized exchange, and no agency is looking over the shoulder of the firms hawking these deals.

The Commodity Futures Trading Commission (CFTC), one of those obscure regulatory agencies tucked away in some corner of Washington, DC, has precise rules defining what a leverage contract is, how it should work, and who is allowed to offer it. The definition, in fact, is crucial. Dealers contend that what they are selling is *not* something that falls under the CFTC's regulatory powers. So they go on selling.

Back in the 1970s federal watchdogs declared a moratorium on the number of firms that would be allowed to sell leverage contracts in precious metals. That meant the four firms doing so at that time (only three still exist) could continue, and no others would be allowed to compete against them for that same business. Those four firms gained, in effect, official "approval" from the government to keep selling the contracts. And, to this day, they boast that they are fully registered with the CFTC to trade. Indeed they are. In 1984 the commission issued a lengthy set of new regulations governing the sale of leverage contracts in gold, silver, platinum, and bulk coins. The rules prohibit leverage firms from claiming to guarantee any investor losses and force them to provide prospective leverage customers with a disclosure statement. The guidelines also give investors a limited right to cancel out of the first leverage contract within three days.

The Privileged Four

The four precious metals firms that made it into the leverage contract business before the government shut the door are Monex International (Newport Beach, California); First National Monetary Corporation

(Southfield, Michigan); International Precious Metals Corporation (IPMC, Fort Lauderdale, Florida); and Premex, a now defunct California firm that went bankrupt in 1984 after continuing run-ins with the government. All of these firms, in fact, have had lengthy battles with the CFTC over leverage contracts.

In early 1982 an administrative law judge for the CFTC ruled that Premex and its president, Samuel Zack, had "violated various federal commodity laws." That ruling found that Premex had (among other things):

> fraudulently prepared and disseminated materially false and misleading promotional material . . . filed materially inaccurate financial statements . . . failed to make and keep accurate general ledger records . . . willfully omitted to state material facts in applications for re-registration [with the CFTC].

Zack was fined $250,000, and Premex was ordered to "cease and desist from soliciting or accepting funds from the public." *But for over a year, while the proceedings against Premex glaciated their way through the bureaucracy, the firm continued to run its advertisements, and unwary investors continued to send in their checks.* After several years of legal wrangling and appeals, the firm was ordered liquidated. Investors were the big losers.

International Precious Metals Corporation (IPMC), one of the surviving leverage firms, was charged with violating anti-fraud provisions of CFTC regulations and settled for a $200,000 fine in December 1982. The original complaint against the Fort Lauderdale firm alleged that "IPMC account executives engaged in fraudulent sales practices in connection with the marketing of IPMC's leverage contracts for the purchase of gold and silver bullion or coins, copper and platinum."

The firm's sales practices, according to the CFTC, included claims of nearly certain profits, statements that understated the risk of loss involved in the purchase of these contracts, failure to explain margin requirements, and failure to liquidate contracts in accordance with customer directives.

Back in 1979 and 1980 Monex International Ltd. and First National Monetary Corporation were involved in disputes with the CFTC concerning their leverage programs. Both are well known, even respected, in the precious metals business. Both offer a variety of other ways to buy precious metals, including bullion purchases, certificates, and options.

Leverage contracts have become to the precious metals industry what the skin magazines are to magazine publishing.

In one publicized operation the CFTC and FBI swooped down on what they later described as "a nationwide network of precious metals boiler rooms accused by the Commission with selling illegal off-exchange futures contracts." In other words, the government said they were hawking illegal leverage contracts, and the Feds nabbed them. According to the CFTC, some of the dealers involved in that sting operation were Atlantic Gold Coins, Inc. and Compusoft, Inc. (both in Fort Lauderdale); Gulf-Atlantic Gold Coins, Inc. (New Orleans); Pacific Gold Coins, Inc. and Northwest Gold Coins, Inc., in Irvine, California.

In separate actions, the following firms were charged with "fraudulent sale of unauthorized leverage contracts":

- Cromex Inc. (also known as The Jefferson Mint)
- Discount Bullion Reserve
- Vero Beach Funding Corp.
- Brazier Corporation Inc., which during 1983 and 1984 was charged with "actively marketing to the public unlawful leverage contracts under its Brazier Capital Plus program."

AVOIDING LEVERAGE CONTRACT AND OTHER MARGIN DEALS

The parade of bucket shops should be enough to dissuade most investors from attempting a killing in leverage contracts. Buying on leverage or margin can look enticing—tenfold profits on a small down payment. But unless you are expert at margin-type account trading, and are at least dealing with one of the "legitimate" leverage contract firms, it's an area to avoid like the plague.

Precious metals investing is risky enough. Don't take chances on "too-good-to-be-true" deals or on dealers you are not certain you can trust.

ERSATZ METALS: SPOTTING AND AVOIDING COUNTERFEIT COINS

Rare coin and precious metals dealers are none too anxious to admit it, but counterfeit coins *are* a problem. Investors *do* run a risk of getting stuck with fakes. That risk is far greater with certain types of coins than with others, and careful investing can cut the risk. But it is there nonetheless, even though the extent of the problem remains controversial.

Recognizing the problem, and learning a little about how to spot spurious specimens, has become standard "training" for coin investors today.

Bullion Fakes and Numismatic Fakes

Just as there are distinctions between *bullion* coins, and *numismatic* coins, there are also differences between the fakes in both of these areas. Krugerrands, Maple Leafs, Mexican gold coins, and most major investment gold bullion coins have been counterfeited. The British gold Sovereign, once the most popular gold coin among European investors, was so widely faked that dealers quoted a separate price for the counterfeit coins.

Every year scores of unwary investors are burned by these counterfeits. Countless more individuals own fake coins and don't yet know it. Some experts claim that investors are bilked out of more money by counterfeit coins than are bilked through bogus dealers or firms that go bankrupt. It makes buying from reputable dealers that much more important.

One of the biggest-selling little "peripherals" for precious metals investors in recent years has been a counterfeit bullion coin detection device that goes by a variety of names. It looks a little like a large bottle opener—small enough to carry around easily in your pocket.

It works like this, according to the manufacturer of one such fake-gold identification gauge:

Gold is much more dense (thus heavier) than metals that are commonly used to make counterfeit bullion coins, such as lead, brass, copper, and steel. They are rather easy to spot.

- If the fake coin is the correct size of the original it will not be the correct weight (because real gold is so much more dense).
- If the fake coin is the correct weight, it must be oversized.
- Or it might be both the wrong size *and* the wrong weight.

A counterfeit coin made out of lead to precisely the same diameter and thickness of a real Krugerrand would be 35 percent lighter than a genuine gold coin. If the ersatz coin were made to the exact weight specification, it would have to be 54 percent thicker than the real thing.

Each one of the little detection devices is made for a specific coin. You need a separate device for a Krugerrand, Maple Leaf, Mexican 50 Peso, Austrian 100 Corona, and so forth. The device has three simple tests:

- It has a round depression that should exactly fit the diameter of the coin. If not, the coin is a fake.
- There is a slot that checks for thickness. If the coin won't fit through the slot, it must be a fake.
- The device has a tiny fulcrum on the bottom which makes it into a miniature teeter-totter when the coin is placed in the round depression. If it is the correct weight, it should balance precisely.

Some amateur sleuths are at this point saying, "Yes, but what about metals that are more nearly the same density as gold?" There are indeed such metals—including tungsten and metals from the platinum group. But making counterfeits with these metals shows little sense since they cost nearly as much as gold (if not more) and are much harder, brittle, and difficult to work with. Making a good fake simply wouldn't be worth the trouble.

One leading firm that sells the detection devices is Fisch Instruments (P.O. Box 160332, Sacramento, CA 95816, [916] 447-5317). The devices are available for about twenty different types of coins and small ingots, priced at about $40. Many coin dealers have taken to using this simple instrument themselves, and according to Kenneth Rutherford, president of Fisch Instruments, it's replacing the more costly, harder-to-use electronic scales and calipers (the thing that looks like a pregnant draftsman's compass, used to measure the thickness of an object).

WHAT'S SAFE?

Although a few counterfeits seem to turn up for nearly all types of valuable coins sooner or later, they are most prevalent with the most popular and most expensive coins.

There is not much to worry about with silver bullion coins. Their low cost per coin discourages the counterfeiters from attempting fakes. But as soon as you move into rare or numismatic silver coins—where the premium above the actual silver content is high—the chance of fakes increases dramatically.

Fake "uncirculated" Morgan and Peace U.S. silver dollars are one danger spot. Real coins of top grade sell for huge premiums over and above the silver content, and these coins are more difficult for the casual observer to detect as fakes. This is one more reason to buy only from reputable dealers and get a guarantee. The vast majority of dealers would not *knowingly* sell a customer a fake, and would indeed be horrified at the prospect. And as slim as the chances are, they are human and can be fooled too, or perhaps simply have not taken the time to check.

The private mint coinlike medallions have not encountered much of a counterfeiting problem. Since so few are made in comparison with the big-name coins, and the private firms would probably spot the fakes easily, they too don't seem worth the bother.

One particularly high-risk area is jewelry made with gold coins. Since these coins are encased in some type of mount, they are more difficult to inspect and, according to some experts, are an attractive way for counterfeiters to unload their wares.

DOUBLE TROUBLE WITH DOUBLE EAGLES

Coin experts say that one of the most widely faked coins in recent years has been the U.S. $20 Double Eagle, often considered a semi-numismatic coin. It's easy to see why the crooks would pick this particular coin. It is a super-popular coin among precious metals investors and coin collectors alike. It sells for a huge premium over the value of its gold bullion content.

Why has it become such a sticky area for investors? Because counterfeit Double Eagles are usually made out of *real gold*. That's right. The premium above actual gold content of these coins makes it worthwhile for the counterfeiters to use real gold, since they can still double or triple their money, or more, with a well-done fake.

And that's what makes this particular counterfeit so insidious and hard to detect. That is also what has spawned efforts to assure investors that they are getting genuine coins when they buy the $20 Double Eagle, also popularly known as the St. Gaudens. One new development is the guaranteed coin product offered by A-Mark Precious Metals, a large Beverly Hills wholesale firm. (This unique twist on gold coin investing is covered in greater detail in Chapter 13 on rare coins.) Each coin is certified and sealed in plastic. As long as the seal is not broken, the guarantee from A-Mark is good.

One further tip about these and other gold and silver semi-numismatic coins: If you purchase in large quantities—in sealed bags or rolls—don't be shy about opening the bags and tubes to have each coin inspected. There often is no other reason for the impressive-looking seal than that the dealer wants it to look impressive, but check first.

The Science of Counterfeit Detection

If you read the chapter about rare coins, you know about the American Numismatic Association Certification Service (ANACS) and a little about how it grades coins. ANACS is really a two-pronged service. It grades and *authenticates* coins. ANACS will check any coin to make certain it is not a counterfeit and will issue a certificate of authentication if it's real.

The process is highly detailed, not something the novice coin buyer could hope to even approximate at home. ANACS will place the coins under electron microscopes and combine years of experience and the collective wisdom of looking at countless coins to spot the tiniest flaws.

The ANA has compiled a good deal of this knowledge into the booklet *Counterfeit Detection*, which the association sells for $7.50. It's not exactly light reading, however, and gets highly technical about the flaws that give away counterfeits. It is illustrated with many specific examples and lots of black-and-white blowup photos of real and fake coins they have caught over the years. I'd recommend it only if you have an abiding interest in numismatics, and grading and counterfeit detection in particular.

AUTHENTICATING YOUR COINS

The easier, though more expensive way is to send in your coin for authentication and wait for the results. ANACS will render an opinion on whether the coin is genuine and if so will issue a photo certificate with a registration number that belongs only to that coin. You will receive the certificate when the coin is returned. All of this costs money, of course, so here is the schedule of fees published by ANACS. *(Note:* ANACS does not assign a value to coins. The coin's value, which decides the fee, is estimated by you, the coin owner.)

Authentication and Grading Fees for Rare Coins

	MEMBERS		NON-MEMBERS	
Owner's Value	*Auth.*	*Grading*	*Auth.*	*Grading*
Up to $150	$7.00	$5.50	$8.00	$6.50
$151–$300	$10.00	$5.50	$11.50	$6.50
$301–$550	$14.00	$5.50	$16.00	$6.50
Over $550	2.7%	1%	3%	1.5%
Maximum Fee	$300	$20	$325	$25

For more information write or call:

ANACS
818 N. Cascade
Colorado Springs, CO 80903
(303) 632-2646

You might want to consider a membership in the American Numismatic Association ($21 per year). In addition to discounts on coin grading and authentication services, ANA provides continuing educational support for individual members and has several publications of interest. It is not, however, a policing agency for numismatic dealers, and you should not look to the ANA for that purpose. The Professional Numismatists' Guild (P.O. Box 430, Van Nuys, CA 91408) serves the role of "enforcer" much better and requires its coin dealer/members to comply with a strict code of ethics. Firms that fall astray get the boot.

If you are interested in finding out more about coin-grading standards, the *Official A.N.A. Grading Standards for United States Coins* has been published in book form by the ANA. The illustrated book sells for $6.95 and contains descriptions of grading considerations for each coin.

Another helpful authentication service is offered through the International Numismatic Society for fees ranging from $7 to $250, depending on the value of the coin in question. This group's address is: P.O. Box 66555, Washington, DC 20035.

CHAPTER 15

Precious Metals Stocks: Investing in Shares of Gold, Silver, and Platinum Mines

- **The Mining Stock Bonus**
- **Modern-Day Gold Rush**
- **Different Types of Mines**
- **Some Tips on Investing in Precious Metals Mining Shares**
- **Mining Company Close-ups**
- **A Silver Lining: U.S. and Canadian Silver Stocks**
- **Platinum and Palladium Mining Shares**
- **Mining Shares: An Investor's Checklist**
- **Mining Stocks: Information Sources**

I think it was Mark Twain who described a gold miner as "A liar standing next to a hole in the ground." In some corners of the precious metals mining business, Twain's observation isn't far off the mark—especially the here-today-gone-tomorrow North American penny mining companies.

But set aside the stereotypes of gold and silver mines, and consider mining corporation stocks as a legitimate way to invest in precious metals. Mining company stocks, much like stocks of other industries, come in a wide assortment. They include dependable, "blue-chip" corporations that have been digging gold since the 1800s. There are also scores of smaller firms trading on the Wild West mining shares markets in Vancouver, Canada; Spokane, Washington; Salt Lake City; and Denver. (A new mining company appears on the Vancouver Stock Exchange nearly every day.)

THE MINING STOCK BONUS

When you buy mining shares, you are making a stock market investment. How well your stocks perform will depend largely on precious metals prices, and to a lesser extent on how well the mining company is run. A well-managed, diversified mining company's stock might do well even if the price of gold is falling, but it will only do very well if gold does very well.

Because you are buying stock in a corporation whose business is to mine a mineral, there are many other variables.

• Investing in mining shares can be a good way to diversify a large stake in precious metals. You should never put a large portion (over 20–30 percent) of your entire investment portfolio in precious metals or *related* assets. But the money that you do invest in this area can itself be diversified among different metals and different methods of holding those metals to cover the risk. Mining shares are one such alternative.

• The big attraction of mining stocks is the supercharged profit potential they offer. When gold and silver prices rise, the mining shares almost always go up even more.

• Some mining stocks pay a dividend—perhaps the only way to invest in precious metals and still receive a regular return on your investment before you sell.

• Except for some foreign and penny mining shares, you can buy and sell gold stocks through a regular stockbroker.

If you plan to explore the booming market in mining shares, do so with your eyes wide open. Just as mining stocks can reward the lucky few with phenomenal profits, they can tumble in the flash of an electronic stock quote machine. Except for the highest-quality blue-chip mining corporation stocks, this is high-risk investing. Gamble no more than you can afford to lose.

A safer approach to mining shares is to invest in a precious metals mutual fund. These funds (discussed in Chapter 12) invest mostly in the mining shares covered in this chapter. Most focus on South African shares. But there are now funds that invest exclusively in gold mines outside that country, mostly in North America. Through a mutual fund, you get instant diversification of even a small investment and receive the benefits of professional management of the fund's assets.

MODERN-DAY GOLD RUSH

The early 1980s saw a gold mining boom in North America, a boom that spread to such unlikely environs as northern Michigan and the Virginia foothills. Between 1982 and 1985 gold production in the United States leaped 75 percent.

The sudden gold rush in Canada and the United States in those years was unexpected, since it came at a time when prices were dropping. Miners were placing their bets on the side of higher gold prices to come. Investors followed, snapping up many of the highest-quality mining issues as they came along. Mines started reopening in Montana, Utah, Wyoming, Colorado, the Dakotas, and even Georgia and the Carolinas.

Environmentalists are dismayed by the trend. With emphasis shifting to the low-grade ores, and deposits that are nearer the surface (easier and cheaper to get to), many new ventures were open-pit or strip mines.

As new ventures, or firms bent on reopening long abandoned mines, most of the gold mining firms that sprout are risky. Few will ever earn a dime.

DIFFERENT TYPES OF MINES

Mining shares fall into neat age/experience categories:

• The newest, most speculative firms are engaged in "exploration." These are the true penny mining stocks that so many investors get

TECHNOLOGY OF MINING

The technology of wrenching gold from Mother Earth's clutches has come far since the days when crusty old gents panned for it in rivers or dug tunnels with pickaxes. Most of the world's easy-to-reach gold is long gone. Today what passes for a gold deposit can be completely invisible to the naked eye. In some cases the gold particles are so sparsely distributed in the rock that mines have to crush it up, lay it out in huge beds, and let a sodium cyanide solution soak through the pile. The cyanide solution dissolves the gold, and the "miners" collect it in the gold-laden runoff called pregnant solution. The name for this process is heap leaching.

Heap leach mines process the super-low-grade ores. Their stocks are more highly leveraged against the price of gold, and when the market swings up these shares are expected to outperform conventional mines. Three examples of heap leach mines (all traded over the counter) in the United States are: Pegasus Gold, Glamis Gold, and Wharf Resources.

The amount of gold mined this way in the United States has soared. In 1979 only about 50,000 ounces were produced by heap leach mines. By 1985 that figure was over 325,000 ounces.

The one mining term with which most of us are familiar—ore—can even be misleading. It's not a mining term at all, but an economic one. A mineral deposit is only a true "ore" if the cost of getting it out of the rock is less than what the gold is worth on the open market. It's not an ore if the gold cannot be extracted at a profit. In that case, it's a rock—but a rock with a difference since it could become an ore if the price of gold rises.

worked up about. They dream of the 15,000 percent profits some mining shares produced back in the boom times of the early 1960s and again in the 1970s. If exploration bears no fruit, however, there will be no development (the next stage) at all.

• Development comes after successful exploration. This involves further test mining, drilling, designing the mine, and building around the site. All of this takes millions of dollars, which will be paid back only if and when the mine starts producing.

• Producing mines are actually turning out gold, silver, or other metals. But all producing mines are not created equal. The amount of money it costs a mine to produce an ounce of bullion is crucial, and the differences can be huge. It may cost some mines two to three times as much as others to produce one ounce of pure metal. There are many reasons, including ore quality, equipment, depth of the mine, labor costs, quality of management, and interest rates. Shares in producing mines are less risky, but the price may be high already, and the shares will not provide the huge rewards.

Whatever type of mining shares piques your interest, be prepared to hold these shares for at least a year, and probably longer. Just as you shouldn't expect to make a quick buck investing in precious metals bullion, you should have no similar delusions about mining shares. This is a speculative investment that requires patience and a long-term view.

Mine Exhaustion

Owning shares in a blue-chip gold mine isn't *quite* like owning IBM. A standard corporation can keep expanding and making its product or providing its service for an indefinite period. *Gold mines run out of gold.* Some sooner, some later. Most producing mines have an estimated lifespan, based on their proven reserves or expert estimates of what is out there.

In the case of South African gold mines, for example, a *long-life* mine has a remaining life of over twenty years. *Medium-life* mines are expected to last eleven to twenty years; *short-life* mines could fold up in six to ten years; and *break-up* mines are expected to remain in business only another one to five years. When a mining concern nears exhaustion, it may begin liquidating its assets and distributing the funds to shareholders.

SOME TIPS ON INVESTING IN PRECIOUS METALS MINING SHARES

The same rules of wise investing apply here as elsewhere. Buy the best quality you can find and spread your risk. A portfolio of mining shares should include some of the old reliables, such as Homestake Mines, a South Dakota mine that has been producing and expanding for over a century; Campbell Red Lake; Dome Mines; Hecla Mining; ASARCO; Sunshine Mining; Callahan Mines; and others.

Only then should you even consider the crap-shoot penny mining shares. You'll need $5,000 to start since you should invest in at least ten or twelve different stocks. The more stocks you own, the better your chances of hitting a winner. (You should assume there will always be losers.)

But there are limits. If you want any chance of selling those shares later, you will have to buy in "round lots," which is to say, blocks of 100 or 1,000 shares, depending on the price of the stock. The really cheap stocks, selling literally for pennies, are bought in 1,000-share lots. Those that sell for dollars per share come in round lots of 100 shares.

Owning odd numbers of shares (anything other than round lots) can cost you dearly later on. If you can find a buyer at all, you may have to sell at a lower price and pay a broker a larger commission to handle the deal.

Once you make your choices, you'll want to hold on. Trading in and out too often will make the broker rich, not you. If you do get lucky, don't get greedy. Old-timers are full of stories about investors who watch their stocks soar, then watch them fall all the way back down again. Don't forget the second half of the investment formula—you have to sell in order to realize a profit.

As out of the way as this market may seem, it's full of promoters, brokers, mining entrepreneurs, mining stock newsletters, and investment advisories all waiting to take your money. Traditional means of assessing a stock's worth don't apply here. And aside from the major high-quality mining companies, these stocks have little or no following among analysts at the big Wall Street brokerage firms. Don't expect advice on penny mining stocks from Merrill Lynch. The specialists in these shares get out there and rub elbows with the bears, tromp through the spring mud, and pore over the mumbo jumbo of geological reports.

Some of the most respected voices in the mining shares arena, especially the penny stocks, claim that throwing darts is as good a method as any to choose which ones to buy. One of the classic books in the field, *Small Fortunes in Penny Mining Stocks,* first published in 1973, endorses this "random walk" (dart throwing) method of selecting stocks. The premise is this: There simply is too little information about most of these firms to make an informed choice. Penny mining stocks are true speculations where *your* opinion is just as valid as the next guy's.

MINING COMPANY CLOSE-UPS

North American Gold and Silver Mines

Thousands of mining company stocks are traded in the United States and Canada, from the major producers to the tiny exploration outfits. In one remote region of northern Idaho alone, called the Coeur D'Alene mining district, there are more than a hundred silver mining concerns. This is the richest silver-producing region of the United States, yielding over 40 percent of the nation's output.

Canadian gold mines with lengthy track records have been popular, although the prices of these stocks are usually rather high. They've been "discovered" by larger numbers of investors.

The "undiscovered" penny gold and silver stocks, and some of the junior producing mines, are traded on the Vancouver Stock Exchange (VSE). In fact, over 2,500 mining company stocks trade on the VSE at any given time. They come and go rapidly.

The Toronto Stock Exchange (TSE), Canada's main stock market, also claims to be one of the world's largest markets for gold shares. Nearly fifty gold mining company stocks trade on the Toronto Exchange, including major producing mines as well as exploration and development firms and junior producers.

The Toronto Exchange calculates a gold shares index that includes twenty-one gold stocks, together worth over $6 billion (Canadian). Options on that gold index which began trading in 1984, are the latest gold investment invention. (In the United States a similar option on an index of gold and silver shares is available on the Philadelphia Stock Exchange.)

An index option is a way to invest in the direction of the gold mining market as a whole. If the index goes up within a certain period of time, the value of your option can also go up and you can make a tidy profit on a small initial investment. But if the index does not go up enough for you to profit, or goes down, you will lose the entire amount of money you paid for the option. (See Chapter 16 for a more detailed look at options.)

These are some of the major Canadian gold mining companies counted in the TSE index:

Major Canadian Gold Mining Companies

Company	Stock Exchange Symbol
Agnico Eagle Mines	AGE
Camflo Mines	CMF
Campbell Red Lake Mines	CRK
Carolin Mines	CLL
Dickenson Mines	DML
Dome Mines	DM
Echo Bay Mines	ECO
Giant Yellowknife Mines	GYK
Kerr Addison Mines	KER
Lac Minerals	LLC
Pamour Porcupine Mines	PAM
Pegasus Gold	PGU
Rayrock Resources	RAY
Sigma Mines	S

Other Selected Gold Stocks Listed in Toronto

Company	Stock Exchange Symbol
Aiguebelle Exploration	AIG
Bachelor Lake Gold Mines	BLG
BP Canada Inc.	BPC
Canada Development Corp.	CDC
Cominco	CLT
Equity Silver Mines	EST
Erickson Gold Mines	EGM
Hudson Bay Mining & Smelting	HBM
INCO	N
Kiena Gold Mines	KGM
Lacana Mining Corp.	LCA
Noranda Mines	NOR
Northgate Exploration	NGX
Pennzoil Co.	PZL
Placer Development Ltd.	PDL
Queenstake Resources	QTR
Roynex Gold Mining	RGM
Sherritt Gordon Mines	SE
Teck Corp.	TEK
United Siscoe Mines	USO
Westmin Resources	WMI
Whim Creek Consolidated	WCC

Here is a brief snapshot of ten of the largest North American mining operations with publicly traded stocks.

Dome Mines

Dome, which trades on the New York Stock Exchange, is a large mining conglomerate. It runs second only to Homestake Mines in total sales and is the largest Canadian producer. Dome has its own gold mine but also controls more than half of two other major Canadian mines: Campbell Red Lake (about 57 percent) and Sigma Mines (about 66 percent). From 1979 to 1985 the stock was as high as $33 and as low as $5 per share. Dome also owns a large interest in gold properties in the United States.

Homestake Mines

Homestake, America's largest homegrown gold mining operation, also owns interest in silver-producing properties and gold projects in several states and Australia. Between 1979 and 1985 the stock price was as high as $44 per share and as low as $8.50. Homestake is an unusual entity, with very little debt and gold reserves that seem to keep expanding each year.

Campbell Red Lake Mines

This stock also trades on the New York Stock Exchange, reaching a high in the 1979–85 period of about $35 and a low of around $5.75 per share. Campbell brags one of the lowest cost-per-ounce production figures in North America (a little over $100) and has been one of the most profitable mines. About 57 percent of this company is owned by Dome Mines.

Echo Bay Mines

This is a relatively new mine, but one of North America's richest properties and now Canada's fifth largest gold producer. The mine's operating cost is a little over $200 per ounce produced, and the stock trades on the American Stock Exchange.

Hecla Mining Company

Hecla Mining is considered a premier *silver* stock in the United States. Its shares trade on the New York Stock Exchange (also in Spokane and on the Pacific Exchange). Between 1979 and 1985 the shares traded for as high as $53 per share and as low as $6. Hecla owns interests in many silver-producing properties in the United States. The company made a disastrous entry into the copper market in the 1960s. It recovered from that caper only in the 1980s, when it undertook an aggressive strategy of acquisitions in the silver business.

Lac Minerals

This mine is now the largest producer in Canada, churning out some 250,000 ounces in a year's time. Lac owns interests in Canada's Hemlo (Ontario) district, which has been described as "North America's largest gold discovery of the last 50 years . . . which could propel Canada into the forefront of world gold production by the end of this century." Shares are traded on the Toronto Stock Enchange.

Agnico Eagle Mines

This firm produces both gold and silver in Canada. Shares trade in Toronto and over the counter. Between 1979 and 1985 the price ranged from below $5 per share to $21. The company is youthful and aggressive.

Sunshine Mining Company

In the United States, Sunshine means silver. As the nation's largest producer, the company even sells the metal to investors with its own name stamped on the bars and coins (the firm's retail arm operates in Texas; see the Dealer Directory in Chapter 11). Shares, which are traded on the New York Stock Exchange and in Spokane, ranged from under $5 per share to over $33 per share between 1979 and 1985 (with a two-for-one stock split along the way). Sunshine's richest silver properties are in the legendary Coeur d'Alene district of Idaho.

Giant Yellowknife Mines

This is another leading Canadian gold producer, with a smattering of silver production to boot. Giant Yellowknife's shares are listed on the American Stock Exchange and in Toronto.

Placer Development Ltd.

Placer recently ranked as fourth leading gold producer in Canada, with about 135,000 ounces per year. Since it too is listed on the American Stock Exchange as well as in Toronto, its shares have been popular among U.S.-based investors. Placer owns both gold and silver mining interests in Canada, the United States, the Philippines, and Mexico.

South African Gold Mining Stocks

South Africa is the world's largest gold-producing nation by far. Its gold mining companies are considered among the best, most consistently profitable in the world. When investors around the globe discovered these stocks back in the 1970s, many people profited handsomely.

Politics aside, the view in the 1980s has shifted. South African mining shares are considered ''mature.'' It's in North America that investors can still hope for fantastic riches.

When you consider the South African government's repugnant racial policies, political and economic instability, and the added pitfalls of purchasing foreign shares, the South African mining stocks have lost their luster. Institutional investors and mutual funds like them for their dividends, their long life, and stable management. But many individual investors, eyeing the gold mining boom in Canada and the United States, see little reason to invest elsewhere.

Others throughout the world see things differently, however. South African mines still produce more gold than those of any other country and can't be completely ignored. According to the London brokerage firm Strauss, Turnbull & Co., these are ten of the highest quality South African gold mines:

> Vaal Reefs Exploration & Mining Ltd.
> Southvaal Holdings Ltd.
> Western Deep Levels Ltd.

Kloof Gold Mining Ltd.
Driefontein Consolidated Ltd.
Buffelsfontein Gold Mining Co., Ltd.
Hartebeestfontein Gold Mining Co., Ltd.
The Randfontein Estates Gold Mining Co., Ltd.
Kinross Mines Ltd.
President Steyn Gold Mining Co., Ltd.

A Gold Mining and Bullion Hybrid

Among the more unusual new methods of investing in gold is The Gold Company of America, a joint venture of Prudential-Bache Securities and the Canadian gold mining firm Barrick Resources. Shares in Gold Company trade like a stock, on the NASDAQ over-the-counter market, but the company is technically a limited partnership. A main attraction of this rather complex setup is that Gold Company shares are designed to pay a dividend in gold bullion—even when gold prices are flat or falling. If gold rises, so does the value of your shares *and* the dividend. The Gold Company of America is a middle ground between owning either bullion or mining shares directly.

A SILVER LINING:
U.S. AND CANADIAN
SILVER STOCKS

The heartbeat of trading in U.S. silver shares is a stock market few have even heard of—Spokane, Washington. When silver prices are on the upswing, and the market is active, the heart beats wildly. When silver prices are depressed, Spokane's market for silver shares goes comatose.

Why should this seemingly offbeat location be the nucleus of silver mining stocks? Simple geography. The silver-lined Coeur d'Alene valley is only seventy-five miles to the east. Unlike other silver mining areas in the United States, where the main line of business is really copper, the mines here are keyed exclusively to the white metal.

The highs and lows of some silver mining stocks since 1968 show why so many fortunes have been made and lost here:

American Silver	6 cents to $7.50
Bismark	21 cents to $6.25
Canyon Silver	10 cents to $4.75
Coeur d'Alene Mines	$2 to $28
Consolidated Silver	61 cents to $10
Midnight Mines	75 cents to $8.10
Royal Apex Silver	7 cents to $6.00
Silver King Mines	75 cents to $10.50

In addition to the major silver mining companies already mentioned, these are a few of the better-known silver stocks (some also mine gold, copper, or related metals), including the exchanges on which each stock trades:

Abot Mining Co.
(Spokane, OTC)

Agnico Eagle Mines
(TSE, OTC)

American Silver Mining
(Spokane, OTC)

ASARCO
(NYSE; a giant copper producer)

Atlas Mining Co.
(Spokane, OTC)

Avino Mines & Resources
(Vancouver, OTC)

Callahan Mining Co.
(NYSE, Spokane Stock Exchange)

Clayton Silver Mines
(Spokane and Pacific stock exchanges)

Coeur d'Alene Mines Corp.
(Spokane, OTC)

Consolidated Silver Corp.
(Spokane, OTC)

Equity Silver Mines
(TSE)

Metropolitan Mines Corp.
(Spokane)

Royal Apex Silver
(Spokane, OTC)

Silver King Mines
(OTC)

Terra Mines Ltd.
(TSE, OTC)

PLATINUM AND PALLADIUM MINING SHARES

Only one pure platinum producer really counts in the Western world (it's in South Africa), and a handful of others are partially linked to platinum and palladium. In fact, with palladium, the opportunities to invest in any kind of "pure play" mining concern are zilch. The USSR has the market locked up.

The one firm that constitutes a pure stock market investment in platinum is Rustenburg Platinum Holdings Ltd. This single South African corporation accounts for most of the Western world's platinum supply (some 56 percent of South Africa's total output). Impala Platinum Holdings is the second leading South African producer, with about 38 percent of the market. A firm called Western Platinum is a distant third, with about 6 percent, followed by a tiny share for the mining firm Atok. One other company in the field is Lydenburg Platinum Ltd. Shares of Rustenburg trade on the stock exchanges in London and Johannesburg.

Several Canadian mining and natural resources firms also have significant holdings in the platinum arena, but they tend to be dwarfed by the firms' other holdings. These stocks include INCO, Noranda Mines, UMEX, and Falconbridge.

MINING SHARES: AN INVESTOR'S CHECKLIST

• Penny mining stocks can be enticing, especially when newsletters, brokers, and other promoters keep telling you about the great potential that awaits. But anyone who is serious about building a portfolio in precious metals should take care of the essentials first. Own some bullion . . . purchase a few blue-chip mining stocks . . . hedge your investment with top-grade numismatic coins . . . get instant diversification with a gold mutual fund. Only after you own the *quality* investments in gold, silver, platinum, and palladium should you even consider the penny gold stocks.

• Thin markets and shady manipulation are a real danger with penny mining shares. Prices for these little stocks can jump quickly on the recommendation of a single well-known investment advisor. Investors read, run out and buy, and the price shoots up because there is so little of the stock to trade. Often the price comes tumbling back down a short while later.

• If you purchase low-priced mining shares from small brokerage firms that specialize in this field, you should have the stock certificates in your possession. When making standard stock market purchases through major brokerage firms, it's often easier to let the broker hold the certificates. But in the gold market, with its wild swings, brokers can go bust right along with precious metals prices. Gold will rise again. Brokers might not.

• Be wary of transaction costs. Commissions (averaging around 7 percent) are already higher for penny stocks than for other types of stock. The bid/ask spread—the dealer's markup on the shares—can also be larger with penny shares. Those two items combined can make transaction costs for penny gold stocks six to eight times more expensive than a standard stock purchase. Your stock might have to go up 40 to 50 percent *just so you can break even on your investment.*

• A key reason to consider mining shares is for the leverage. (This was covered in Chapter 12: Precious Metals Mutual Funds, but here it is again, slightly altered.) If it costs a mining company $250 to produce an ounce of gold and the price is $350, there is a $100 profit. If the price of gold climbs to $550, the profit to the mine increases *200 percent* to $300, while the price of gold itself has gone up only *57 percent.*

The percentage increase would be even *greater* if you start with a mine that has a *higher* production cost, say $300 per ounce. This mine's initial profit with gold at $350 is only $50 per ounce, so a jump in the gold price to $550 would put the profit per ounce instead at $250, or 400 percent higher.

Here is an example of what happened to the price of one gold stock during a gold price run-up. Between June and December 1982 the price of gold went from $300 to $450, an increase of 50 percent. During that same six months, shares of Pegasus Gold Inc., a junior gold mine that trades OTC in the United States, leaped from $2 (Canadian) to $12—a gain of 500 percent. The greater increase in the mine's profits compared to the profits of owning the gold directly represents the leverage and should be reflected by a large increase in the price of the mine's shares. Remember that leverage works just as well on the way down.

• If you own penny mining shares, and you find yourself in the middle of a big price increase, remember: These are not stocks to hold forever. Part of the reason that prices of penny issues increase by those phenomenal amounts is because frantic buyers during a bull market begin to throw money at any stock that has gold or silver in its name. Those may be unrealistic levels and might not last.

• Diversify your holdings of penny mining stocks but don't over-diversify. If you buy too many different stocks with too little money (figure no less than $1,000 per stock, probably a little more), transaction costs will eat you alive. But you will want to own a selection of mining stocks so your chances are better of hitting that one big winner in the penny mining stock lottery.

• In the penny stock arcade, if you make a big purchase ($5,000 and up) don't accept as gospel the commission or price of the stock you are first quoted. You may be able to negotiate price and commission on larger orders.

• In most stock trades, you should stipulate the highest price you are willing to pay or the lowest price you are willing to accept. Too many investors buy at "market price," which is to say, they accept whatever the broker can get when the deal is made. Instead, consider a different type of order called a limit order. In this case, you set a limit on what you will accept, and if the broker cannot find a buyer or seller to meet it, the trade will not be made.

• Gold mining, especially in Canada, is somewhat seasonal. Prices of the exploratory and development firms can drop in winter when interest wanes (and the promoters fly south) and pick up again in the spring. This is a minor influence, however, since gold and silver prices will always dictate the direction mining shares go.

Mining Shares on the Vancouver Stock Exchange (VSE)

For some good old-fashioned, bare-knuckled investing in penny mining stocks, nothing can beat the stock exchange in the bejeweled West Coast city of Vancouver, Canada. It must be the only major city in the world where the hottest-selling publications on the airport newsstand are gold mining handbooks.

Vancouver's stock market has long had a none-too-saintly reputation. The rules for listing shares on this exchange have been beefed up in recent years, but they are still designed—by admission of the exchange's own officials—to attract the startup gold mining operations. It is a venture capital market, a venture capital town.

Deals to launch new mining exploration the world over are struck in Vancouver. The money is raised through the Vancouver stock market. Over 2,500 mining company stocks trade here. Hundreds are exploration companies that haven't a prayer of earning a dime for at least three to six years—if they are lucky.

Mines that outgrow Vancouver often move to the Toronto Exchange, and to the U.S. over-the-counter market. But in recent years, the trend has been for stocks to maintain double or triple listings in all three markets. So much the better to snare investors. The Canadian mining companies especially like to tap into American cash via the NASDAQ over-the-counter market. When gold prices hit an upswing, they know that investors in the United States will buy just about anything that glitters.

The liberal economics of the VSE have produced their share of scandals. Quick profits turned here often end up in the hands of fast-talking promoters and venture capitalists, not investors. Seeking to rid itself of its reputation as a giant bucket shop, the VSE has sought reforms in recent years, and now has such safeguards as a computer surveillance system to detect suspect trading patterns.

If this sounds like your kind of action, try a little reading first. A monthly Vancouver Stock Exchange publication, *Review,* carries extensive information about stocks traded here. One handy feature is a list of brokerage firms that are members of the VSE.

MINING STOCKS: INFORMATION SOURCES

Where to Find More Information on Precious Metals Mining Stocks and Related Topics

State of California
Division of Mines and Geology
2815 "O" St.
Sacramento, CA 95816
(916) 445-5716
Offers an extensive list of free or low-cost publications about how to prospect for gold. Write or call for their list of available publications.

The George Cross Newsletter
1710-609 Granville St.
Box 10363
Stock Exchange Tower
Vancouver, BC, Canada
V7Y 1G5
(604) 683-7265

Daily mining news sheet.
$300/year

Gold Stock News
HMR Publishing
P.O. Box 471
Barrington, IL 60010
(312) 428-6633

Coverage of North American
and Australian gold stocks.
$95/year

Independent Survey Company
Box 10334
Pacific Centre
Vancouver, BC, Canada
V7Y 1G5
(604) 682-7868

Monthly charts on Canadian
mining stocks. $200/year

International Asset Investor
HMR Publishing
P.O. Box 471
Barrington, IL 60010
(312) 428-6633

Worldwide view of metals and
mining stocks. Monthly,
$120/year

*International Investor's
Viewpoint*
P.O. Box 447
160 Stafford Plaza
Wilsonville, OR 97070
(503) 682-2750

Monthly newsletter on
international investments, with
emphasis on gold mining
shares. $175/year

Johannesburg *Gold and Metal
Mining* Advisor
Box 11634
Birmingham, AL 35202

Quarterly publication on South
African mining stocks.

The Mining Record
311 Steele St., Suite 208
Denver, CO 80206
(303) 355-3571

Weekly mining shares
information. $24/year
Also publishes *The Western
Mining Directory* annual ($45).

North American Gold Mining Industry News
P.O. Box 662
Wilsonville, OR 97070
(800) 547-3428

Biweekly newspaper with extensive mining stock quotes on all U.S. and Canadian exchanges. $45/year

North American Gold Mining Stocks
P.O. Box 871
Woodside, NY 11377
(718) 457-1426

Monthly newsletter on junior gold mining stocks. $50/year

The Northern Miner
7 Labatt Ave.
Toronto, Ontario, Canada
M5A 3P2
(416) 368-3481

Weekly, $40/year (Canadian). Also publishes The yearly *Canadian Mines Handbook* ($24).

Penny Mining Stock Report
Target Publishing
P.O. Box 25
Pleasanton, CA 94566
(415) 463-2215

Monthly newsletter recommends penny gold and silver stocks. $90/year

Personal Finance
1300 N. 17th St.
P.O. Box 9665
Arlington, VA 22209

General investment newsletter, periodic articles on gold and silver mining shares. Biweekly, $94/year

Jerry Pogue's Penny Stock Report
National Securities Corp.
500 Union St., Suite 240
Seattle, WA 98101
(800) 426-1608 or
(206) 622-7200

National Securities Corp. is a brokerage firm that specializes in mining shares.

The Terex Report
110-50 71st Road
Forest Hills, NY 11375

Monthly newsletter on North American gold and silver mining companies. $75/year

Today's Market Line
626 W. Pender, Suite 702
Vancouver, BC, Canada
V6B 1V9
(604) 684-8888

Daily information on VSE-listed shares. $315/year

Vancouver Stock Exchange Review
Stock Exchange Tower
P.O. Box 10333
609 Granville St.
Vancouver, BC, Canada
V7Y 1H1

Monthly review of VSE dealings. $55/year. Write to VSE for list of other exchange publications.

The Wallace Miner
506 Sixth St.
Wallace, ID 83873
(208) 556-1561

Weekly newspaper covering U.S. mining stocks. $30/year second class, $59 first class

Western Mining News
North 3019 Argonne Rd.
Spokane, WA 99212
(509) 922-4184

Weekly stock quotes and news. $55/year

CHAPTER 16

Precious Metals Options: Playing for the Big Hit . . . or (Gulp!) Miss
(The Beginner's Guide to a Temporary Paper Promise)

- Precious Metals Options: Some Basics
- What's It All Mean?
- Inside the Options Contracts
- Other Option Choices
- The Main Options Menu
- An Options Q & A
- Options on Silver and Gold *Futures*

PRECIOUS METALS OPTIONS: SOME BASICS

Today the letter carrier brought a form letter from Western Federal Corporation, a precious metals dealer I had once called for information:

Dear Investor:
    If you're willing to risk losing $1,000 (all of it), you can control

as much as $20,000 worth of silver or gold. Don't be frightened. The potential profit is truly astonishing: Yet I [the Western Federal broker who signed the letter], guarantee there is NO additional risk. Here's a recent example:

In mid-1982 silver was depressed . . . and stood at $4.88. For $1,037 you could have bought a silver call option . . . and you *could* have lost it all. But, in fact, silver rose to $14.71 and you would have made $10,279 (an 890 percent profit) by selling your option in February 1983.

Even more remarkable is the fact that your profit potential, if silver moves down can also be extraordinary.

From its peak of $14.71, silver dropped—more than $5 per ounce—in just three weeks. If you had purchased a silver put option for less than a thousand dollars early [that] February— again you could have lost every penny. Instead, you would have made more than $21,000 (a 2,100 percent profit) if you'd sold it only 30 days later.

These examples were the extremes (top and bottom) of the market and were used only to show what *can* happen *if your timing is right on target,* but paradoxically, they also show what is perhaps the single most important advantage of silver and gold options . . .

Loss Limitation

As with any investment, silver and gold options have an element of risk. If your timing is off, you could lose all that you invest. However, unlike futures contracts—or other leveraged investments—you could never lose a penny more. With silver and gold options, *your risk is limited—to an amount you choose—in advance.*

> Sincerely,
> Your Friendly Dealer

As junk mail goes, this was tame. It chose the most convenient examples to show those big profits (the vast majority of investors who bought options during those periods weren't as lucky), but it did correctly point out that you can lose your money in options—all of it.

Riverboat Gamblers Gather Round

By now you may already be lost. Just what is an option, and what does it have to do with investing in precious metals? And if it's just for riverboat gambler types, why should you consider it as a legitimate precious metals investment alternative?

First things first. An option, although largely unknown to most folks, looks far less mysterious and forbidding after a moment's study. Options have been used in business for centuries, although they were only reinvented for precious metals in recent years.

This is how it basically works, using silver as an example:

There are two types of options. You buy one type—a call option—when you expect the price of silver (or gold or platinum) to go up; you buy the other—a put option—when you expect the price to drop.

A call option gives you the *right* to purchase silver anytime within, say, nine months (time periods will differ), at a specific price. If the price goes up anytime during those nine months, you have the right to buy the silver at the lower option price or simply sell your option to somebody else at its now increased value. That's how you make money.

When you exercise or sell the option, assuming the price has gone up and you want to, you don't actually have to buy the silver. You can simply pocket the difference between what the new price of silver is and the price at which your option gives you the right to buy it. Just tell the broker or dealer to cash it in and walk away with the profits.

An option offers the possibility of great riches because it uses big leverage. That means you can control lots of gold or silver with a relatively small amount of money. An investor receives *all* of the profit potential of holding that larger pile of silver or gold, but not all of the risk. The risk is always limited to the price you pay for the option.

Suppose silver is selling at $10 per ounce today, and you think it is grossly undervalued given current economic conditions. You could purchase a call option granting you the right to buy 1,000 ounces of the metal at $11 per ounce for the next nine months.

Of course that doesn't come free. You pay a price for that option, which is called a premium. Assume the option is selling for a $1 premium. That means $1 per ounce, and since the option represents 1,000 ounces of silver, your investment would be $1,000.

So here's what we have so far:

- Current price of silver: $10.00 per ounce.
- An option that gives you the right to buy 1,000 ounces of silver at $11.00—which, incidentally, is called the strike price.

- The option is good for nine months to an exact date. After that, it expires and becomes totally worthless. (The object is to exercise that option at a profit sometime before the contract expires.)
- The premium is $1 per ounce, making your cost to buy the option $1,000.
- Add the premium you paid ($1) to the strike price ($11) and you get your break-even price: $12.00 per ounce.

WHAT'S IT ALL MEAN?

Here's what must happen for you to make a profit . . . or easily lose that entire $1,000. Some different possibilities:

(1) The price of silver drops. This is easy to follow. If the price of silver moves below where it was when you bought the option ($10), and stays there for the entire nine-month duration of your option, you will lose all of your money—in this case, $1,000. Once the option expires, it's dead. Worthless. Even if silver were to double the very next day, it would do you no good. If you have no stomach for this type of risk, this first case is a clear argument for using that $1,000 to buy physical silver instead. That way you'd really own something—not just a temporary paper promise.

(2) Say the price of silver does rise, but only a little, to $10.90. You still lose everything, since it hasn't quite made it to your strike price.

(3) Once the price goes *above* your strike price—$11—you are "in the money." Now you start making back your original investment. If the price of silver rises to only $11.50, you will make back half of your original investment. Remember, your strike price is $11 and your break-even price is $12. If it reaches $12, you get back your original $1,000 investment, no more.

(4) Only when the price of silver passes the $12 mark does the fun really begin. Since you own control of 1,000 ounces of silver, for every 10-cent upward move in the price beyond $12 an ounce you would make $100 profit. For every 50-cent move up, you make $500. And you would make a profit of $1,000 for a $1 move to $13 per ounce. If the price of silver were to increase 50 percent over this option's nine-month duration (other time periods range from a few days to a year)—from $10 to $15—you would make a $3,000 profit, a gain of 300 percent on your investment. That's leverage at work in an options contract, and it's the reason options attract investors seeking the fast buck or some added investment excitement with a limit on how much they can lose.

What About Those Losses?

The broker from Western Federal was right. You *can* lose every penny of what you pay to purchase a gold or silver option. *But that's all you can lose.* That may sound ridiculous to some people, but it's the only reason many investors even consider gambling money on options. With some other types of leveraged precious metals investments— commodity futures contracts, margin purchase plans, and deferred delivery schemes—not only can you lose your initial investment *but you might also be on the hook for more.* Such "unlimited loss" investments can add insult to injury. After you lose your initial outlay, they send you a bill for more! Some deal.

INSIDE THE OPTIONS CONTRACTS

With options (call options in this case), however, you buy the *right* to buy those 1,000 ounces of silver, not the *obligation*. You don't have to buy it if you don't want to. That's why you never risk more than the premium you pay.

Put Options: Betting on a Drop

For real gamblers, the beauty of options is the ability to bet *either way* on the market—up or down. It's one of the few chances you'll have to turn a handsome profit betting that prices of gold, silver, or platinum will *drop*.

The way to do it is with a put option, which is the opposite of the call. This second type of option grants you the right to *sell* a precious metal at a set price within a specified period of time.

Using silver again as an example, suppose the price today were $15 per ounce and you think that's just too high and that the market is about to drop. You could run things in reverse. Buy a nine-month put option, with a strike price of $14 per ounce. Assuming that option was selling at a $1 premium—again a $1,000 price tag—you'd have a break-even price at $13 per ounce. If you were wrong about silver, and the price didn't drop during those nine months, you'd have lost the $1,000. If you were right, and it dropped to, say, $10 per ounce, and you sold out at that point, once again you'd reel in a $3,000 profit for your prescience.

OTHER OPTION CHOICES

The silver example only scratches the surface. There are lots of different breeds of options for gold, silver, and platinum. Here are some of the major types and other considerations:

• Options come with different maturity dates. In the previous example, the length of the option was nine months. That's rather long in the world of options. You could just as well have bought a shorter option—30, 60, 90, 120, or perhaps 180 days. The range could be from as short as a day to as long as a year and even longer in special cases.

• All else being equal, the shorter option will cost less. There is less time for gold or silver to go up or down and for you to make money on the deal.

• Options are available at many different strike prices—your choice. If you choose a strike price that's far away from what gold is selling for at the time (called far out of the money), it will have a much lower premium and will cost you less. The trade-off is that the price must rise much higher before you start to make a profit. On the other hand, the lower price means you put up very little money and still have unlimited profit potential if you've guessed right and there is a big swing in the market.

• The most common size for gold options is 100 ounces; 1,000 ounces for silver. They do come in larger amounts, however, with equally higher premiums. The large options work just like the small ones. Sizes are the same for both puts and calls.

• You must exercise your option before you can realize a profit. That sounds obvious, but it doesn't work automatically (well, in some cases it does, where the dealer will automatically exercise it for you on the expiration date if you are in the money and you have not yet done so). If you own a call option and the price shoots up, you may have some impressive profits—*on paper*. If you wait longer, it might go up more . . . it might not. You will realize profits only when you cash in the option.

• "Limited loss" is touted by dealers as an attraction of options. That depends on your perspective. *How do you consider a 100 percent loss of your invested capital a "limited loss"?* Many intelligent individuals in this world would consider that a major loss, a total wipeout, a disaster—anything but a limited loss. It's all psychology. Some people feel that risking $1,000, $2,000, or more is worth it for the potential big hit. But if the prospect of watching that kind of money disappear because you guessed wrong is more than a little upsetting, this is not the place for you.

When you invest in physical gold and silver—the real stuff, not a paper surrogate—if the price drops it's no big deal. You can hang on for the long term and have confidence it will come back. Barring some disaster for gold (that is, the alchemists finally achieve their long-sought-after breakthrough), there is little chance it would become worthless.

• Be prepared to recognize the options market vernacular. A $500 November Gold Call is a call option on gold with a $500 strike price that expires in November.

• With some types of option contracts, you may have to inform the dealer by a certain time that you want to exercise the option. The length of time (usually a few days) will vary, and some options do not have this requirement.

• There is no set formula to determine the price (premium) of an option. These factors play a part:

> • The difference between the strike price you choose and the current market price of the gold or silver. As a general rule, the greater the difference the lower the premium.
> • The length of time the option will run. Longer costs more.
> • The amount of activity—supply and demand—in the option.
> • Track record of price swings (volatility) of the metal. Silver, for example, is more volatile than gold, so option premiums might be higher.

• You can also *grant* options, instead of simply buying and selling them. It works like this. In any options transaction, there is a buyer and a seller. You can *buy* call options . . . you can *buy* put options . . . and you can also *grant* put and call options on gold and silver you already own. You sell an option to somebody else, giving him the right to buy *your* gold, silver, or platinum at a set price until some time in the future. *You* get the premium. And if the person who bought the option from you guessed wrong, you keep your gold or silver—and the other guy's money. If it goes the wrong way (from your point of view), you will have to give up your metals at the agreed price. But at least you still have the premium. Granting options is a way to generate income on your holdings during periods you expect precious metals prices to be flat.

THE MAIN OPTIONS MENU

Just as there are different brands of precious metals bullion, and different brands of gold and silver certificates, so too are there different brands of gold and silver options. But the choices are more limited.

They fall into two broad categories:

(1) Options that are created and sold by precious metals dealers (dealer options). These are options to buy or sell physical metals, bought and sold for cash.

(2) Options that are created by an organized stock market or commodity futures exchange, such as the Commodity Exchange, Inc., in New York (COMEX) or the American Stock Exchange (AMEX). These are called exchange-traded options, and there are now two varieties of these as well.

At COMEX they are technically options to buy or sell a *futures contract* for gold or silver, instead of the physical metal itself. COMEX options on gold futures have traded since October 1982, and silver options were introduced in October 1984.

The AMEX exchange-traded option, on the other hand, is an option to buy physical gold (no silver yet)—also called a cash-settlement option.

The difference can be confusing for investors looking into options for the first time. Don't let it bother you too much. The way it works, and the net result, will be nearly the same for most investors. You can still lose all (but not more than) your investment if the price goes the wrong way, and upward profits are unlimited. The differences are mostly technical—but there are differences.

For example: A dealer (cash-settlement) call option on 100 ounces of gold gives you the right to buy that amount of metal at the option's strike price anytime before the option's expiration date. And for this privilege you pay a premium. Exchange-traded options also carry a premium, but since they trade auction-style, those premiums tend to be a bit lower than with dealer options, where the dealer sets the price.

Here's another difference. Instead of giving you the right to buy the physical gold, the exchange-traded option gives you the right to buy a futures contract representing a certain amount of gold, which in turn is tantamount to owning the gold itself. It's an extra layer of paper that makes it more confusing but really changes the mechanics for the individual investor very little. Since most investors simply liquidate the option, rather than demand delivery of the underlying asset (gold or the futures contract on gold), the difference between owning the gold or owning the futures contract never has a chance to occur. Markups might vary, but if the price goes against you, both options will expire equally worthless.

Still, the subtle difference makes some investors wary. That's one reason the American Stock Exchange created the first exchange-traded option based on physical gold. It is offered through a new subsidiary, the AMEX Commodities Exchange, and began trading in 1985. Until that point, all options on physical gold were dealer-granted options (such as Mocatta). The AMEX option, as the first government-approved option on physical gold, could generate a sizable following among cautious individual investors who shun anything remotely connected with the risky futures market. The AMEX option is for 100 ounces of gold and is available through brokers cleared to trade options. For more information on AMEX gold options, contact the AMEX Commodities Corp., 86 Trinity Place, New York, NY 10006, (800) THE-AMEX or (800) 462-AMEX.

One widely recognized dealer option on precious metals is offered by Mocatta Metals Corporation, a well-known name in the world metals market. Mocatta offers options on gold, silver, platinum, and even copper. But, as with Mocatta precious metals certificates, the options can be bought through a network of metals dealers, and not directly from Mocatta. Just as you would go through a broker to buy IBM stock, you would also go through a middleman to buy a Mocatta option.

Two other widely recognized options are offered by Valeurs White Weld, S.A., a Swiss firm; and Continental Ore Europe, Ltd., a British company. Both of these options are sold through a variety of precious metals dealers in the United States. Monex International Ltd., a large California-based metals merchant, also offers an options program of its own for gold and silver. Unlike Mocatta, however, Monex (and only Monex) sells the options itself.

In the final analysis, some experts believe the exchange-traded options hold a slight edge because they offer greater liquidity, lower premiums, and are backed by an exchange clearinghouse rather than an individual dealer.

Also in the exchange-traded sphere are the International Options Clearing Corporation (IOCC) gold and silver options. They trade through a multinational linkup of stock exchanges in Montreal, Vancouver, Amsterdam, the Netherlands (the European Options Exchange), and Sydney, Australia. One attraction for smaller investors who don't mind dealing via foreign exchanges is the small minimum size of the contract—only 10 ounces for gold and 250 ounces for silver. That compares with standard minimums elsewhere of 100 ounces for gold and 1,000 ounces for silver. (More on this later.)

Inside Options

When considering Mocatta's option menu, you will see the name of another firm, Metals Quality Corporation, an affiliate of Mocatta Metals. Although they are separate companies, independently responsible for backing what they sell, when dealers refer to Mocatta Options they often include both.

These are some of the precious metals options offered by Mocatta:

- Put and call options on gold bullion.
- Call options on gold coins.
- Put and call options on silver bullion.
- Call options on U.S. silver clad coins.
- Put and call options on platinum (Metals Quality Corporation).
- Call options on U.S. 90 percent silver coin bags.
- Call options on U.S. silver dollar bags.
- A hybrid type of option that Mocatta calls a Lookback, available in both puts and calls for gold, silver, and platinum bullion.

AN OPTIONS Q & A

What different strike prices are available? Strike prices for gold options can usually be set in $10 per ounce increments ($450, $460,

$470); silver strike prices can be set in 25-cent increments; platinum in $20 per ounce steps; and bags of silver coins in $50 increments per bag.

What are the different delivery months? Different types of options have different standard delivery months. This is somthing you will have to ask about before you buy.

Are there other ways to take a profit in a precious metals option other than to exercise it? Yes, you can simply resell the option. It's a way to make a profit on an option *before* the price of the gold, silver, or platinum reaches your strike price. For example, if you bought a silver option when the price was $9.00 per ounce, and your option had a strike price of $10.50 per ounce, you'd have to wait until the price hit $10.50 before you'd be "in the money," and it would have to go beyond that before you'd hit your break-even point and start making a profit.

But what if that option is for nine months, and after just three months the price of silver jumps to just under $10.50 per ounce? At that point, the value of your option (the premium you paid when you bought it) has probably gone up as well. You could make a profit—albeit a modest one—by reselling the option itself.

Reselling, however, is not allowed in some types of options. Monex, for example, a California dealer that offers its own option plan, says that its options are "non-tradeable." In their words, "There is no market in which an option purchased from Monex can be resold, nor can Monex repurchase it." If you want the flexibility of being able to resell, you'll have to look elsewhere. One special feature the Monex option offers is automatic profit protection. If your option is in the money at the time it expires, this dealer will automatically exercise it for you (heaven knows how you'd "forget" about your option, but I suppose it could happen).

How do they figure the charges? The price you pay for the option from the dealer—the retail purchase price—includes the option premium, plus commissions and fees. As long as you do not take delivery of the metal when you exercise your option (*if* you get a chance to do that) there are no storage, insurance, or other charges. There should be no hidden charges on an option of this type—no charges to maintain the account, no charges for interest or anything like it. Ask, to make certain about this when you invest. And if the dealer tells you there are charges, be skeptical. They might be unloading some other type of investment on you that you don't want.

When do the options expire? Mocatta options expire at "high noon," East Coast time, on the first banking day of the option's delivery month. Call options from Valeurs White Weld and Continental Ore Europe are a little tougher to figure. They expire at 11:00 A.M. *Geneva, Switzerland, time* on the expiration date of the option. Monex International options expire at 1:00 P.M. Pacific Coast time on the last trading day of the option, or if that's a weekend or holiday, on the next business day.

What information should I receive before investing? You should receive something called a Commodity Option Disclosure Statement, specifically for the type of option that you are considering, such as a Silver Option Granted by Continental Ore Europe, Ltd. Here is the standard introduction to an options disclosure statement:

> BECAUSE OF THE VOLATILE NATURE OF THE COMMODITIES MARKETS, THE PURCHASE OF COMMODITY OPTIONS IS NOT SUITABLE FOR MANY MEMBERS OF THE PUBLIC. A PERSON SHOULD NOT PURCHASE A COMMODITY OPTION UNLESS HE OR SHE IS PREPARED TO SUSTAIN A TOTAL LOSS OF THE PURCHASE PRICE OF THE COMMODITY OPTION. SUCH TRANSACTIONS SHOULD BE ENTERED INTO ONLY BY PERSONS WHO ARE AWARE OF THE POTENTIAL LOSS AND WHO UNDERSTAND THE NATURE AND EXTENT OF THEIR RIGHTS AND OBLIGATIONS. THESE COMMODITY OPTIONS HAVE NOT BEEN APPROVED OR DISAPPROVED BY THE COMMODITY FUTURES TRADING COMMISSION [a federal agency] NOR HAS THE COMMISSION PASSED UPON THE ACCURACY OR ADEQUACY OF THIS STATEMENT. ANY REPRESENTATION TO THE CONTRARY IS A VIOLATION OF THE COMMODITY EXCHANGE ACT AND THE REGULATIONS THEREUNDER.

A disclosure statement goes on to explain (in less than lucid language at times) how the option works, who guarantees it, how the order will be processed, how the metals are held, and what fees and commissions you will pay.

Before a legitimate dealer will allow you to trade options, you will also be required to state that you have received, read, and understood the disclosures and that you are aware of the risks.

Will I receive a copy of the actual option certificate? Not unless you ask for it. And if you do that, you will be charged a fee, perhaps as much as $100. Don't bother. The vast majority of option buyers let the firm (Mocatta, Valeurs, Continental) hold the option certificate in a custody account at no charge. Why pay for a piece of paper you don't need? You'll receive a statement instead.

What's a naked option? If you *write* an option against precious metals that you do not currently own, that's a naked option. It's dangerous. Unless you are a pro, stay away from this strategy.

What is staying power? Since you can never lose more than the price you pay for a precious metals option, even if the price goes against you soon after you invest, options let you hang on and hope for a reversal. It's different in futures contracts (explained in next chapter) and with margin-buying schemes. With futures you are on the hook for even bigger sums. If the price goes the wrong way, you'll have to act fast to get out lest you lose your shirt . . . and your pants.

Are there any other advantages or disadvantages to dealer options compared to exchange-traded options? To get a price quote on a dealer option, you must call the dealer—prices are not widely published as they are with exchange-traded options. Since there is no competitive auction system, prices are set by the dealer, who is also not obligated to buy back your option. Exchange options, such as those traded on COMEX, offer a readily available market to unload your option before its expiration date, if that's what you want to do.

But ask a *dealer* the same question and you get different answers. Mocatta claims that it provides a well-greased two-way market for its precious metals options and that obtaining a current price quote from the dealer you bought it from is no big deal. What's more, say Mocatta officials, "The quotes must be fair, because the broker, when asking for a quote, doesn't indicate to Mocatta whether he means to buy or sell, and the bid/offer price he receives for you from Mocatta is good for either buying or selling." And while COMEX closes shop at 2:30 P.M. in New York, Mocatta says it will buy and sell its own options until 10:00 P.M., New York time (if your broker is still open).

Are there more reasons to invest in options other than to try to make a profit? Sure, but most of them involve techniques used mostly by very large investors or professional traders. Options can also be used to *protect* the value of bullion you already own or to protect a futures position. It's usually called hedging.

OPTIONS ON SILVER AND GOLD FUTURES

In October 1982 COMEX—the Commodity Exchange, Inc., New York—introduced the first exchange-traded option that moves up and down with the price of gold. In the years that followed, this option on COMEX gold futures caught on nicely. By 1985 COMEX had also introduced an option on silver futures, which it hoped would emulate the gold option's success.

From the investor's viewpoint, COMEX options on gold and silver futures work much like any other option. As the exchange itself notes, "With options on COMEX gold futures, any investor can trade this important precious metal while limiting risk exposure to a predetermined dollar amount. Someone who buys a COMEX gold futures option can lose no more than the cost of the option, commonly known as the premium. Yet, because gold futures options are highly leveraged an investor can make substantial profits if the gold price moves in his favor."

COMEX options have a premium, a strike price, and an expiration date, and are exercised at the sole discretion of the buyer—just like the options already covered. These options, however, are traded on a commodities exchange, just as stocks are traded on a stock exchange.

So what, you ask? Good question. The bottom-line difference is slight. In an exchange-traded option, you have lots of maniacs out on the trading floor conducting a pushing, shoving, and shouting match that passes for a free market auction. All this competition is supposed to ensure you a better price. Maybe yes, maybe no. You also can be assured that the option you are buying has an active resale market and that it is backed up by one of the world's leading commodity exchanges.

Because this is an option on a gold *futures contract*, and not physical metals, the jargon and paperwork tend to be even more confused. The advantage is accessibility. A larger number of investment firms can sell you a COMEX option.

COMEX gold futures options trade between the hours of 9:00 A.M. and 2:30 P.M. Silver options trade on the COMEX between 9:05 A.M. and 2:25 P.M. COMEX silver and gold options contracts expire on the second Friday of the month *prior* to the expiration of the underlying futures contract. That means May silver options, for example, expire on the second Friday in *April*. They are available for 100 ounces of gold; 5,000 ounces of silver.

A Winning Example

Here is one example of how a COMEX call option on silver can work if you are living right:

On September 1, with COMEX December silver futures trading at $9.95 per ounce, an investor who believes silver is about to rise buys a $10 call option on December silver futures at the current premium of 40 cents per ounce, or $2,000. By early November, December silver futures are trading at $11 an ounce, and the $10 December call is trading for a premium of $1.02 per ounce. The investor sells his option for $5,100 and a profit of $3,100. Had silver gone down, the investor's $2,000 would have been wiped out.

Reading Up

Competition for investor attention is fierce among the exchanges and metals firms. Most of them offer your weight in free or low-cost booklets and other printed matter about what they sell. COMEX is no exception. The exchange offers several free publications that take you through gold and silver options (as well as futures). One booklet, *COMEX Gold Futures Options: Strategies for Investors*, offers a detailed series of examples showing sophisticated options-trading strategies. It covers every contingency, from raging bull strategies to strongly bearish moves. Be forewarned. This is heavy-duty reading. It assumes you are already well versed in the basics of options and doesn't bother to explain such terms as a "bull put spread—vertical" or what it means when you "short the lower strike put" and then "long the higher strike put." The charge for this publication is 50 cents. While you're at it, ask for a free copy of the COMEX Information Kit (only the first one is free) and a slick little booklet, *Options on COMEX Gold Futures: A New Way to Trade Gold with Limited Risk*.

If you are interested in silver, ask for *Options on COMEX Silver Futures: An Introduction*, which is also free from COMEX at 4 World Trade Center, New York, NY 10048 (212) 938-2900.

Options Round the Clock

If the options action in the United States isn't enough to suit your taste, consider IOCC silver and gold options traded on the Montreal Stock Exchange, Vancouver Stock Exchange, Sydney Stock Exchange (in Australia), and the European Options Exchange, in Amsterdam. IOCC stands for International Options Clearing Corporation, which is jointly owned by the different exchanges.

These are options on actual bullion—pure and simple gold and silver bullion—not futures contracts, coins, stocks, certificates, or anything else. Trading started in Amsterdam in 1981. The other markets joined in later.

This is a single option that can be traded identically on any of the participating exchanges around the world. You could buy it in Montreal (through a broker of course) and sell it in Amsterdam or Vancouver. Because of the time differences between these different international markets, the effect is to create an almost continuous round the clock market in precious metals options.

For the real nail biters who follow the prices of metals around the globe, that's an advantage over, say, COMEX, where trading is confined to five and a half hours a day. IOCC options also come in smaller bite-size pieces—10-ounce contracts for gold and 250-ounce contracts for silver. As with nearly all precious metals trading around the world, prices are quoted in U.S. dollars. Contracts are also settled in U.S. currency, so there is no foreign exchange headache to worry about.

Except for trading outside the United States, the IOCC options work much the same as their stateside cousins. They offer the same profit and loss potential from buying and selling puts and calls.

For more information on IOCC continuously traded gold and silver options, write to:

Options Department
The Montreal Stock Exchange
P.O. Box 61
800 Square Victoria
Montreal, Quebec
Canada, H4Z 1A9
(514) 871-2424

or,

Options Department
Vancouver Stock Exchange
P.O. Box 10333
609n Granville St.
Vancouver, BC
Canada, V7Y 1H1
(604) 689-3334

I'd Rather Be in Philadelphia

Top honors for the most obscure precious metals option go to the Aux Gold/Silver Index option traded via the Philadelphia Stock Exchange. Stock index options as a group were one of the hottest financial products of the early 1980s. This one is based on an index of seven major gold and silver mining stocks, including firms such as Dome Mines, Campbell Red Lake, Homestake, and Sunshine Mining.

For more information on this one you can contact the Philadelphia Exchange at 1900 Market Street, Philadelphia, PA 19103 (215) 496-5000. But be warned. This choice is so obscure even the people who work at the exchange seem to know little about it.

Mocatta Options with a Twist

Not content to leave well enough alone with its standard precious metals options, Mocatta Metals Corporation concocted a laundry list of variations—hybrids that even let you be a Monday morning quarterback with your options.

The Mocatta Investment Option goes regular options one better. It is a call option on a metal with a strike price that is already much lower than the metal's current market price. That means that when you buy it, it's already a long way "in the money." The idea is to combine the limited risk of an option with the even higher profit potential of a leveraged investment such as futures or margin accounts.

Mocatta Metals Corporation says it will extend the term of the option (typically for three months) for an added charge. That lets you buy more time for the option to become profitable, and you pay only the carrying charge. At the same time, the option will automatically terminate if the price plunges to below your already low strike price, thus avoiding any loss beyond your initial premium.

The Mocatta Lookback Option offers yet another twist, allowing an investor to look back over the length of the option and choose the most favorable price to buy or sell. This strategy works best when prices are going up or down rapidly.

The lookback option is a call or put option that differs from the standard option in one major way: Its strike price is set *at the time you sell or exercise the option*. You get whatever price was best over the term of the option. That advantage does not come free. You pay for it in a higher option premium. Lookback options are available on 100 ounces of gold, 1,000 ounces of silver, and 50 ounces of platinum.

CHAPTER 17

Futures Contracts: Legalized Theft?
(The Beginner's Guide to the Wild and Woolly Market in Precious Metals Futures)

- **How a Precious Metals Futures Contract Works**
- **Where Futures Are Traded**
- **Risks and Pitfalls of Futures Trading**
- **Contract Particulars**
- **Trading Tips**
- **A Guide to Futures Exchanges**

The title sounds drastic. But not when you stop to consider that up to *90 percent of the average investors who play the commodity futures game lose money.* Those are not enticing odds—and for most rational individuals, this is a crazy way to invest in precious metals.

The volume of contracts traded on the futures exchanges is mind-boggling. Contracts representing more gold than there is on earth are traded in a single year. The Commodity Exchange of New York (COMEX) accounts for 98 percent of U.S. gold futures trading volume. Over 12 million gold contracts, each one representing one hundred ounces of the metal, have traded on COMEX in a single year. Total value: over $500 billion.

HOW A PRECIOUS METALS FUTURES CONTRACT WORKS

This is a market where you can put up the "modest" sum of, say, $4,000 and if things go against you, you can end up losing $20,000 or more. That's because when you "invest" in a commodity futures contract (the term "invest" is used loosely here), you agree to buy or sell a set amount of gold, silver, platinum, or palladium before some specific date in the future, at a set price. It is a firm commitment. You are legally bound to pay and accept the price stated in the futures contract.

If gold today is selling for $400 an ounce and you believe it is headed up, you could buy a futures contract to purchase 100 ounces of gold at, say, $420 per ounce six months from now. That contract might cost you a few thousand dollars. It means you have agreed to buy 100 ounces of gold at $420 per ounce—you are on the hook for an investment of $42,000.

You can also play the futures market by agreeing to *sell* a precious metal sometime in the future at a fixed price. You don't actually have to own a single ounce of the metal to do this—but your profits or losses will add up as if you did. This is what traders call selling short.

This is *not* like an option where you have the *choice* of buying or not buying, selling or not selling. Here you are committed to the gold at that price. You profit handsomely if the price goes up. But you get scalded if it doesn't.

If the price simply stays at $400 per ounce, you lose another $2,000. If it drops to $380, you've lost $4,000 more. The more it drops, the more you lose. And that's money you must keep posting as the price drops.

That's not all. If the price drops, as long as you continue to hold your futures contract, you will be forced to cough up more money. That's a margin call, the phone call most dreaded in this business. (Most experienced traders don't wait for that to happen: If the price moves against them, they get out immediately and live to speculate another day.)

Putting in Your Ante

Anyone who buys a futures contract must deposit a down payment with his or her broker. That serves as collateral, or margin money. It must be an amount large enough to, in the words of COMEX, "cover losses that might normally occur in the course of a day's trading."

When any trader first buys a futures contract (in the market's jargon, this is called establishing a position), he must ante up the initial margin amount. That's considered good faith money and serves as evidence that you stand ready to meet the obligations under the futures contract—in other words, that you have the money to buy what you've said you will buy.

For example, an investor who buys a 100-ounce gold futures contract at $400 per ounce might be asked to post original margin of $4,000—10 percent of the $40,000 total contract value. If the price jumps 10 percent, you make your money. If it drops 10 percent, you must put more cash into your margin account immediately or it will be liquidated at a loss to you. If this sounds suspiciously like gambling, it is.

All gains and losses on your futures contract are settled in cash *every day*. This is called a mark to the market. That's so there will be no big surprises later on. Instead of losing one gigantic amount later, you lose smaller amounts every day for a longer period. But you can get out anytime.

Each commodity exchange sets a minimum margin amount that its dealer/members must charge you when you take a futures position. Each dealer, however, is free to require a greater amount of margin, and some do. Initial margin requirements usually range between 5 and 15 percent of the value of the contract, according to the Chicago Board of Trade (CBOT), a major futures exchange. Some brokers recommend that speculators never meet a margin call because it simply means you are perpetuating a losing position—throwing good money after bad.

According to experts at the commodity exchanges, a unique attraction of futures contracts is their ability to offer an efficient "affordable" way to participate in the precious metals markets without the problems of owning the physical metals—storage, insurance, delivery, etc. Hardly anyone who invests in a futures contract actually delivers or takes delivery of the gold, silver, or whatever. As with options, most buyers simply trade the paper, pocket the profits, or swallow hard and eat the losses. According to COMEX figures, only about 3 percent of all futures contracts traded each year result in delivery of the commodity.

WHERE FUTURES ARE TRADED

Where does all of this "legalized theft" take place? In the two commodity exchange meccas: New York and Chicago. (No letters please, some people *have* made profits, and precious metals futures contracts *do have* many legitimate institutional uses.)

• Gold and silver futures are traded on the Commodity Exchange, Inc., in New York (COMEX). This is the biggest.

• Platinum and palladium futures trade on the New York Mercantile Exchange (NYMEX). This is a much smaller market than COMEX or the Chicago Board of Trade, and trading in platinum and palladium futures is not nearly as active as for gold and silver. That would make an investment there even more risky, since you might not be able to get in or out as quickly as you would like.

• The American Board of Trade (ABT), also in New York, is a kind of quasi-exchange that offers futures trading in gold, silver, and platinum bullion and silver coins. ABT portrays itself as a "grass-roots" organization that offers something similar to a futures contract in smaller bite-size pieces.

• The Chicago Board of Trade (CBOT), a big rival of COMEX, also trades futures contracts on gold and silver bullion.

• Trading in gold futures also takes places on the International Monetary Market (IMM), a division of the Chicago Mercantile Exchange.

• Rounding out the field is the MidAmerica Commodities Exchange, also in Chicago, where gold and silver futures contracts are traded in much smaller numbers.

These commodity exchanges compete against one another. They trade claims of being the biggest or best, or offering some advantage to futures traders. They also like publicity, since few Americans understand the controlled insanity that goes on there.

If you are ever in New York or Chicago, and you're looking for something out of the ordinary to see, try visiting COMEX or the CBOT during trading hours. You'll see a gigantic room divided up into informal pit or bull ring–type areas where different commodities are traded.

You will see a crushing mass of people in brightly colored jackets (colors represent different commodities) who look like an out-of-control mob of fans trying to buy tickets to a Michael Jackson concert. These people might be a little older, but not much. Working in the constant din of the exchange floor every day is so stressful that trader burnout keeps the faces mostly youthful. These are the traders who will actually execute a deal on a futures contract you buy.

A Membership Organization

A commodities exchange is a big club. The exchange floor is where members meet to make their trades. The exchange itself does not buy or sell anything. Members do. The CBOT describes itself as a barometer, reflecting the effects of worldwide supply and demand factors on prices.

RISKS AND PITFALLS OF FUTURES TRADING

Also keep in mind that futures were not invented with individual investors like you in mind. They were first created back in the nineteenth century to help provide a more orderly market for farm products. Today, pork bellies, soybeans, heating oil, plywood, and other commodities trade alongside gold and silver. A commodity is a commodity in the eyes of the futures market. They'd be happy to create a contract for future delivery of gumballs if they believed there was a market for them.

The mechanics of trading a futures contract (as opposed to the mechanics of the market itself) are little more difficult than investing in stocks or bonds. But then again, stocks and bonds can look overwhelmingly complicated to anyone unfamiliar with how stocks and bonds work. Just as you must buy stocks through a stockbroker who taps into the stock exchange for you, so too must you open an account with a commodities dealer in order to trade futures.

If you do that, you will receive scary-sounding risk disclosure statements. They *should* scare you. Here is point number one on the Customer Risk Disclosure Statement from Clayton Brokerage Co., a large St. Louis–based commodities brokerage firm:

> You may sustain a total loss of the margin funds you deposit with your broker to establish a position in the commodity futures market. In addition, if the market moves against your position, you

may be called upon by your broker to deposit a substantial amount of additional margin funds on short notice, in order to maintain your position. If you do not provide the required funds within the prescribed time, your position may be liquidated at a loss and you will be liable for any resulting deficit in your account.

Customers at this firm are also asked to complete a detailed account-opening application form that requires information on personal finances and their ability to handle the risks.

CONTRACT PARTICULARS

The CBOT is the oldest commodity exchange. Its menu today includes two futures contracts tailored for smaller speculators. Those are:

(1) a one-kilogram gold contract, representing 32.15 ounces of gold
(2) a 1,000-ounce silver contract. You need less money to get into these contracts, and the margin amount will initially be lower. But don't let that fool you. Your losses could still be large.

COMEX gold and silver futures are larger—100 ounces for gold; 5,000 ounces for silver. Here's how you could either make or lose $3,000 in two weeks' time, based on an initial outlay of $4,000:

On May 1 you buy a futures contract for purchase of gold in August at $450. You post $4,000 margin with the broker. On May 15 gold has moved to $480 per ounce. You sell the contract and receive back your $4,000 margin, plus $3,000 in profits (you'll have to subtract commission and other trading costs from that amount). That's the good news. If the price drops to $420 instead, and you get out at that point, there's only $1,000 left in your margin account. After subtracting transaction costs, you would get back less than $1,000 of your original $4,000. You could put up more money and hang on, but you could lose that and more if the market keeps going down.

Platinum and Palladium Futures

For platinum and palladium futures, the key exchange is NYMEX—the New York Mercantile Exchange. The platinum contract here represents 50 ounces; the palladium, 100 ounces. These contracts are less popular than gold and silver and it is a little harder to find a dealer. For a list of NYMEX member firms that serve individual accounts, you can write to the NYMEX Department of Research and Education.

The American Board of Trade, a membership organization of commodities brokers and dealers, claims that its "forward" (same as futures) contracts are designed with small individual investors in mind. This upstart "exchange" likes to call its product a forward contract instead of a futures contract to avoid hassles with government regulators. The effect is the same. This is ABT's lineup:

• Gold bullion in contract sizes of 1, 2, 5, 10, and 32.15 ounces (one kilo).
• Silver bullion in contract sizes of 10, 20, 50, 100, 500, and 1,000 ounces.
• Silver coins in contract sizes of $100, $200, $500, and $1,000 face value bags of dimes, quarters, or half-dollars.
• Platinum in contract sizes of 1, 2, 5, 10, and 50 troy ounces.

The ABT has been around since 1969. It has aggressively sought the individual investor market in futures trading and claims to have the lowest commissions, fees, and other costs of all the exchanges. (ABT refers to its competitors as the "old-line" exchanges.)

Unlike the big exchanges where you must work through a broker/dealer, you can open an account directly with ABT or through one of its 200 or so members around the country. Customers are allowed to place orders directly with the floor of the exchange via a toll-free telephone line set up to receive and record orders from investors outside New York.

TRADING TIPS

Futures trading, with its big risks, complex trading strategies, and moment-to-moment price changes, comes with its own set of general rules for speculators. If you study the field further, you'll see them again and again. They are worth heeding:

• Casual investors stay away. This is a speculator's market, and if your interest in precious metals is to help secure a financial future for you and your family, erase futures from your list. Investors must study prices constantly. While you sleep, a political crisis in some far corner of the globe could change the price of precious metals, causing you to lose thousands of dollars—a nightmare you won't even know about until you awake the next morning.

• Timing is everything in futures trading. If you buy bullion, you can wait out a price dip. With a futures contract, a drop in prices will probably force you out—and you will lose, even if prices head up a short while later.

• Be realistic. In other words, *thinking* that you are prepared to lose $1,000, $3,000, $5,000, or more is one thing. *Dealing* with your emotions when it really happens is quite another. Don't risk money you want or need for other purposes . . . and even if you have a small portion of your overall holdings set aside for speculation, you'll want to conserve that too.

• You might think, after extensive study, that you know what will happen to prices. You don't. You might be wrong, and if you are, the *last* thing you want to do is be stubborn and hang on. Professional traders preach this point time and again. Cut your losses. If the market moves against you, get out.

• To help prevent losses, set limits for yourself. When those limits are reached, get out. A way to do this is to place a ''Stop Loss'' order with your broker. This doesn't mean he will be able to get you out at exactly that spot. The market can move a long way overnight, and you can get stuck with that additional loss.

• Ask for a rundown of the possible transaction costs. Some of those charges can be ''hidden'' among bid/ask spreads, different opening and closing prices, and other little tricks not spelled out unless you ask.

• An ounce (maybe a kilo) of skepticism is healthy. There are many slickly produced, glowing accounts of the great things you can do in the futures market. Don't be fooled into thinking this is anything but a gamble.

A GUIDE TO FUTURES EXCHANGES

The American Board of Trade, Inc.
9 South William St.
New York, NY 10004
(212) 943-0100

Ask for package of information on opening an ABT account.

Chicago Board of Trade
Market Planning and Support
LaSalle at Jackson
Chicago, IL 60604
(312) 435-3558
(800) 621-4641
(800) 572-4217 (in Illinois)

CBOT has a series of booklets on its different types of futures contracts. Available for the asking.

Chicago Mercantile Exchange
(International Monetary Market)
30 S. Wacker Drive
Chicago, IL 60606
(312) 930-3048

**Commodity Exchange, Inc.
(COMEX)**
4 World Trade Center
New York, NY 10048
(212) 938-2900 (main number)
(212) 928-2914 (marketing dept.)
(800) 255-5202

COMEX has slick booklets on all of its precious metals futures and options products, plus some other publications about trading strategies and price histories. Some are free, others have a nominal charge. Ask for the current Publications List. Comex Goldline, real-time gold price quotes: (900) 976-GOLD.

**MidAmerica Commodity
Exchange**
175 West Jackson Blvd.
Chicago, IL 60604
(312) 435-0606

New York Mercantile Exchange
4 World Trade Center
New York, NY 10048
(212) 938-2222

Write for a booklet on platinum and palladium futures contract specifications, and for a list of NYMEX member firms. For recorded 24-hour information on platinum and palladium futures prices call (212) 938-8014.

Note: Precious metals forward (futures) investments are also available through the big Swiss bank, Crédit Suisse. See the Dealer Directory in Chapter 11 for addresses and phone numbers of CS offices in the United States.

PART III

Winning Strategies

CHAPTER 18

Tax Tips for Precious Metals Investors

- **Precious Metals for IRAs**
- **Reporting to the IRS**
- **Sales Tax on Precious Metals Purchases**

Taxes—the first (chronologically) of life's two grand inevitabilities—are as much a concern with precious metals as they are with most other investments today. Here is a rundown of key tax considerations facing precious metals investors:

PRECIOUS METALS FOR IRAs

You once could invest tax-deferred retirement account funds directly in precious metals. You could, for example, buy gold and hold it in your Individual Retirement Account (IRA). But in 1981, Congress banned physical metals and other tangible assets from IRA portfolios.

The battle to bring them back has raged ever since. If you've had your eye on a gold accumulation plan as part of your IRA, hoping to capture the tax write-off for that investment as well, forget it. Precious metals in physical form are taboo for IRAs.

But there's still a way to link part of your retirement grubstake to precious metals—through a precious metals *mutual fund*. Most of these funds are eligible and offer special IRA plans, even if the fund invests partially in bullion. If you want to inject gold into your IRA, mutual funds are the way to do it.

REPORTING TO THE IRS

If you buy a Canadian Maple leaf or other gold *bullion* coins, when you sell them back to a dealer, that dealer is now required by law to report the sale to the IRS. Tax collectors want to know if you made a profit, so they'll be sure to collect their share.

But if you take a U.S. $20 Gold Double Eagle—an even more valuable coin—and sell it back to that same dealer, the transaction need not be reported to the IRS. You are still legally bound to report your profit, of course, but the dealer won't tell on you. When this rule took hold in 1984, there was a boom in sales of numismatic gold coins. Somehow it's difficult to imagine that when those coins are sold for a profit, their previous owners will dutifully report the capital gain on April 15.

According to IRS documents, the reporting rule specifically exempts any coin as long as "the gross proceeds from its sale exceed by more than 15 percent its value as a commodity." Net result: Any numismatic or semi-numismatic precious metals item that sells for a premium of over 15 percent above its bullion value falls outside the IRS reporting rules. At least that's for now. Congress and the IRS have a habit of changing the rules with the frequency of guest hosts on *The Tonight Show*.

In order to define which commodities are subject to reporting, the lawmakers decided to include anything that is deliverable under a government-approved commodity futures contract. That certainly includes gold, silver, platinum, and palladium bullion. But it seemed to leave out bullion coins. Then in December 1983 the CFTC up and approved a futures contract for gold coins. The IRS promptly fired off a press release gleefully "stressing" that brokers also had to report sales of Krugerrand, Maple Leaf, and Mexican Peso gold coins now that there was an approved commodities contract for these items. The IRS pointed out that this rule applied even though futures contracts on gold coins were not actively traded on any exchange. And since there is also an approved futures contract for U.S. silver coins, sales of those items must be reported to the IRS as well.

"Well, if you're going to take it literally," the dealers shot back, "then it's our opinion that reporting need only be done for sales that are of the minimum size required on CFTC-approved commodity futures contracts." That would be 32.15 ounces of gold, 1,000 ounces of silver, or 25 gold coins.

But the IRS didn't buy that argument. It announced that ". . . an information report is required on the sale of a single gold coin . . . even though all CFTC contracts for gold coins call for a minimum delivery of 25 coins." And the tax agency added this: "Contracts for pre-1965 U.S. silver coins have been approved for trading by the CFTC since July 1, 1983. Brokers are required to file information reports on sales of such coins."

When you buy and sell bullion, you should expect the dealer to ask for your social security number. Even though firms report only on a sale, not a purchase, many collect that number up front to protect themselves later.

SALES TAX ON PRECIOUS METALS PURCHASES

A major concern to any buyer of precious metals is sales tax. But dealers have made this easy to avoid—as long as you do not take delivery of your investment or you buy from a dealer in another state.

If you live in a state that does not have a state sales tax, you don't have a problem. Congratulations (from someone who pays the highest sales tax in the nation).

If not, you can purchase any of the precious metals through one of dozens of different certificate, storage, or accumulation plans and not have to worry about paying any sales tax either. Most dealers store precious metals in a state without a sales tax. Delaware has become the mecca for this purpose. Avoiding sales taxes can be a strong incentive to invest through a certificate plan.

CHAPTER 19

Strategies and Tips for a Happy Journey

- **Rolling with the Ratios**
- **Swapping Silver for Gains**
- **Rolling with Platinum**
- **The Platinum/Palladium Price Ratio**
- **Precious Metals Tips: A Grab Bag for Investors**

Buy and hold is about the simplest investment strategy anyone can employ. You decide what to buy, buy it, and settle back for a long ride. And it's probably the course taken by the greatest number of gold investors; a bit less so with silver, since the metal is not as lovingly thought of as a replacement for money; and even less for platinum and palladium, which are considered more speculative by most individuals.

Dollar cost averaging is the classic buy-and-hold strategy. This chapter is about some of the more esoteric ways to grab an investment edge in precious metals—specific trading strategies and general trading tips.

ROLLING WITH THE RATIOS

Whenever prices change there is opportunity for profit. Since the prices of gold, silver, platinum, and palladium rise and fall with confounding ease, you can profit from those swings.

The price of each metal also changes in a different way—*in relation to the other three metals*. The price of gold, for example, has sometimes been fifty times greater than that of silver. And at other periods it has sold for only seventeen times more than the price of the white metal. This is what dealers call the gold/silver ratio.

If you know how to read it, this ever-changing ratio is another way you can profit from the changing prices of gold and silver. It also applies to each of the metals in relation to the others. But the key ratios for market watchers are gold/silver, gold/platinum, and lately also platinum/palladium and silver/platinum.

Here's How It Works

Over the years, the average price ratio of gold to silver has been about 34 or 35 to one. To illustrate simply, that means if gold is selling for $350 per ounce, and the historical gold/silver ratio is working, silver is selling at $10 per ounce. But it doesn't always work that way.

As I write, in fact, the price of gold compared to that of silver is a little more than 44 to one. The sages who follow this ratio have been saying that because it is so high, silver must be cheap, or at least it looks cheap in comparison to the price of gold.

Using the familiar water-glass analogy, that's the half full point of view. It comes from precious metals investors biased toward thinking prices simply *must* be headed up soon. The half empty view could just as easily say, "No, silver is not cheap, gold is expensive," thus blowing the strategy to bits.

In order to understand how this strategy is supposed to work, you must think in terms of total ounces of metal owned—*not* in terms of how much it is all worth in dollars. To score in this game, you want to rack up more ounces, not dollar signs.

Here's how you do it. No magic, no mystery. When silver is "cheap" (high gold/silver ratio) switch out of gold and into silver. Do the reverse when the gold/silver ratio is low, and keep doing it whenever the ratio appears to be way out of line (either high or low). Even if you don't invest another dime, you can walk away owning more ounces of metal because you have switched your holdings from "expensive" gold to "cheap" silver (to use one possible case).

A Switch Example

Say my brother Jim buys 10 ounces of gold when the ratio is at its average of 34 to one. Some months later that ratio has broadened to 40 to one, so Jim switches to silver and now owns 400 ounces of that metal instead. (Ignore commissions for the moment.) A year later the pendulum has swung back, and gold is selling at only thirty times the price of silver. Jim switches back into gold again to take advantage of that shift. *Now he owns 13.3 ounces of gold.* Without having invested any more money (other than transaction costs), and even if the price of gold has not changed one iota, he has made a profit of 3.3 ounces of gold—whatever it happens to be worth. If the price has since dropped, that "bonus gold" can cut his losses. It could even turn what would have been a losing investment into a winner. Or added on to a price increase, it could dramatically boost his overall profit.

Fly in the Ointment

Don't rejoice too quickly, however. There are a few glitches in this money-making machine. You can't switch back and forth between gold and silver bullion for nothing. You will have to pay somebody a commission. And there is also the "spread" to worry about—the difference between the price the dealer charges when you buy and the price he offers when you sell to him. Those will differ depending on how, when, and where you buy. But you can be certain they will severely sully the attraction of rolling with the ratios. Still, if you are in a certificate plan that holds your "round trip" (buy and sell) transaction costs below, say, 4 or 5 percent, it may still be worth exploring.

This is not for every tiny swing up or down in the ratio. Save it for the big moves—when the ratio tops 40 to one or dips below 30 to one.

Here's more food for thought on the topic. Just because the experts say there is such a thing as a normal gold/silver ratio doesn't mean it's so. Things change. The market certainly does. What was a normal relationship between the prices of gold and silver over the last ten or twenty years might now be resolutely abnormal. So don't count on it always heading back home to the 34-to-one region as the benchmark ratio. It might not happen.

SWAPPING SILVER FOR GAINS

A similar strategy can even work between two different forms of the same metal. Junk silver and silver bullion are a good example. At times the market, in its mystical wisdom, will send the price of junk silver coins to a higher than usual premium above the actual bullion value of the silver in those coins. That can happen when silver prices are severely depressed and may reflect the unique "floor" that junk silver coins—since they are currency—offer as an investment.

At times the junk silver premium has reached 25 percent or more above the bullion price of silver. When that happens, many investors will swap their bags or rolls of junk silver coins for bullion bars. *Personal Finance,* an investment newsletter, offered this example of how it worked at one point: With the spot price of silver at $7.10, a typical low-overhead bullion dealer was offering to buy bags of junk coins (face value $1,000) for about $6,000. (Each bag contains about 715 ounces of silver.)

In exchange for a bag, an owner could have bought 782 ounces of silver in bar form—a pickup of 67 ounces, or 9.4 percent by weight. "Conversely," added *Personal Finance,* "when the price of silver is high and the premium on coins shrinks, you'll want to switch your bars for coins—because coins typically hold their value better in a declining market."

These types of trading opportunities won't come up and bite you. To catch them, you will have to keep your eyes open, follow prices, and bring out your pocket calculator to figure a ratio once in a while. It's simple. To figure the gold/silver ratio, for example, divide the price of gold by the price of silver.

ROLLING WITH PLATINUM

You can put similar strategies to work between gold/platinum and platinum/palladium. Platinum's hair-trigger supply/demand balance, for example, can send its price in different directions compared to gold.

At times the price of platinum closely tracks the price of gold. It has been more and less expensive than gold. The accompanying chart illustrates how wide those chasms were from the mid-1970s to the mid-1980s. Consider a switch to platinum when its price is cheap compared to gold and out of platinum to gold when the opposite is true.

THE PLATINUM/PALLADIUM PRICE RATIO

There's also a moving price ratio that investors watch between platinum and palladium. This one is trickier. Only in recent years has palladium been viewed even marginally as an investment metal, and in 1982–83 its fabulous price breakout made the other metals look rather anemic.

From a low of $48 per ounce in mid-1982, the price of palladium exploded almost 260 percent, to pass $172 per ounce in late 1983, before backing off slightly. While gold, silver, and platinum were weak, palladium showed superhuman strength. By 1984, palladium looked so strong that many metals experts felt the only thing holding it back was the low price of the other metals. In other words, the market was reluctant to let the price ratio of palladium to the other metals get too far out of hand.

According to J. Aron & Company's research on this metal, the critical price ratio between platinum and palladium is 2 to one. "... [S]ince an ounce of platinum goes twice as far as an ounce of palladium (in industrial uses such as electronics) it begins to make economic sense for the manufacturer to switch back to platinum when the price of palladium exceeds half the platinum price." So when it is less than that, palladium looks good as an investment played off against platinum.

Platinum's Price Relationship to Gold

Weekly Data

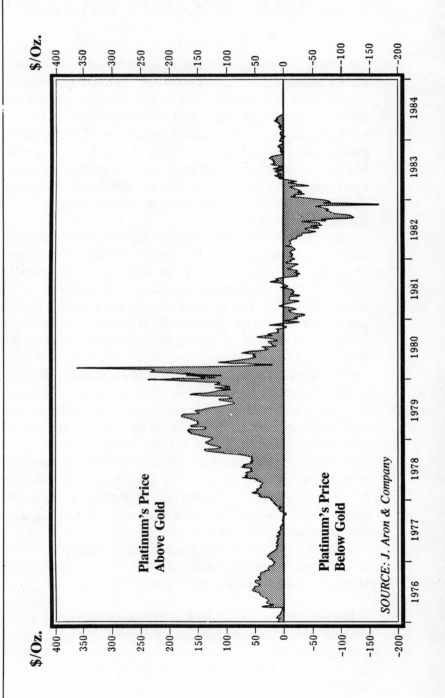

$/Oz.

400
350
300
250
200
150
100
50
0
-50
-100
-150
-200

Platinum's Price Above Gold

Platinum's Price Below Gold

1976 1977 1978 1979 1980 1981 1982 1983 1984

SOURCE: J. Aron & Company

PRECIOUS METALS TIPS:
A GRAB BAG FOR INVESTORS

• *Don't overtrade*. You can be an involved investor without constantly buying and selling. A good cure for overactive traders is simply to keep track of transaction costs. Add the phone bills, commissions, delivery charges, and taxes, and see what they come to. You may be surprised. If you've established a system for regularly adding to your precious metals holdings, stick with it. Look for opportunities, but don't be pressured into making trades you are not prepared for. God knows there will be plenty of brokers, dealers, and advisory services with their screaming headlines telling you to "Buy Now." The best advice is to ignore them.

• *Be independent*. The precious metals investment field can get clubby if you let it. There is a herding instinct at work here. When things are not going their way, too many gold "believers" have the frustrating habit of seeking out positive reinforcement—a shoulder to cry on. And there is no shortage of groups willing to tell you anything you want to hear. That doesn't make it good advice. Sorting out all of the recommendations to accomplish your personal goals will be the difficult part.

• *Treat precious metals investment like a business*. It's your money —your financial future. It makes sense to treat a portfolio like a small business you own. It won't become a success by itself. It takes hard work on your part. Take the time to do it right. Find out the tax implications of a move you plan to make *before* you make it. Keep good records (even more important now that the IRS has clamped down on taxpayer record-keeping rules). A small business owner controls his company's risks and recognizes how important it is to provide maintenance and follow-up. The same rules apply to keeping tabs on your own investment portfolio in precious metals.

• Finally: *Don't overextend*. Gold and the other precious metals can be addictive. There are so many ways to invest—such enticing profits. Often they seem right at your fingertips—if only . . .

Because of the strong pull of the precious metals as investment choices, it's all the more important that you know your limits going in. Start conservatively. It's not important how much you start with. Establish "core" holdings before you try out (*if* you try out) the speculative choices.

CHAPTER 20

Computer-Aid for Precious Metals Investors

- **What a Computer Can Do for You**
- **Tracking Options with a Computer**
- **Computer-Aid Sources**

One of today's most perfect marriages is the link between investors and their personal or home computers. Precious metals investors crave information fast. The personal computer, along with the right software and linkups, can oblige as never before.

If you already own a personal computer, or have considered buying one, there are many ways you can now use it to help in your precious metals endeavors. Even the smaller, less expensive home computers, outfitted with the right software programs and a link to an outside financial database, can turn your den into a mini metals-trading room.

Computerized investing, virtually unheard of a few years ago, is now big business. The field has its own specialized magazines and newsletters. Literally hundreds of electronic library services (that's all a database really is) are selling every type of financial information you can imagine, including information on precious metals.

With your computer, you can follow what's going on in the market, keep track of your own constantly changing holdings, and even play "what if" games to help you make precious metals investment decisions.

The ability to retrieve and manipulate precious metals and other investment information with your personal computer right at home has come far in recent years. Not long ago, all you could do was put the prices on the screen and stare at them. Now computers are smart. They can "download" the information (snatch it out of the database and store it in your computer's own memory). Thus captured, that information can help you make investment decisions.

WHAT A COMPUTER CAN DO FOR YOU

Here are some of the financial feats you can now accomplish through your personal computer:

Feed in current precious metals prices and instantly determine the value of your holdings. If your holdings are small, you don't need a computer to do this for you. A $2.95 pocket calculator will suffice.

But if you have reached a more advanced point—with investments spread among bullion, coins, mutual funds, options, and perhaps individual mining shares—keeping track of it will be a snap with a portfolio management program. Dozens are now available.

Prices for these software packages range from as little as $25 to over $600, and they are available for every type of computer—from the Commodore and Atari home varieties to Apples, IBMs, TIs, and AT&Ts, among others. Most are intended to help individual consumer/investors track a general investment portfolio. But the idea is usually adaptable to precious metals.

These programs let you add in your original costs, including commissions, premiums, and the like, and keep track of all the ups and downs in the market. Some will even help figure the tax angles. If nothing else, these computer programs can serve as simple record-keeping devices, allowing you to store and regularly update important investment details such as dates, prices, commissions, dividends, maturity dates, expiration dates, and many others.

Probably the single largest use of the computer for precious metals investing is to track prices. There are many ways you can do that. How you do it will determine how much it costs.

For most people, paying for access to "real-time" (as they happen) prices of precious metals would not be worthwhile. Using one of the many services that now offer this can cost you several hundred dollars to start and another hundred or two per month. You'd be far better off investing that money in a precious metals accumulation plan every month. But there are also some less expensive, pay-as-you-go database services.

Stock market investing has received the most attention from the computer folks. Scores of software packages now offer to help investors find the route to riches. They offer different stock selection systems, as well as historical databases through which you can learn a thousand times more about any company than you'd ever care to know.

For precious metals investors, the stock selection tools can help choose mining shares. You probably *won't* find information on penny mining stocks through a stock market database. But you will be able to find the major North American mines and some of the junior producers.

The touch of a few keys summons up a mining stock's dividend history. You can track the stock's price/earnings ratio over a period of years if you desire, find out what portion is held by institutions, chart the company's earnings over different time periods, and, of course, see how the price of the stock has performed. Those are just a few of the fifty or more "screens" that some types of stock database/software packages offer.

TRACKING OPTIONS WITH A COMPUTER

For precious metals options investors, there are new software packages to help analyze the effects of an investment decision under different market conditions. In other words, you can ask the computer, "What will happen if I buy now, and the price does this?" These "what if" scenarios can help you make more informed investment decisions. One firm (Blue Chip Software) has even developed a computer game patterned on the commodities market. It lets you "risk" millions without ever losing a cent and can help you learn how the market works.

Since breaking news can affect precious metals prices, you might consider a service that offers the latest business and financial stories, delivered right to your computer. The leader is Dow Jones News Retrieval, which draws on the vast resources of the Dow Jones/*Wall Street Journal* financial empire.

COMPUTER-AID SOURCES

Here's a sampling of financial database services, and a few software packages and other services of interest to precious metals investors.

ADP Comtrend
1345 Washington Blvd.
Stamford, CT 06902
(800) 451-1511
(203) 357-1611

Through this financial database you can get commodities and futures prices, including information on precious metals. Expensive.

ADP Network Services
175 Jackson Plaza
Ann Arbor, MI 48106
(313) 995-6400

One of the world's largest. Most users are corporations. ADP's commodities section contains ten years or more of prices for gold, silver, platinum, palladium, and silver coins. Although many ADP users pay a yearly subscription charge, some information is available on a "time spent" basis. Available 24 hours a day, 7 days a week. Expensive.

Bonneville Telecommunications
669 North/10th West
Centerville, UT 84014
(800) 453-9404

Offers access to commodity futures prices (including precious metals) for charges ranging from $180 to $400 per month; and also Daily Metals Report, from News-a-tron Market Reports.

Commodity Communications Corp.
420 Eisenhower Lane North
Lombard, IL 60148
(800) 621-2628

A leading supplier of real-time commodity futures prices to financial institutions and individual investors. Information available includes news, charts, technical studies.

Commodity Systems, Inc.
200 West Palmetto Park Rd., Suite 200
Boca Raton, FL 33432
(305) 392-8663

CSI's Quicktrieve software lets you retrieve and work with precious metals options information. This is one of the lower-priced services. The initial software charge is $135, with monthly rates for tapping into the data beginning as low as $29.

CompuServe
Information Services Division
5000 Arlington Center Blvd.
Columbus, OH 43220
(800) 848-8199
(614) 457-0802

CompuServe is one of the Big Three in the business (Dow Jones and The Source are the other two), offering a vast range of information— not all financial. Very little deals with precious metals. The consumer version has a one-time $40 charge, plus time charges on the system. There is also an "executive" service for $90, or $140 with the software to communicate with an IBM computer. Hourly rates range from $6 to $12.50

Dataspeed, Inc.
1900 South Norfolk St.
San Mateo, CA 94403
(415) 571-1800
(800) S-MARKET

Dataspeed invented QUOTREK, a hand-held stock market quote device. The latest invention is Modio, a cross between a computer modem (telephone hookup) and a radio. It lets you receive stock commodity (precious metals) prices via FM signal and display them on your computer screen. All this high technology costs you $550 for the Modio device, plus a minimum of $60 per month for the information. Even comes with a built-in alarm that you can set to go off when the price of gold, silver, or whatever reaches a predetermined point.

Dow Jones News Retrieval
Dow Jones & Co.
P.O. Box 300
Princeton, NJ 08540
(800) 257-5114
(609) 452-1511 (in New Jersey)

The most popular financial news and information database. Only spare information on precious metals. After $75 sign-up charge, you pay by the minute. It's most expensive during peak hours, roughly 9 A.M. to 6 P.M. Prices range from 15 cents per minute in off-peak times to $1.20 per minute.

Interactive Data Corporation
303 Wyman St.
Waltham, MA 02154
(617) 895-4300

A huge financial database, includes information on commodities such as precious metals. Expensive.

Market Data Systems, Inc.
3835 Lamar Ave.
Memphis, TN 38118
(800) 432-4413
(901) 363-0500

Pricing and volume information on commodity futures. Costs $295, plus exchange fees.

NewsNet
945 Haverford Rd.
Bryn Mawr, PA 19010
(215) 527-8030

Texts of investment newsletters on-line, including some that cover precious metals. NewsNet charges a $15 per month minimum. Hourly rates range from $24.

PC Quote, Inc.
401 S. LaSalle St., 16th floor
Chicago, IL 60605
(800) 225-5657
(312) 786-5400 (in Illinois)

You can use PC Quote with your IBM PC or compatible computer at home to get as-they-happen price quotes, via satellite, on precious metals and other items. Also news and portfolio management help. But it's not cheap. Software costs $195, plus about $500 for installation, $490 security deposit, and monthly charges starting at $245. The two-foot satellite dish should impress the neighbors. PC Quote officials say the service reaches anywhere in the U.S.

Pocket Quote Pro
Telemet America, Inc.
515 Wythe St.
Alexandria, VA 22314
(800) 368-2078
(703) 548-2042

Hand-held device that receives stock and commodity prices by radio signal. Basic subscription $299 per year, plus other charges for the information you want. For $199, also has Radio Exchange, which will feed price quotes directly into your personal computer. Available only in certain cities.

The Source
1616 Anderson Rd.
McLean, VA 22102
(800) 336-3366
(703) 821-6666

Calls itself an "information utility." The Source Investor Series includes information on precious metals. Hourly time charges range from $7.75 to $34.75, depending on time and speed of transmission.

Wall Street On-Line, Inc.
11 Hanover Square, Suite 1300
New York, NY 10005
(212) 514-5780

A real-time price quote service, charging a flat fee of $135 per month. Includes commodity prices from COMEX, CME, and CBOT.

Membership Organizations

American Association of Individual Investors (AAII)
612 N. Michigan Ave.
Chicago, IL 60611
(312) 280-0170

A nonprofit support group for investors in all fields, including precious metals and computerized investing. AAII publishes a bimonthly newsletter, *Computerized Investing*. Subscription is $44 per year, or $22 for members. A membership costs $44 per year. Also publishes *The Individual Investor's Microcomputer Guide*, a compendium of software and financial databases (comes with the newsletter). Offers software discounts to members.

American Association of Microcomputer Investors
P.O. Box 1384
Princeton, NJ 08542
(609) 737-3972

AAMI also publishes an extensive listing of investment software, included with the $49 membership. Discounts also available.

Also of Interest

Blue Chip Software
6740 Eton Ave.
Canoga Park, CA 91303
(818) 346-0730

Sells investment computer games. Tycoon program is a commodities market simulation game that lets you practice trading precious metals, complete with price histories and graphs. Price: $60.

CHAPTER 21

The Precious Metals Sideshow: Information Galore

- **Advisory Service Madness**
- **Can They Really See the Future?**
- **A Short (Very Short) Directory of Precious Metals Publications**
- **Other Helpful Sources of Precious Metals Information for Investors**

ADVISORY SERVICE MADNESS

There is no shortage of newsletters and other publications that claim to offer "inside dope" on precious metals investing. But there *is* a critical shortage of good ones. Even bad ones are expensive.

A "short" list of investment advisory newsletters purporting to offer guidance on precious metals could easily reach fifty. They range from one-man or -woman operations with a post office box and Xerox machine to large organizations that publish to serve their own business interests. The sad fact is precious few have the interests of their *readers* in mind.

One thing is apparent if you look at large stacks of these publications all at once. It's largely an incestuous crowd. Newsletter publishers interview other newsletter publishers and publish the interviews—charging you big sums for that information. They put on seminars of all varieties and invite each other to speak (you're invited to attend for a fee), at which point they plug each other's companies or products or publications. If Senator William Proxmire gave out Golden Fleece awards for private publishing, there would be plenty of winners here.

Some precious metals newsletters are put out by hard assets fanatics. They rant and rave about impending government confiscation; they preach imminent economic doom for the United States (and have for years) unless the lawless band of hooligans running Washington sees the light and puts the nation back on the gold standard.

You'll see endless claims about conspiracies—to take away your gold, manipulate the price, or other related themes. Some people take these conspiratorial ravings seriously. They pay money to hear it, over and over again. (Better they should buy rare coins with that cash!) Precious metals are a *commonsense* type of investment. But strangely, many of their most strenuous supporters make little sense at all.

CAN THEY REALLY SEE THE FUTURE?

It's astounding how many of the folks who publish advisories blatantly claim to see the future—and expect people to follow their whimsical advice. What's far more astounding, however, is that *people do*. Is it the old "what's in print must be believable" bugaboo?

The promotional materials are even more outrageous. If you invest in precious metals, sooner or later you are bound to end up on a mailing list. When that happens, break out the shovels.

The most tried and true hook to draw in a potential subscriber to an investment newsletter is the ubiquitous "Special Report" offered free or—get this—for a "special reduced rate." I sent for a dozen to have a look. Hooey.

Don't be fooled. If ever you have the urge to shell out the $29, $39,

$49, or more for one of these reports, take that money and buy as much silver with it as you can. The silver will absolutely be a better investment.

Hotline Hooey

There are some precious metals advisory firms that try to sell a recorded telephone commentary for sums of up to $600. That's $600 for a *phone number* (you pay the long-distance charges, of course) so you can listen to someone give you the same predictions orally.

The unsettling part is the sheer volume of this draff spewed forth daily in an unending stream. Meaningless prediction after meaningless prediction. You can't blame consumers for biting, at least once in a while. Everyone would dearly love to think that maybe just one of these fortune-tellers is really on to something.

If you were looking for advice on whether to buy a car, and which car to buy, would you ask your local Chevy dealer for that advice? I doubt it. His answers would surely be, "Yes, buy a Chevy."

The equivalent of the "Yes, buy a Chevy" line in the precious metals business is the newsletter published by a precious metals dealer or brokerage firm. There are many of them around. Some of the straight-forward information, such as historical prices, is fine. But all too often, dealer newsletters are self-serving house organs.

It will be a long time before a precious metals dealer recommends that you stay *out* of precious metals because the market stinks and appears to be getting worse. Dealers will write about the items they have in stock and want to push. That's good business for them, not good investment advice for you.

If you want independent opinions, go to an independent source. That, however, is a commodity more rare than the metals themselves, though not entirely unheard of. If you don't want politics or dealer sales pitches or pages of charts that amount to little more than elaborate tea leaf sets, don't read precious metals newsletters published by politically motivated groups, by dealers, or by publishers or individuals who claim they can predict the future price of any precious metal. They can't.

The Sampler: Beware

Still, I don't expect you to take my word for it. The best way is to order a crop of these publications for yourself. And a great way to do that is through an outfit called Select Information Exchange (2095 Broadway, New York, NY 10023). SIE is a big subscription agency that handles some 400 investment newsletters, including many in the precious metals field. For about $11.95 to $18 (prices vary) you can order a sample "subscription" to as many as thirty different metals publications. (It's usually a single sample, not a real subscription.)

But if you do, be warned. A torrent of junk mail will follow for months, or years to come, the likes of which you have never seen. Every financial group in America seems to buy SIE's mailing lists.

A SHORT (VERY SHORT) DIRECTORY OF PRECIOUS METALS PUBLICATIONS

I started this section intending to provide an extensive list of precious metals newsletters and related publications. When I got to fifty (not including the mining and coin publications listed in other chapters) it was getting out of hand. Besides, what was the point in listing publications I've just ravaged as worthless twaddle?

To be fair, however, there are some highly professional, well-done, worthwhile publications on precious metals. Here are just a few that I think stand above the crowd in one way or another. Even these have their weak points. This doesn't mean there aren't other worthwhile publications.

Also included is a listing of general interest personal finance and investment publications that cover precious metals from time to time or may carry regular price information or stories about new investment products and services in gold, silver, platinum, and palladium.

Silver & Gold Report
P.O. Box 40
Bethel, CT 06801
(203) 748-2036

This newsletter, published twenty-three times a year, calls itself "An Independent And Impartial Precious Metals Newsletter." Best evidence that it's true is that many dealers seem to hate the newsletter for refusing to be a cheerleader for the business ("a sure sign that we must be doing something right," as an old editor of mine at a newsletter group in Washington, DC, always said). The full rate is $144 for one year, but introductory rates are sometimes advertised.

Green's Commodity Market Comments
Economic News Agency
P.O. Box 174
Princeton, NJ 08542
(609) 921-6594

This biweekly sheet (the paper really is green) is a bit pricey at $240 for a year's subscription and is focused primarily on futures and options trading. It has a solid reputation in the field and has been around for a long time. Publisher Charles Stahl is one of the respected names in commodities publishing.

The Metals Investor
Newsletter Mgmt. Corp./Sub. Fulfillment
10076 Boca Entrada Blvd.
Box 3007
Boca Raton, FL 33431
(800) 231-2310

If you are interested only in the four precious metals, you will get more than you bargain for with this monthly twelve-page newsletter. *The Metals Investor* calls itself "the independent advisory letter devoted to investment opportunities in industrial metals" and covers everything from aluminum to zinc. Still, it's well thought out and packs much more information into those pages than most other letters. Priced at $250 per year, but special offers as low as $48 have been available at times.

Deliberations
P.O. Box 182
Adelaide St. Station
Toronto, Ontario
Canada, M5C 2J1
(416) 926-0995

This twice-monthly newsletter, subtitled *The Ian McAvity Market Letter* after the editor, is a "technical analysis" publication. That is to say, it is chock-full of charts and graphs and commentary about this cycle or that. Price: $215 per year.

The Financial Success Report
Target Publishing
P.O. Box 25
Pleasanton, CA 94566
(415) 463-2215

This is a weekly newsletter published by financial activist Howard J. Ruff. Doesn't seem to offer much in the way of practical "how-to" information, but if you read beyond some of the hype for this group's massive financial get-togethers, Ruff has a knack for making some good clean financial common sense. And it's weekly, so you feel as if you're getting more. Price: $99 per year.

Young's International Gold Reports
Young Research & Publishing, Inc.
366 Thames St.
Newport, RI 02840
(401) 849-2131

Published by Richard C. Young, this monthly report is an extract of Young's heftier (and more expensive) publication *Young's World Money Forecast*. It's basically a four-page synopsis of Young's current analysis of the gold market from an international perspective. This is broad-brush material. If you are seeking specific information on trading the different precious metals products, it's probably not for you. Price: $150 per year.

Personal Finance
KCI Communications, Inc.
1300 N. 17th St., Suite 1660
Arlington, VA 22209
(703) 276-7100

This eight-page newsletter, published every two weeks, is not specifically a precious metals newsletter but does cover the field regularly. Authors tend to promote their own special interests, but the publication still manages to pack useful information into each issue. And *Personal Finance* always seems to uncover a new angle on investing in one thing or another. Price: $94 per year.

Fact, The Money Management Magazine
305 E. 46th St.
New York, NY 10017

A general-interest monthly magazine on personal investing. Includes periodic features on precious metals, rare coins, and related areas. Price: $24 per year.

Barron's
National Business and Financial Weekly
Dow Jones & Co.
200 Burnett Rd.
Chicopee, MA 01021

Barron's is a weekly of general interest to investors. Its main focus is the stock market, and there are extensive charts including gold stocks and other precious metals prices, as well as commodities coverage that includes metals. Price: $39 for six months; $77 for one year.

OTHER HELPFUL SOURCES OF PRECIOUS METALS INFORMATION FOR INVESTORS

Publications and Organizations of Interest but Not Mentioned Elsewhere

American Bureau of Metal Statistics, Inc.
400 Plaza Drive (Harmon Meadow)
P.O. Box 1405
Secaucus, NJ 07094-0405

Publishes statistical reports on all metals.

American Metal Market
7 East 12th St.
New York, NY 10003
(212) 741-4000

Trade publication in metals industry.

Industry Council for Tangible Assets
214 Massachusetts Ave., N.E., Suite 560
Washington, DC 20002
(202) 544-1101

Trade association of metals and coin dealers.

Investment Seminars Inc. (ISI)
The Heritage Building
1859 Main St.
Sarasota, FL 33577

Regularly sponsors investment conferences around the world.

Metals Week
McGraw-Hill Publishing
1221 Avenue of the Americas
New York, NY 10020
(212) 512-6126

Metals trade publication.

National Committee for Monetary Reform
4425 W. Napoleon Ave.
Metairie, LA 70001

Gold advocacy organization. Sponsors numerous precious metals investing conferences and is a major publisher of hard assets books and newsletters.

National Futures Association
200 W. Madison
Chicago, IL 60606
(800) 621-3570
(312) 781-1300

Organization of futures dealers. Enforces standards and investor protections.

The Role of Gold in Consumer Investment Portfolios
Salomon Bros. Center for the
Study of Financial Institutions
90 Trinity Place
New York, NY 10006

70-page monograph on the topic, $5.

Index

United Precious Metals, Inc., 152
United Services Gold Shares, 173–75, 190
United Services Prospector Fund, 173, 175–76, 190
United States:
  dollar, 24–25, 28
  gold coins minted by, 104–5
  gold stockpiled by, 14
  institutional investment in, 25–27
  platinum and palladium stockpiled in, 59–60
  regulations, 6, 23, 70, 88, 96, 150, 153, 209
  silver dollars of, 68–69, 109–10, 200–202, 214
  silver stockpiled in, 42–44
  wholesale gold operations in, 14
USA Today, 183

Valeurs White Weld, S.A., 168, 246, 248
Vancouver Stock Exchange (VSE), 224, 233–34, 253, 254

Vancouver Stock Exchange Review, 237
Vanguard Group, 182, 190
vaults, private, 114–15
volatility, market, 73–74
"voodoo economics," 8–9

Wallace Miner, 237
Wall Street Journal, 171, 183
Wall Street On-Line, Inc., 283
warehouse receipts, *see* certificates, precious metals
Western Federal Corporation, 164
Western Mining News, 237
Western Platinum, 231
wholesale purchases, 90
Wood Gundy Ltd., 166

Young, Richard C., 290
Young's International Gold Reports, 290

Zack, Samuel, 210
Zurich, Switzerland, 33, 49